AF882126

IT Audit Fundamentals

Official Study Guide

IT AUDIT
FUNDAMENTALS
An ISACA® Certificate

ISACA®

About ISACA

For more than 50 years, ISACA® (*www.isaca.org*) has advanced the best talent, expertise and learning in technology. ISACA equips individuals with knowledge, credentials, education and community to progress their careers and transform their organizations, and enables enterprises to train and build quality teams. Among those credentials, ISACA advances and validates business-critical skills and knowledge through the globally respected Certified Information Systems Auditor® (CISA®), Certified in Risk and Information Systems Control® (CRISC®), Certified Information Security Manager® (CISM®), Certified in the Governance of Enterprise IT® (CGEIT®) and Certified Data Privacy Solutions Engineer™ (CDPSE™) credentials. ISACA is a global professional association and learning organization that leverages the expertise of its 145,000 members who work in information security, governance, assurance, risk and privacy to drive innovation through technology. It has a presence in 188 countries, including more than 220 chapters worldwide.

Disclaimer

ISACA has designed and created the *IT Audit Fundamentals Study Guide* (the "Work") primarily as an educational resource for professionals. ISACA makes no claim that use of any of the Work will assure a successful outcome. The Work should not be considered inclusive of all proper information, procedures and tests or exclusive of other information, procedures and tests that are reasonably directed to obtaining the same results. In determining the propriety of any specific information, procedure or test, professionals should apply their own professional judgment to the specific circumstances presented by the particular systems or information technology environment.

Reservation of Rights

© 2022 ISACA. All rights reserved. No part of this publication may be used, copied, reproduced, modified, distributed, displayed, stored in a retrieval system or transmitted in any form by any means (electronic, mechanical, photocopying, recording or otherwise) without the prior written authorization of ISACA.

ISACA
1700 E. Golf Road, Suite 400
Schaumburg, IL 60173, USA
Phone: +1.847.660.5505
Fax: +1.847.253.1755
Contact us: https://support.isaca.org
Website: www.isaca.org

Provide Feedback: To comment, please visit *https://support.isaca.org*.
Participate in the ISACA Online Forums: https://engage.isaca.org/onlineforums

Twitter: http://twitter.com/ISACANews
LinkedIn: www.linkedin.com/company/isaca
Facebook: www.facebook.com/ISACAGlobal
Instagram: www.instagram.com/isacanews/

ISBN 978-1-60420-940-2
IT Audit Fundamentals Study Guide
Printed in the United States of America

Acknowledgments

ISACA would like to recognize:

Expert Reviewers

Muhammad Abul Kalam Azad, CISA, CISM, CRISC, CDPSE, CISSP, Bangladesh
Paul Ellis, CISA, CISM, CDPSE, UK
Ashish Gupta, CISA, CRISC, CDPSE, Netherlands
Leighton R. Johnson III, CISA, CISM, CGEIT, CRISC, CDPSE, USA
Maleeha Masood, CISA, CISM, CDPSE, ITIL-F, PRINCE2, Security+, Pakistan
Syed Aun Muhammad, CISA, Canada
Mercy Omollo, CISA, CRISC, CDPSE, Kenya
Anand Ramachandran, CISA, CISM, CRISC, SABSA Foundation SCF, UK
Anamika Roy, CISA, CISM, USA
Wadim Wesolek, CISA, CIPP/E, UK

Board of Directors

Gregory Touhill, Chair, CISM, CISSP, Director, CERT Division of Carnegie Mellon University's Software Engineering Institute, USA
Pamela Nigro, Vice-Chair, CISA, CGEIT, CRISC, CDPSE, CRMA, Vice President, Security, Medecision, USA
John De Santis, Former Chairman and Chief Executive Officer, HyTrust, Inc., USA
Niel Harper, CISA, CRISC, CDPSE, CISSP, Former Chief Information Security Officer and Privacy Officer, United Nations Office for Project Services (UNOPS), Denmark
Gabriela Hernandez-Cardoso, Independent Board Member, Mexico
Maureen O'Connell, Board Chair, Acacia Research (NASDAQ), Former Chief Financial Officer and Chief Administration Officer, Scholastic, Inc., USA
David Samuelson, Chief Executive Officer, ISACA, USA
Gerrard Schmid, President and Chief Executive Officer, Diebold Nixdorf, USA
Veronica Rose, CISA, CDPSE, Founder, Encrypt Africa, Kenya
Asaf Weisberg, CISA, CISM, CGEIT, CRISC, Chief Executive Officer, introSight Ltd., Israel
Tracey Dedrick, ISACA Board Chair, 2020-2021, Former Chief Risk Officer, Hudson City Bancorp, USA
Brennan P. Baybeck, CISA, CISM, CRISC, CISSP, ISACA Board Chair, 2019-2020, Vice President and Chief Information Security Officer for Customer Services, Oracle Corporation, USA
Rob Clyde, CISM, ISACA Board Chair, 2018-2019, Independent Director, Titus, and Executive Chair, White Cloud Security, USA

ISACA. All Rights Reserved.

Page intentionally left blank

ISACA. All Rights Reserved.

Table of Contents

ISACA. All Rights Reserved.

ISACA. All Rights Reserved.

ISACA. All Rights Reserved.

ISACA. All Rights Reserved.

ISACA. All Rights Reserved.

Page intentionally left blank

ISACA. All Rights Reserved.

LIST OF FIGURES

Chapter 1. The Audit Function: Purpose and Organization

Chapter 2. Controls, Risk and Audit

Chapter 3. Performing an Audit

ISACA. All Rights Reserved.

Chapter 4. IT Environment and Components

Chapter 5. Specific Audit Subjects

Chapter 6. Overview of Newer Technologies

ISACA. All Rights Reserved.

IT AUDIT FUNDAMENTALS
An ISACA® Certificate

Chapter 1:

The Audit Function: Purpose and Organization

The Audit Function

ISACA. All Rights Reserved.

The Audit Function

1.1 Learning Objectives

This chapter provides an overall look at the IT audit function and how it contributes to the enterprise's mission and strategies.

After completing this chapter, learners will be able to:

- Define the purpose, roles and responsibilities of the IT audit function.
- Describe the purpose, intent and contents of the audit charter.
- Explain how strategic business goals relate to IT and the audit function.
- Describe how the overall governance process relates to IT audit.
- Explain how independence applies to the audit function.
- Describe relationships that auditors have with enterprise functions and oversight activities, such as governance, risk management, compliance and information security.
- Explain IT department roles and responsibilities.
- Explain how lines of defense and internal audit relate to risk management.
- Articulate the difference between internal and external auditing and describe how the two functions work together.
- Describe how the audit function incorporates the work of other auditors and experts.

1.2 Audit Purpose, Roles and Responsibilities

The purpose of the audit function is to provide the board of directors and senior management independent assurance of the enterprise internal controls, governance and risk management activities. Management is charged with executing the enterprise mission and strategy, which are defined by the board of directors and other stakeholders. Auditors play a key role in independently and objectively ensuring that management actions are aligned with the enterprise objectives.

Audits are the formal examination and/or testing of information systems to ensure that effective operations, compliance with various regulations, and functioning business operations are prepared to meet potential challenges. Most significantly, an audit can assure stakeholders of the financial, operational and ethical well-being of the enterprise. Audits are conducted either internally by staff within an enterprise (internal audit) or externally by a third party, such as an independent accounting firm, regulatory body or consulting firm. Audits are performed for a variety of reasons.

Specifically, an IT audit can determine whether:

- Information systems comply with applicable laws, regulations, contracts and/or industry guidelines.
- Information systems and related processes comply with governance criteria and related and relevant policies and procedures.
- Data and information are managed with appropriate levels of confidentiality, integrity, availability and privacy.
- IT operations are efficient and effectiveness targets are met.

Given support for these outcomes and the integrated role of the audit function in the enterprise, the responsibilities of the audit function, related to information and technology, are to:

ISACA. All Rights Reserved.

- Develop and implement a risk-based IT audit strategy in compliance with IT audit standards to ensure that known risk is assessed and addressed (accepted, avoided, mitigated or transferred).
- Plan specific audits (formal examination and/or testing) to determine whether information systems are protected and controlled, and provide value to the enterprise. Consideration should also be given to emerging and newer technologies.
- Conduct audits in accordance with IT audit standards to achieve planned audit objectives.
- Report audit findings and make recommendations to key stakeholders to communicate results and effect change.
- Lead remediation efforts (i.e., follow up on audit reports) to ensure that management takes appropriate actions in a timely manner.

In fulfilling these responsibilities, auditors should remain aware of the numerous internal and external threats levied against enterprises. These threats range from IT resource abuse to cyberthreats, ransomware attacks, fraud, and errors and omissions. An IT auditor should be aware of these threats when performing IT audits and assessments.

Throughout this study guide, two foundational terms (risk and control) are used. The following definitions frame the context in which these terms are used:

- **Risk**—A potential uncertain event that may be harmful or may negatively impact objective achievement.
- **Control**—The means of managing risk, including policies, procedures, guidelines, practices and organizational structures. Controls can be of an administrative, technical, management or legal nature.

1.2.1 Audit Charter

The role of the audit function is established by an audit charter. An audit charter is a document approved by those charged with governance that defines and documents the purpose, authority, responsibility and accountability of the IT audit function.

An audit charter:

- Establishes the position of the internal audit function within the enterprise.
- Authorizes access to records, personnel and physical properties relevant to the performance of IT audit and assurance engagements.
- Defines the scope of audit activities.

In establishing the internal audit function position, the audit charter should clearly state the function's authority to perform IT audits and reviews. This mandate should be approved by the board of directors and/or audit committee. If an audit charter exists for the audit function as a whole, the IT audit and assurance mandate should be incorporated.[1]

The charter should clearly state management responsibility and objectives for, and delegation of authority to, the audit and/or IT audit function.

An audit charter should document the following for the IT audit and assurance function:[2]

- Independence, code of ethics and standards
- Protocols that the IT audit and assurance practitioner will follow in the performance of engagements, including but not limited to communication and escalation
- Roles and responsibilities of the auditee during the IT audit or assurance engagement

[1] ISACA, *IT Audit Framework (ITAF™): A Professional Practices Framework for IT Audit, 4th Edition*, USA, 2020, Guideline 2001.1, *https://store.isaca.org/s/store#/store/browse/detail/a2S4w000004Ko91EAC*. In this publication, subsequent references to *IT Audit Framework* guidelines will be cited with the ITAF acronym followed by the guideline's numeric identifier (e.g., ITAF 2001.1).

[2] ITAF 2001.2.1

ISACA. All Rights Reserved.

- Role in reporting irregularities and illegal acts
- Purpose, responsibility, authority and accountability (described in the following sections)

Purpose

The audit charter should describe:[3]

- Aims/goals of the audit function
- Objectives of the audit function
- Audit function mission statement
- Scope of the audit function
- Work performed by the audit function

Work performed may include different types of audits, e.g., IT, compliance, financial, operational, integrated, administrative or specialized (e.g., fraud audits or forensic audits). Work may also include nonaudit services, such as advisory services on projects.

Responsibility

Audit responsibility describes the role, scope and objectives of the audit function.

The audit charter should describe:

- Implementation of the independence requirement
- Relationships with external audit firms (reliance strategy with the external auditor)
- Auditee expectations (services and deliverables that the auditees can expect from the audit function)
- Auditee requirements (responsibilities of the auditee, e.g., requirement that all auditees make themselves available and assist the audit function and practitioners in fulfilling assigned responsibilities)
- Professional standards and compliance standards that detail the requirements to which the audit function and practitioners will adhere (e.g., enterprise standards or ISACA standards)

Authority

Audit authority describes the audit function position within the enterprise, including lines of reporting and rights of access.

The audit charter should describe:[4]

- Right of access to relevant information, systems (i.e., logs, activities and controls built into systems), personnel and locations by practitioners performing an audit engagement
- Limitations of authority of the audit function and practitioners, if any
- Processes to be audited that the audit function is authorized to audit (e.g., freedom of the audit function to determine the processes that it will audit, based on the risk-based audit plan)

[3] ITAF 2001.2.3
[4] ITAF 2001.2.4

ISACA. All Rights Reserved.

Accountability

Accountability of the audit function is demonstrated through its reports to those charged with governance and oversight of the audit function. The reports may include, but are not limited to, results of management progress on agreed-on implementations and summaries of the audit department performance metrics. The responsibilities through which accountability is determined may be included in the audit charter. For example, the audit charter could describe:[5]

- Required reporting to those charged with governance and oversight of the audit function on the independence of the function and any potential impairments to independence
- Quality assurance process
- Staffing rules for audit engagements[6]

The audit charter should be communicated to executive/senior management. Relevant elements of the audit charter may be shared with groups being audited.[7] The audit charter should be reviewed periodically to ensure that the purpose and responsibilities in practice align with the purpose and responsibilities documented and that the charter aligns with the enterprise mission and strategies. An immediate review of the audit charter should be conducted if the enterprise mission or strategies change or if the audit function responsibilities change. This review should take place on at least an annual basis and also when responsibilities change.[8] Once established, the audit charter should be changed only if the change is thoroughly justified.

ADDITIONAL GUIDANCE

For additional guidance, see ISACA Standard 1001 Audit Charter and Guideline 2001 Audit Charter.

1.2.2 The Business, IT and IT Audit

An IT auditor should have a strong understanding of the business and goals of the enterprise. This includes understanding business processes, internal controls and IT mechanisms for supporting the business strategy.

Strategic Business Goals and IT

When an enterprise decides on a strategy, achievement of the strategy requires support from a variety of functions across the enterprise. IT plays a two-pronged role. Its support of the strategy may be through customer-facing activities, e.g., creating a new customer website, or its support of the strategy may be through supporting the enterprise operations. Either way, the goals established by the business line drive the priorities of IT. The role of the IT auditor in the alignment of business goals with IT is providing assurance. When an IT auditor performs an IT audit or assessment, the auditor provides assurance to the enterprise of IT's contribution to business goals.

IT Strategic Planning

Strategic planning is the process of determining the enterprise objectives, changes to the objectives, and policies to govern their adoption and use. Strategic planning from an IT standpoint is how an enterprise wants to leverage IT in the long term to improve its business processes. Generally three to five years in duration, strategic plans should be fully aligned and consistent with overall enterprise goals and objectives. IT department management, the IT steering committee, and the strategy committee (which provides valuable strategic input related to stakeholder value), play

[5] ITAF 2001.2.5
[6] ITAF 2001.2.6
[7] ITAF 1001.3
[8] ITAF 1001.4

ISACA. All Rights Reserved.

key roles in the development and implementation of the plans. Given the IT strategic plan's alignment with the overall business strategy, an IT auditor should understand the importance of strategic planning. Considerations include management control practices and, in particular, the need to assess how operational, tactical or business development plans are considered in IT strategy formulation. Attention should be given to requirements for updating, communicating, monitoring and evaluating plans.

Three Lines Model

The Institute of Internal Auditors® (IIA®) updated its governance and risk management guidance, the Three Lines Model (formerly Three Lines of Defense) in 2020.[9] **Figure 1.1** shows the Three Lines Model. Six principles and the core roles of management, internal audit and the enterprise governing body constitute the updated model guidance for helping enterprises "identify structures and processes that best assist the achievement of objectives and facilitate strong governance and risk management."[10]

Figure 1.1—IIA's Three Lines Model

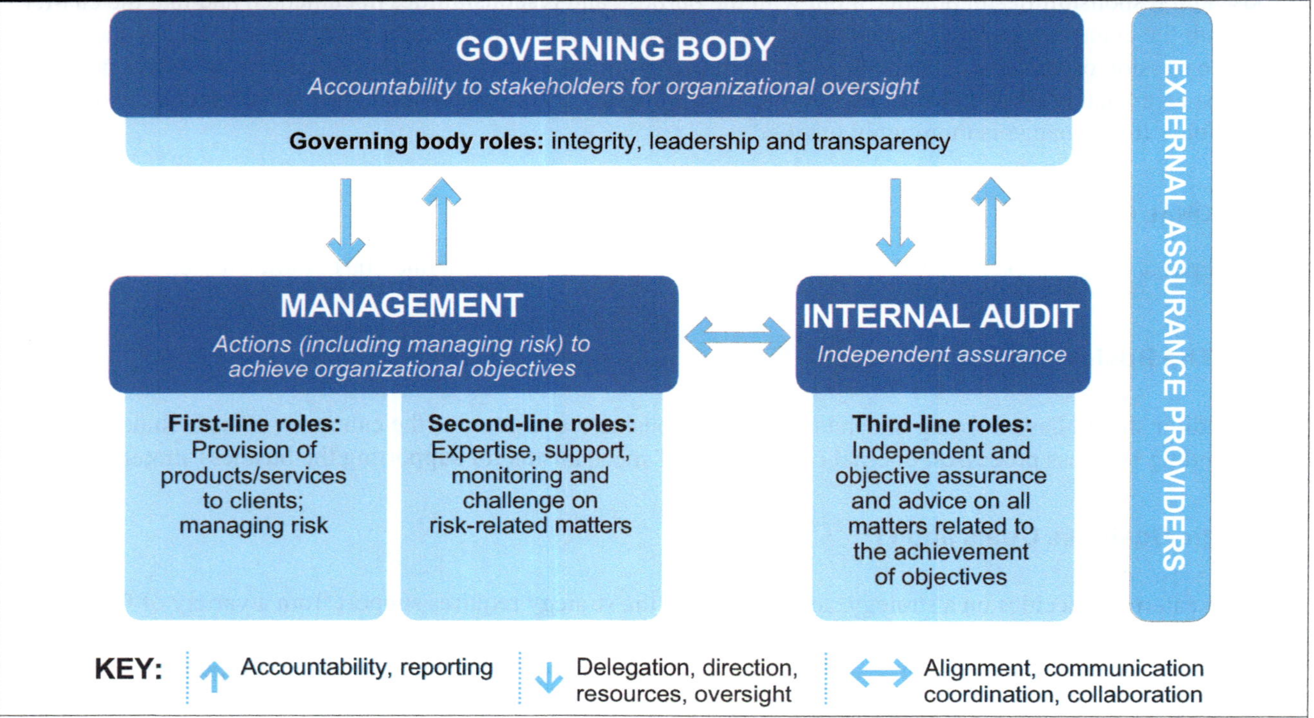

Source: Copyright © 2022 by The Institute of Internal Auditors®, Inc. (IIA®). All rights reserved. Permission was obtained from IIA to publish this reproduction, which is the same in all material respects as the original, unless approved as changed. See The Institute of Internal Auditors, "The IIA's Three Lines Model: An Update of the Three Lines of Defense," July 2020, *www.theiia.org/globalassets/documents/resources/the-iias-three-lines-model-an-update-of-the-three-lines-of-defense-july-2020/three-lines-model-updated.pdf*.

In the Three Lines Model, the governing body, management and internal audit perform the following roles and activities:[11]

[9] The Institute of Internal Auditors®, "The IIA's Three Lines Model: An Update of the Three Lines of Defense," July 2020, *www.theiia.org/globalassets/documents/resources/the-iias-three-lines-model-an-update-of-the-three-lines-of-defense-july-2020/three-lines-model-updated.pdf*

[10] Poulton, L.; "The New Three Lines Model: a step forward for risk and compliance," Thomson Reuters Practical Law In-House Blog, 30 July 2020, *http://in-houseblog.practicallaw.com/the-new-three-lines-model-a-step-forward-for-risk-and-compliance/*

[11] *Ibid.*

ISACA. All Rights Reserved.

- **Governing body**—Accountability (e.g., establish the internal audit function and ensure alignment of organizational objectives/activities with stakeholders' interests)
- **Management (first and second lines)**—Action (e.g., manage risk, achieve organizational objectives)
- **Internal Audit (third line)**—Assurance (e.g., assure adequacy and effectiveness of governance and risk management)

Further, the IIA describes the interactions of all core roles. Specifically for internal auditors, the guidance highlights the following for core interactions with management and the governing body (**figure 1.2**).

Figure 1.2—Core Interactions for Auditors in Three Lines Model

Core Role	Interaction With Internal Audit Should Reflect Internal Audit's:
Management	• Collaboration and communication with management to prevent duplication • Independence from management that supports the internal audit function by giving it the latitude to perform its work without hindrance[12]
Governing body	• Accountability to the governing body • Receipt of governing body approval and resources provided in support of the audit plan[13]

Source: ISACA, *CISA® Review Manual, 27th Edition*, USA, 2019, figure 2.5, *www.isaca.org/bookstore/cisa-exam-resources/crm27ed*

1.3 Audit Function Organization and Enterprise Relationships

Audit services should be managed to establish and maintain the organizational independence of the audit function. Organizational independence is best understood when considering internal relationships and functions that drive IT activities and govern the enterprise and external relationships that provide further audit and assurance services.

1.3.1 Organizational Independence

Overall, the IT audit function should be independent of the area or activity being reviewed to permit objective completion of the audit and assurance engagement. Independence entails:

- Self-governance (i.e., an audit department that is established by an audit charter and that functions outside an operational department)[14]
- Freedom from conditions that threaten objectivity or the appearance of objectivity. (Threats to objectivity must be managed at the individual auditor, engagement, functional and organizational levels. Independence includes independence of mind and independence in appearance.)

Independence may be supported when the audit function:

- Reports to a level within the enterprise that provides organizational (enterprise) independence and enables the IT audit function to perform its responsibilities without interference, e.g., the audit department reports functionally to the board of directors and administratively to the chief executive officer (CEO).
- Discloses the details of the impairment to the appropriate parties if independence is impaired in fact or appearance.
- Does not perform nonaudit roles in IT initiatives that require assumption of management responsibilities because such roles could impair future independence.

12 *Op cit* The Institute of Internal Auditors
13 *Ibid.*
14 *Op cit* ISACA, *IT Audit Framework (ITAF™): A Professional Practices Framework for IT Audit*

ISACA. All Rights Reserved.

- Addresses independence and accountability of the audit function in its charter and/or engagement letter.

To ensure organizational independence, the audit function should reside outside any operational department reporting to the head of an operational department or being assigned any operational responsibilities or activities that can compromise organizational independence.[15]

Independence should be assessed by the audit function at least on an annual basis and confirmed with those charged with governance and oversight of the audit function.[16]

ADDITIONAL GUIDANCE

For additional guidance, see ISACA Standard 1002 Organizational Independence and Guideline 2002 Organizational Independence

1.3.2 Enterprise (Internal) Relationships

An IT audit function supports relationships with many departments and functions within an enterprise. An IT auditor must be aware of the purposes, responsibilities and roles that these relationships and functions play that are applicable to IT-related activities. Descriptions of these departments and functions follow.

Board of Directors and Senior Management

The board of directors is accountable and liable for the enterprise. Pertaining to IT-related activities, a board of directors is responsible for the stewardship of IT resources and assigns senior management with the responsibility for implementation of necessary IT systems and controls. Board members and senior management need to be aware of the enterprise IT assets and their criticality to ongoing business operations. The board of directors and senior management are responsible for ensuring that the enterprise IT department sustains and extends the enterprise strategies and objectives.

In the US, there are instances in which federal legislation (e.g., Foreign Corrupt Practices Act, Fair Labor Standards Act) creates individual accountability for those serving on boards. Globally, this individual liability for board members also exists under the EU General Data Protection Regulation (GDPR). A claimant usually pursues the financial resources of a corporation over those of an individual, however, exposure may exist for individuals.

Business Process Owners

A business process is a set of interrelated cross-functional activities or events that result in the delivery of a specific product or service to a customer. A business process is controlled by policies, procedures, practices and organizational structures designed to provide reasonable assurance that a business process will achieve its objectives.

A business process owner is the individual responsible for identifying process requirements, approving process design and managing process performance. A business process owner must be at an appropriately high level in the enterprise and have authority to commit resources.

Some examples of business processes include:

- **E-commerce**—Buying and selling of goods online using technology to process transactions

[15] ITAF 2002.2.1
[16] ITAF 2002.4.1

ISACA. All Rights Reserved.

- **Electronic Data Interchange (EDI)**—Transmission, translation and storage of transactions initiated by or destined for application processing
- **Point-of-Sale Systems**—Process of capturing data at the time and place that the transaction occurs
- **Electronic Funds Transfer**—Electronic transfer of funds between a buyer and seller via their respective financial institutions

IT Strategy Committee

An IT strategy committee is at the level of the board of directors and ensures that the board is involved in major IT matters and decisions. The committee is primarily accountable for managing the portfolios of IT-enabled investments, IT services and other IT resources, and is the owner of the portfolios. The committee focuses on current and future strategic IT issues and advises the board of directors and senior management on IT strategy.

IT Steering Committee

An IT steering committee is an executive management-level committee that assists in the delivery of the IT strategy, oversees day-to-day management of IT service delivery and IT projects, and focuses on implementation. This committee typically serves as a general review board for major IT projects and should not become involved in routine operations. Although IT steering committee responsibilities vary from enterprise to enterprise, examples of primary functions that this committee performs include:

- Reviewing the long- and short-range plans of the IT department to ensure that they align with the corporate objectives.
- Approving and monitoring major projects and statuses of IT plans and budgets, establishing priorities, approving standards and procedures, and monitoring overall IT performance.
- Reviewing and approving sourcing strategies for select or all IT activities, including insourcing and outsourcing, and the globalization or offshoring of functions.

Chief Information Officer

The chief information officer (CIO) is the most senior official of the enterprise who is accountable for conducting IT advocacy; aligning IT and business strategies; planning, resourcing and managing the delivery of IT services and information; and deploying associated human resources. The CIO, along with the enterprise's chief executive officer (CEO), is concerned with how the enterprise can achieve strategic business and IT alignment. The CIO's role is to ask questions that focus attention on important IT issues.

Chief Information Security Officer

The chief information security officer (CISO) is the person in charge of information security within the enterprise. All enterprises have someone responsible for security, regardless of whether anyone holds the CISO title. Due to its scope and breadth, the authority required, and the responsibility that must be assumed, information security leadership is a senior officer or top management role. Legal responsibility, by default, extends up the command structure and ultimately resides with senior management and the board of directors. Failure to recognize this and implement appropriate governance structures can result in a lack of effective alignment of business objectives and security activities.

ISACA. All Rights Reserved.

Risk Management

Risk management is the discipline by which an enterprise in any industry assesses, controls, exploits, finances and monitors risk from all sources for the purpose of increasing the enterprise short- and long-term value to its stakeholders.

Risk management involves the coordination of activities that direct and control an enterprise regarding risk. Risk management requires the development and implementation of internal controls to manage and mitigate risk throughout the enterprise, including financial, operational, reputational, investment, physical security and cybersecurity risk.

Although each IT business opportunity carries the potential to support and enrich enterprise goals and operations, there are various degrees of risk when an enterprise is dependent on IT. Risk management must balance the operational needs of the business with the need for effective controls, while maintaining productivity. The management of IT-related risk must maintain focus on the preservation of value and ensure that the measurement of risk is transparent, showing the impacts and contributions of IT-related business risk optimization.

Risk must be evaluated across the entire enterprise, not just on a system-wide or department-wide basis. Having a grasp of the big picture helps risk managers align their efforts with the enterprise business priorities and culture. Whenever a change to systems or processes is being considered, a prudent risk management assessment can allow the enterprise to avoid unnecessary situations in which high levels of risk may be encountered.

One of the steps of the risk management process is to identify the IT-related business vulnerabilities and assess their impact on stakeholders. A vulnerability is a weakness in the design, implementation, operation or internal control of a process that can expose the system to adverse threats.

An IT vulnerability is a characteristic of an information resource that can be exploited by a threat, causing harm or damage. Examples of vulnerabilities include:

- Lack of user knowledge
- Lack of security functionality
- Poor authentication practices
- Untested technology
- Unprotected transmissions
- Unprotected storage

A vulnerability can exist because of a weakness in design, implementation, operation or internal control. A vulnerability can be increased or decreased by vulnerability events, e.g., the weakening of controls. Exploitation of vulnerabilities can impact the enterprise in many ways. Examples of impacts include:

- Direct loss of value/money
- Breach of legislation/regulations
- Loss of reputation/goodwill
- Endangering staff or customers
- Breach of confidence
- Loss of business opportunity
- Reduction in operational efficiency/performance
- Interruption of business activity

ISACA. All Rights Reserved.

The risk management process should include an assessment to formulate an overall risk view or risk profile for the enterprise, calculating the probability of occurrence and impacts for each threat. Responses to address each identified risk should then be determined. If risk mitigation is chosen to address a risk, then controls can be evaluated to reduce vulnerabilities to an acceptable level.

Compliance

Compliance applies to the adherence to, and the ability to demonstrate adherence to, not only requirements mandated by laws and regulations, but also requirements resulting from voluntary contractual obligations and internal policies.

Compliance includes issues of data governance, data privacy and protection, operational risk, and information security. The complex nature of IT and global connectivity introduced various types of risk within the enterprise information life cycle—from receipt, processing, storage, transmission and distribution, through destruction. To protect stakeholder interests, various legal and regulatory requirements have been enacted.

The IT auditor should review legislative and regulatory requirements pertaining to the access and use of IT resources, systems and data to assess whether IT assets are effectively protected and whether associated risk is managed appropriately.

When determining the compliance level of an enterprise with external requirements, an IT auditor should be aware of:

- Government or other relevant external requirements dealing with:
  - Electronic data, personal data, copyrights, e-commerce, e-signatures, etc.
  - IT practices and controls
  - Data and program storage
  - IT activities and audits
- Applicable laws and regulations that apply to the enterprise geographical area and industry
- External requirements that can affect business plans; setting enterprise policies, standards and procedures; and business application
- IT department activities that address adherence to laws or regulations
- Enterprise procedures that address legal and regulatory compliance requirements
- Contracts or agreements with external IT service providers that contain legal or regulatory requirements related to services provided

Information Security

Information security ensures that, within the enterprise, information is protected against disclosure to unauthorized users (confidentiality), improper modification (integrity), and failure of timely and reliable access to and use of information when required (availability). Information security exists to support and further the business objectives of the enterprise by managing risk, to limit disruptions to acceptable levels. All enterprise processes must be assessed and appropriate security requirements applied, to minimize disruptions and achieve business objectives.

The IT auditor is responsible for the evaluation of information security policies, standards and procedures to ensure completeness, alignment with generally accepted practices and compliance with applicable external requirements. An IT audit can help to determine information security deficiencies from a controls and compliance standpoint and is one of the essential resources in strategy development.

ISACA. All Rights Reserved.

An IT auditor should develop a good working relationship with information-security-related functions to achieve good security governance and compliance. An IT auditor can be instrumental in implementing security standards by providing feedback to senior management through reviews and audit findings that can serve to influence the tone at the top and create high-level support for information security activities.

IT Department

An IT auditor interacts frequently with IT management and staff, and should be familiar with the structure and responsibilities of an IT department. An IT department can be structured in different ways. One such format is shown in **figure 1.3**.

Figure 1.3—Example IT Department Structure

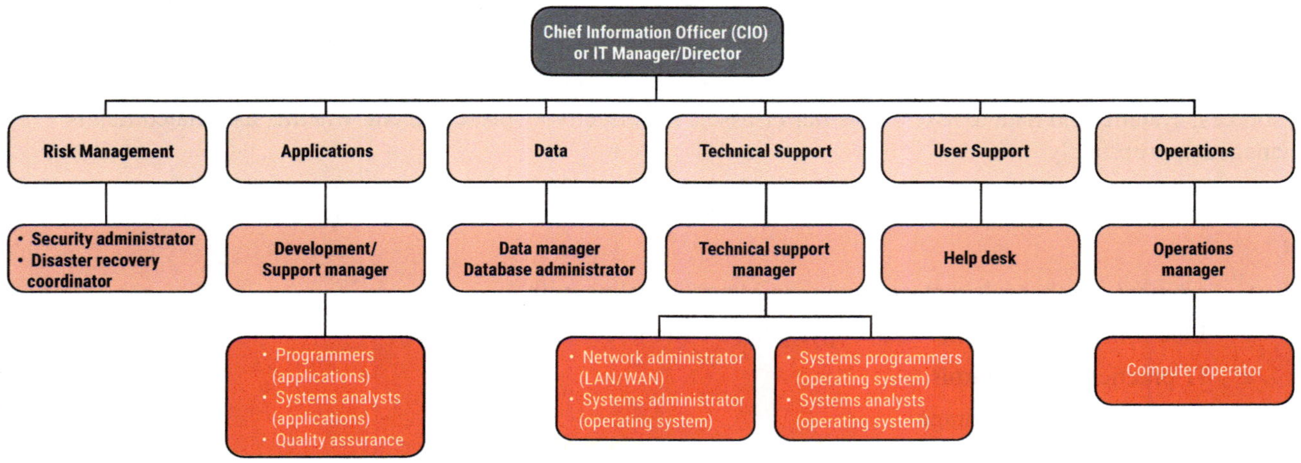

Source: ISACA, *CISA® Review Manual, 27th Edition*, USA, 2019, figure 2.5, *www.isaca.org/bookstore/cisa-exam-resources/crm27ed*

The organizational chart in **figure 1.3** includes functions related to security, applications development and maintenance; technical support for network and systems administration; and operations. The IT department is typically headed by an IT manager/director or, in large enterprises, by a CIO.

It is important for an IT auditor to be familiar with the IT department hierarchy, authorities and roles. Generally, an IT auditor interacts with the following IT roles and should be familiar with the roles and their responsibilities:

- **Systems development**—Implementing new systems and maintaining existing systems, typically performed by programmers and analysts. An IT auditor should be familiar with documentation standards and practices, and be able to review documentation for a given system and determine whether it follows the enterprise documentation standards. In addition, an IT auditor should understand the current approaches to developing systems and how documentation is constructed. An IT auditor should be able to recognize IT documentation components, such as database specifications, file layouts and self-documented program listings.
- **Project management**—Planning and execution of IT projects. Project management staff use budgets assigned to them for the delivery of IT initiatives and report project progress to the IT steering committee. Project managers play a central role in executing the vision of the IT strategy and steering committees by planning, coordinating and delivering IT projects to the enterprise. An IT auditor should have a thorough understanding of the phases of project management.
- **Help desk (service desk)**—Responding to technical questions and problems faced by users within an enterprise.

ISACA. All Rights Reserved.

- **End-user support**—Acting as a liaison between the IT department and the end users. End users are responsible for operations related to business application services. There is a small distinction between the terms end user and user. End user refers specifically to someone who will access a business application. User is broader and can refer to administrative accounts and accounts used to access platforms.
- **Data management**—Building the data architecture in large IT environments and managing data as enterprise assets.
- **Quality assurance (QA)**—Negotiating and facilitating quality activities in all areas of IT.
- **Third-party management**—Providing direction to the outsourcer on issues and escalating internally within the enterprise and IT function; monitoring and reporting on service levels to management; reviewing changes to the contract due to new requirements and obtaining IT approvals.
- **Infrastructure operations and maintenance**—Ensuring efficient and effective computer and data center operations, typically performed by computer operators, librarians, schedulers and data control personnel. The data center includes the servers and mainframe; peripherals, such as high-speed printers; networking equipment; magnetic media and storage area networks. The control group in this area is responsible for the collection, conversion and control of input, and the balancing and distribution of output to the user community.
- **Media management**—Managing all program and data files maintained on removable media.
- **Data entry**—Processing information, including batch or online entry. In most enterprises, personnel in user departments do their own data entry online. In many online environments, data are captured from the original source. An IT auditor should be familiar with the user department and the system application controls to ensure that data are validated, accurate, complete and authorized.
- **Supervisory control and data acquisition (SCADA)**—Controlling and monitoring industrial and manufacturing processes and utility facilities. The term SCADA usually refers to centralized systems that monitor and control entire sites, or complexes of systems spread out over large areas (kilometers or miles). These systems are typical in industrial plants, steel mills, power plants and electrical facilities.
- **Systems administration**—Maintaining major multiuser computer systems, including local area networks (LANs), wireless local area networks (WLANs), wide area networks (WANs), virtual machine/server/network environments, personal area networks (PANs), storage area networks (SANs), intranets and extranets, and midrange and mainframe systems.
- **Security administration**—Ensuring that users comply with the enterprise security policy and that controls are adequate to prevent unauthorized access to enterprise assets, including data, programs and equipment). Security administration typically works with compliance, risk management and audit functions to ensure that security is appropriately designed and updated based on audit feedback or testing.
- **Database administration**—Managing the custody of enterprise data, and the definition and maintenance of the data structures in the enterprise database system. Database administrators (DBA) are also responsible for the security of the shared data stored on database systems. Because the DBA has the capability of gaining access to all data, including production data, the IT department must exercise close control over database administration.
- **Systems analysis**—Designing systems based on the needs of the user.
- **Security architecture**—Evaluating security technologies and design of security aspects of network topology, access control, identity management and other security systems. The security architect establishes security policies and security requirements,, often working with compliance, risk management and audit functions to incorporate their requirements and recommendations into the security policies and architecture.
- **System security engineering**—Providing technical information system security engineering support to the enterprise and interacting with other enterprises on matters concerning acquisition, system management, certification, accreditation and evaluation.
- **Applications development and maintenance**—Developing and maintaining applications, including developing new code or changing the existing setup or configuration of the application. Staff develop the programs or change the application setup that will ultimately run in a production environment. Management must ensure that

ISACA. All Rights Reserved.

staff cannot modify production programs or application data. Staff should work in a test-only environment and submit their work to another group that is charged with moving programs and application changes into the production environment.

- **Infrastructure development and maintenance**—Maintaining the systems software, including the operating system (OS). Infrastructure staff access should be limited to only the system libraries of the specific software they maintain. Use of domain administration and superuser accounts should be tightly controlled and monitored.
- **Network administration**—Overseeing maintenance of key components of the infrastructure (e.g., routers, switches, firewalls, network segmentation, performance management, remote access).

The audit function ability to provide proper oversight and increase operational resilience is supported by auditors:

- Establishing and maintaining a collaborative relationship with the IT department
- Keeping current on changes in technology

An early and ongoing collaboration with the IT department helps the IT auditor to identify and mitigate operational gaps and potential risk. This collaboration can give the IT team advantages, such as staying within budget and getting buy-in from the rest of the enterprise. Although IT is naturally more focused on the technical aspects of project implementations, user training, etc., the fresh, outside perspective of IT audit can spot potential pitfalls and help with timely course corrections.

In addition to maintaining a collaborative relationship with the IT department, IT auditors are charged with being aware of changes in technology. Every adoption of new technology within an organization changes its risk landscape. The auditor's time spent self-educating on emerging and newer technologies facilitates the auditor's ability to have informed discussions with the IT department.

1.4 External Relationships

An IT audit function often maintains relationships with entities outside an enterprise. These relationships may be with:

- An IT auditor from an external firm
- A management consultant
- An expert in the area of the engagement who has been appointed by top management or by the audit team

Other examples of experts with whom the audit function may liaise include government regulators and compliance program assessors.

1.4.1 Relationship with External Audit Firm

An external audit firm typically provides many services. These services include independent audit of enterprise financial statements, risk and regulatory compliance, and managed services, such as controls testing and monitoring. The Public Company Accounting Standards Board (PCAOB) provides guidance on services that the external auditor function can provide, particularly services that are performed concurrently with an audit, in its Ethics and Independence Rules paragraph .05, entitled "Performance of other services."[17]

External IT auditors assess the systems that support transactions that flow to the financial statements. An external IT auditor must understand the IT systems underpinning business processes relevant for financial reporting and how the entity has responded to risk arising from IT. Because the use of IT affects the way control activities are implemented in the enterprise and related financial reporting, an external IT auditor needs to consider whether the entity has

[17] PCAOB, "ET Section 100 Independence, Integrity, and Objectivity," *https://pcaobus.org/oversight/standards/ethics-independence-rules/details/ET101*

ISACA. All Rights Reserved.

responded adequately to risk arising from IT by establishing effective general IT controls and application controls. **Figure 1.4** shows differences between internal and external audit/assurance reviews.

Figure 1.4—Comparison of Internal and External Assurance Reviews

Characteristic	Internal Audit	External Audit
Independence requirements	Independence of internal auditors should be established, verified and maintained.	Independence of the external auditors should be established, verified and maintained.
Interested party (user)	Executive management, audit committee, operational management and enabler owners are involved.	Primarily directed toward the board/shareholders but of importance to the enterprise in general
Responsible party (accountable party)	Management and business enabled owners are involved.	The board and executive management are involved.
Assurance provider (assurance professional)	Internal auditor	External auditor
Reporting format and requirements	Internal consistency is required, in line with professional standards.	Highly regulated/standardized
Governing rules/standards	Standardized approaches are based on good practices. Professional standards and code of ethics are required.	Adherence to applicable codes of ethics and professional standards required
Level of trust (reliability)	Medium—depends on the skill and expertise of the internal audit function and on cooperation of the accountable party.	Maximum—the skill and expertise of the external auditor are essential requirements of all audit assignments.

Source: Adapted from ISACA, *CGEIT® Review Manual, 8th Edition,* USA, 2020, *www.isaca.org/bookstore/cgeit-exam-resources/cgm8ed*

If IT audit services are provided by an external audit firm, the scope and objectives of the services should be documented in a formal contract or statement of work between the contracting enterprise and the firm. In either case, the internal audit function should be independent and report to an audit committee, if one exists, or to the highest management level, such as the board of directors.

Depending on the scope, terms and materiality of the audit engagement and in accordance with relevant IT auditing standards, an external audit firm may rely on the work of IT auditors within the enterprise. After the external auditor has evaluated and tested the internal auditor's work, the work may be relied on.

This work and any other work based on the relationship with an external audit firm should be described in the audit charter or engagement letters.[18] This relationship should be documented with detail on how the internal and external auditor firms may rely on each other's work. Considerations may include, but should not be limited to, how:

- Work will be coordinated to minimize any duplication of effort.
- Audit documentation and evidence will be shared.
- Work planned by the external auditors will affect the audit plan for the upcoming period.[19]

[18] ITAF 2402.10.1
[19] ITAF 2001.2.4

ISACA. All Rights Reserved.

1.4.2 Using the Work of Other Auditors and Experts

In highly specialized areas, in addition to enlisting internal experts from areas such as risk or compliance, an audit department may use external experts when there is a lack of departmental knowledge required to perform a specific IT audit.[20] External experts can include practitioners in emerging or newer technologies, such as blockchain, machine learning (ML) or artificial intelligence (AI). External experts may also have specialized knowledge in specific technologies, such as networking, automated teller machines, wireless, systems integration and digital forensics, or they may be subject matter experts in a particular industry or area of specialization, such as banking, securities trading, insurance or the law. If external experts are used, or there will be a reliance on prior testing performed by other entities (external auditors or regulators), a protocol should be established. The protocol should define:

- Circumstances in which reliance on the work of others is an appropriate strategy
- Initial assessment and ongoing monitoring of the qualifications of those external to the audit function who will perform work for the audit function
- Circumstances that might warrant exclusions from engagements due to reliance on work of others

The following should be considered when determining whether to outsource some or all IT audit services to an external provider:

- Restrictions on outsourcing of audit/security services provided by laws and regulations
- Audit charter or contractual stipulations
- Impact on overall and specific IT audit objectives
- Impact on IT audit risk and professional liability
- Independence and objectivity of other auditors and experts
- Professional competence, qualifications and experience
- Scope of work proposed to be outsourced and approach
- Supervisory and audit management controls
- Method and modalities of communication of results of audit work
- Compliance with legal and regulatory stipulations
- Compliance with applicable professional standards

Based on the nature of the IT audit, the following may also require special consideration:

- Testimonials/references and background checks
- Access to systems, premises and records
- Confidentiality restrictions to protect customer-related information
- Computer-assisted auditing techniques (CAATs) and other tools used by the external audit service provider
- Standards and methodologies for performance of work and documentation
- Nondisclosure agreements

The IT auditor or entity outsourcing the auditing services should monitor the relationship to ensure objectivity and independence throughout the duration of the service. Although some or all of the audit work may be delegated to an external party, the related professional liability is not necessarily delegated. It is the responsibility of the IT auditor or enterprise employing audit services to do the following:

- Clearly communicate the audit objectives, scope and methodology through a formal engagement letter.

[20] ITAF 2206.2.2

ISACA. All Rights Reserved.

- Establish a monitoring process for regular review of the work of the external audit firm with regard to planning, supervision, review and documentation. The work performed and reports issued by external IT auditors or experts should be reviewed to confirm that:
  - The scope specified in the audit charter, terms of reference or letter of engagement has been met.
  - Any significant assumptions used by external IT auditors or experts have been identified.
  - The findings and conclusions reported by external IT auditors have been agreed to by management.
- Assess the usefulness and appropriateness of the work and reports of external IT audit providers, and assess the impact of significant findings on the overall audit objectives.

After assessing the work of other experts, an IT auditor should apply additional test procedures to gain sufficient and appropriate audit evidence if the work of other experts does not provide such evidence. In addition, an IT auditor should consider whether supplemental testing or reperformance of the work of other experts is required.[21]

ADDITIONAL GUIDANCE

For additional guidance, see ISACA Standard 1206 Using the Work of Other Experts and Guideline 2206 Using the Work of Other Experts.

[21] ITAF 2206.6.2

ISACA. All Rights Reserved.

Page intentionally left blank

ISACA. All Rights Reserved.

1.5 Knowledge Check

Review questions are an assessment of knowledge of the fundamentals of IT auditing and related topics.

For individuals intending to earn the ISACA Fundamentals of IT Auditing Certificate, these questions are written to depict the type of questions that may appear on the exam. They do not specifically appear on the exam, but similar ones may appear.

Review Questions

1. The purpose, authority, responsibility and accountability of the audit function and the role of IT audit should be defined and described in an:

   A. Audit program
   B. Audit charter
   C. Audit plan

2. To ensure organizational independence, the audit function should report to those responsible for:

   A. IT operations
   B. Enterprise governance
   C. Compliance with government regulations

3. How often should an IT auditor interact and collaborate with the IT department?

   A. Infrequently, to ensure objectivity
   B. Occasionally, to share results of recent audits
   C. Frequently, to understand IT department responsibilities and upcoming projects

4. Which of the following **BEST** describes the internal audit function role in governance and risk management?

   A. Advises on risk and tests the effectiveness of internal controls
   B. Manages risk and establishes an internal control structure
   C. Monitors risk and challenges the effectiveness of controls

5. When IT audit work is outsourced to an external provider, the entity outsourcing the audit services should:

   A. Require the external provider to establish the audit objectives, scope and methodology that will be used to conduct the audit.
   B. Wait to review the planning, supervision and documentation of the audit work performed by the external provider until all audit work has been completed.
   C. Assess the audit work of the external provider and consider performing supplemental testing if the audit work and results are not sufficient or useful.

Answers on page 32

ISACA. All Rights Reserved.

Chapter 1 ANSWER KEY

Review Questions

1. A. An audit program is a step-by-step set of audit procedures and instructions.

   B. An audit charter is a document approved by those charged with governance that defines and documents the purpose, authority, responsibility and accountability of the audit function and the role of IT audit.

   C. An audit plan is a high-level description of the audit work to be performed in a certain period of time by the auditor or a team of auditors.

2. A. To ensure organizational independence, the audit function should be an independent function or department outside any operational department (e.g., IT operations).

   B. To ensure organizational independence, the audit function should report to those charged with governance (e.g., the board of directors for their input and/or approval).

   C. To ensure organizational independence, the audit function should be independent of any operational responsibilities or activities that could compromise organizational independence (e.g., an activity that is responsible for regulatory compliance that is subject to an audit).

3. A. It is important for an IT auditor to realize that audit objectives and priorities may not always be the same as those of the IT department when it comes to specific IT projects and that an IT auditor must remain objective. However, this should not hinder an IT auditor's ability to interact and collaborate with an IT department to learn about IT projects before they actually occur, to participate in planning sessions or to discuss any risk that the enterprise may be taking on.

   B. An early and ongoing collaboration between the IT auditor and IT department helps to identify and mitigate operational gaps and potential risk. Such frequent interaction can give the IT department a fresh, outside perspective of IT, while IT audit can spot potential pitfalls and help with timely course corrections.

   C. To properly interact with IT department management and staff, an IT auditor should be familiar with the structure and responsibilities of an IT department and should frequently spend time meeting with IT staff to understand their responsibilities, observe their roles and discuss upcoming projects.

4. **A. The audit function responsibilities (third line) include advising the governing body and risk management function on the effectiveness of internal controls and testing internal controls.**

   B. The management function first line responsibilities include managing risk and establishing an internal control structure.

   C. The management function second line responsibilities include monitoring risk and controls and challenging the effectiveness of controls and management of risk across the enterprise.

5. A. It is the responsibility of the IT auditor or enterprise employing audit services to clearly communicate the audit objectives, scope and methodology through a formal engagement letter.

   B. The IT auditor or enterprise employing audit services should establish a monitoring process for regular review of the work of the external audit firm with regard to planning, supervision, review and documentation.

   C. The IT auditor or enterprise employing audit services should assess the usefulness and appropriateness of the work and reports of external IT audit providers and assess the impact of significant findings on the overall audit objectives. Based on the IT auditor's assessment of the work of other experts, the auditor should apply additional test procedures to gain sufficient and appropriate audit evidence if the work of other experts does not provide such evidence. In addition, an IT auditor should consider whether supplemental testing of the work of other experts is required.

ISACA. All Rights Reserved.

IT AUDIT
FUNDAMENTALS
An ISACA® Certificate

Chapter 2:
Controls, Risk and Audit

Controls, Risk and Audit

ISACA. All Rights Reserved.

Controls, Risk and Audit

2.1 Learning Objectives

This chapter delves into the establishment, management and monitoring of internal and IT controls. After completing this chapter, learners will be able to:

- Articulate the purpose of internal controls.
- Describe how controls contribute to the achievement of business objectives.
- Identify different types of controls.
- Distinguish between IT risk and related controls.
- Summarize the intent and difference between preventive, detective and corrective controls.
- Describe common standards and frameworks that apply to risk management and control.
- Define the relationship between control and risk.
- Explain how to monitor and assess controls.
- Describe the purpose and use of continuous auditing.
- Articulate the benefits of risk-based auditing.
- Explain the Agile approach to auditing and what makes it unique.
- Define audit risk and explain how to reduce it.

2.2 Internal Controls and Control Objectives

Each enterprise has a mission and goals that it wishes to achieve. While management plays a role in the actions taken to make these goals a reality, auditors ensure that management's actions are aligned with the mission. Tools that auditors use to provide this assurance are internal controls and control objectives, which are all part of the control environment.

2.2.1 Internal Controls

An internal control is composed of the policies, procedures, practices and organizational structures designed to provide reasonable assurance that business objectives will be achieved. Internal controls operate at all levels within an enterprise to mitigate its exposures to risk that potentially could prevent the enterprise from achieving its objectives.

The two key aspects that controls should address are:

- What should be achieved
- What should be avoided

Internal controls or control activities help ensure that management directives are carried out. They help ensure that necessary actions are taken to address risk, to achieve the enterprise business objectives. Control activities occur throughout the enterprise, at all levels and in all functions. They include a range of activities as diverse as approvals, authorizations, verifications, reconciliations, reviews of operating performance, security of assets and segregation of duties.

ISACA. All Rights Reserved.

2.2.2 Control Objectives

A control objective is a statement of the desired result or purpose to be achieved by implementing control procedures in a particular process. Control objectives may relate to the following concepts:

- Effectiveness and efficiency of operations
- Reliability of financial reporting
- Compliance with applicable laws and regulations[22]

Control objectives apply to all controls, whether they are manual, automated or a combination (e.g., review of system logs). Enterprise management makes choices relative to control objectives by:

- Selecting those that are applicable.
- Deciding on those that will be implemented.
- Choosing how to implement them (frequency, span, automation, etc.).
- Accepting the risk of not implementing those that may apply.

IT Control Objectives

Control objectives in an IT environment do not differ from those in a manual environment; however, the way controls are implemented may differ. Thus, IT control objectives need to be addressed based on their relevance to specific IT-related processes.

Specific IT control objectives include the following:

- Safeguarding assets so that information on automated systems is up to date and secure from improper access.
- Ensuring system development life cycle (SDLC) processes are established, in place and operating effectively to provide reasonable assurance that business, financial and/or industrial software systems and applications are developed in a repeatable and reliable manner to ensure that business objectives are met.
- Ensuring integrity of general OS environments, including network management and operations.
- Ensuring integrity of sensitive and critical application system environments, including accounting/financial and management information (information objectives) and customer data, through:
  - Authorization of the input. Each transaction is authorized and entered only once.
  - Validation of the input. Each input is validated and will not cause negative impact to the processing of transactions.
  - Accuracy and completeness of transaction processing. All transactions are recorded accurately and entered into the system for the proper period.
  - Reliability of overall information processing activities.
  - Accuracy, completeness and security of the output.
  - Database confidentiality, integrity and availability.
- Ensuring appropriate identification and authentication of users of IT resources (end users and infrastructure support).
- Ensuring the efficiency and effectiveness of operations (operational objectives).
- Complying with users' requirements, enterprise policies and procedures, and applicable laws and regulations (compliance objectives).

[22] Committee of Sponsoring Organizations of the Treadway Commission (COSO), *Internal Control – Integrated Framework: Executive Summary*, USA, May 2013, *https://www.coso.org/Shared%20Documents/Framework-Executive-Summary.pdf*

ISACA. All Rights Reserved.

- Ensuring availability of IT services by developing efficient business continuity plans (BCPs) and disaster recovery plans (DRPs) that include backup and recovery processes.
- Enhancing protection of data and systems by developing an incident response plan.
- Ensuring integrity and reliability of systems by implementing effective change management procedures.
- Ensuring that outsourced IT processes and services have clearly defined service level agreements (SLAs) and contract terms and conditions to ensure that the enterprise assets are properly protected and meet business goals and objectives.

When identifying test procedures, an IT auditor should ensure that the test is aligned with the controls, which in turn align with the control objectives.

Control Methods

Controls can be grouped by method as managerial (administrative), technical or physical (**figure 2.1**).

Figure 2.1—Control Categories

Category	Description
Managerial (administrative)	Controls related to the oversight, reporting, procedures and operations of a process. These include policy, procedures, balancing, employee development and compliance reporting
Technical	Controls also known as logical controls and are provided through the use of technology, piece of equipment or device. Examples include firewalls, network or host-based intrusion detection systems (IDSs), passwords and antivirus software. A technical control requires proper managerial (administrative) controls to operate correctly.
Physical	Controls that are locks, fences, closed-circuit TV (CCTV), and devices that are installed to physically restrict access to a facility or hardware. Physical controls require maintenance, monitoring and the ability to address and react to an alert should a problem be indicated.

Source: *CISA® Review Manual, 27th Edition*, USA, 2019, figure 5.4, *www.isaca.org/bookstore/cisa-exam-resources/crm27ed*

Often operational and administrative controls that concern day-to-day operations, functions and activities are included within managerial controls. Technical controls and physical controls, respectively, relate to the use of technology and the use of physical equipment or devices to regulate access.

An enterprise should maintain a correct balance of control types in order to meet its specific needs and help achieve its business objectives. For example, the implementation of a technical control, such as a firewall, requires training for the staff who manage or operate it, correct procedures for its configuration, assignment of responsibilities for its monitoring, and schedules for regular testing. If these coinciding controls are not in place, stakeholders may develop a false sense of security, resulting in unidentified vulnerabilities, an ineffective use of resources and greater risk than anticipated or intended.

IT-Specific Controls and Procedures

A well-designed IT system should have controls built in for all its sensitive or critical functions—for example, the general procedure to ensure that adequate safeguards over access to assets and facilities can be translated into an IT-related set of control procedures, covering access safeguards over computer programs, data and equipment. IT control procedures include:

- Strategy and direction of the IT function
- General organization and management of the IT function

ISACA. All Rights Reserved.

- Access to IT resources, including data and programs
- Systems development methodologies and change control
- Operations procedures
- Systems programming and technical support functions
- Quality assurance (QA) procedures
- Physical access controls
- BCP/DRP
- Networks and communication technology (e.g., local area networks, wide area networks, wireless)
- Database administration
- Protection and detective mechanisms against internal and external attacks

In an integrated application environment, controls are embedded and designed into the business application that supports the processes. Business process control assurance involves evaluating controls at the process and activity levels. These controls may be a combination of management, programmed and manual controls.

2.2.3 Control Classifications and Threat Events

Controls are implemented to provide reasonable assurance to management that the organization business objectives will be achieved, and risk events will be prevented or detected and corrected. Controls can be categorized into the following classes:

- **Preventive**—An internal control used to avoid undesirable events, errors and other occurrences that an enterprise has determined could have a negative material effect on a process or end product.
- **Detective**—Designed to detect and report when errors, omissions and unauthorized uses or entries occur.
- **Corrective**—Designed to correct errors, omissions and unauthorized uses and intrusions, once they are detected.

Figure 2.2 is summary of control classes and functions with examples. Fundamentally, the purpose of a preventive control is to identify problems before they arise or to prevent an error or a malicious act from occurring. Examples of preventive controls (in addition to those provided in **figure 2.2**) include:

- Application whitelisting
- Multifactor authentication
- Firewalls that block all traffic on ports known to be associated with malicious tools

Figure 2.2—Control Classification

Topics	Objective	Recommendations
Inventory	Establish and maintain an inventory	Users are expected to follow standards for managing computers connected to the network and have registered network addresses. The OS and owner should be included along with the data provided.
Malware	Install antivirus software with automatic updating	Antivirus software with an automatic DAT file should be updated at regular intervals—no less than weekly.
Passwords	Recognize the importance of passwords	Users must use only strong passwords. The IT department should provide password guidance. Departmental accounts are created for work groups to prevent/avoid password sharing.
Patching	Make it automatic—less work necessary, less chance for compromise	Each machine should be configured to patch automatically for OS and basic software patching. A process should be set up that works for the department and minimizes disruptions at inconvenient times. Workstations should be more automated to enable system administrators the time to give servers the attention required to minimize the impact on services offered.

ISACA. All Rights Reserved.

Figure 2.2—Control Classification *(cont.)*

Topics	Objective	Recommendations
Minimizing services offered by systems	Eliminate unnecessary services— reducing security risk and saving time in the long run	To improve basic security and minimize effort to maintain systems, workstations should offer only needed services. Many OSs are installed with services turned on. By removing services, the chance that a workstation will be compromised is reduced and security risk is minimized.
Addressing vulnerabilities	Eliminate many vulnerabilities with good system administration	System compromises can be time-consuming and damage credibility and the business integrity. Information from enterprisewide scans helps to identify vulnerabilities on each system and provide a baseline for comparison when system integrity is in question.
Backups	Allow easy recovery from user mistakes and hardware failure with backups	Backups should be made offsite for increased security.

Source: *CISA® Review Manual, 27th Edition*, USA, 2019, figure 1.5, *www.isaca.org/bookstore/cisa-exam-resources/crm27ed*

A detective control does not stop unauthorized uses or entries from occurring, but it indicates that a threat event (any event during which a threat element/actor interacts with an asset in a manner that has the potential to directly result in harm) has happened or is happening. Not everything can be blocked at the moment. However, by detecting a threat event, the enterprise can respond more promptly and limit any potential impact. If a threat event occurs, the purpose of a corrective control is to help an enterprise recover from the effects of an attack. For example, if unauthorized access has been gained to a specific enterprise computer, a procedure is initiated to protect the rest of the network.

In summary, detective and preventive controls are used to reduce the likelihood of a threat event (the probability of something happening), while corrective controls are intended to mitigate the consequences (**figure 2.3**).

Figure 2.3—Control Purpose

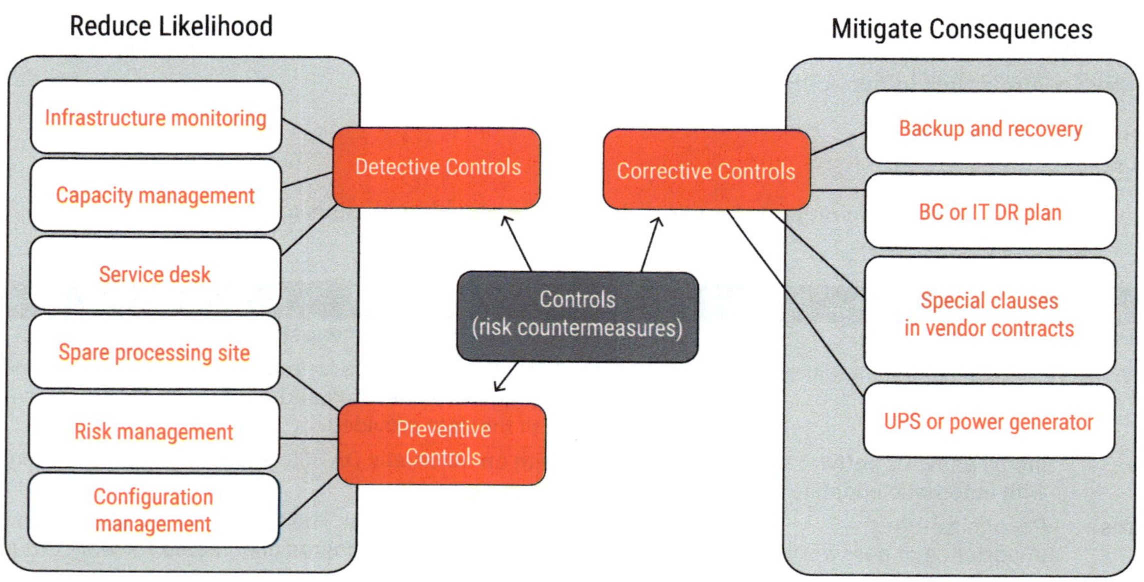

Source: ISACA, *Fundamentals of Information Systems Audit and Assurance* (Facilitator Guide), USA, 2018

ISACA. All Rights Reserved.

Figure 2.4 shows the interaction between control types and how they affect a threat event.

Figure 2.4—Interaction of Control Types and Threat Events

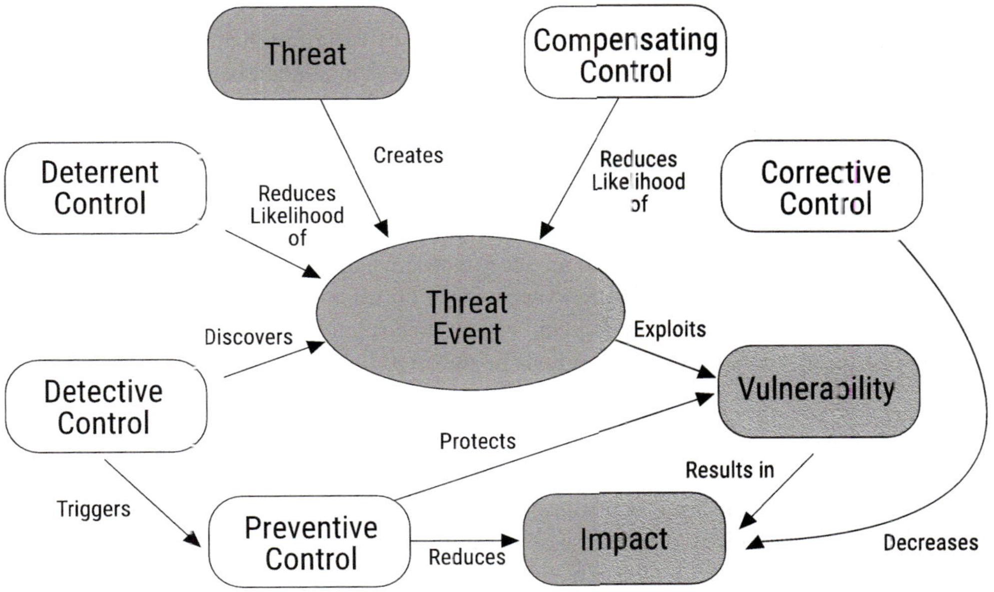

Source: Adapted from ISACA, *CRISC® Review Manual, 7th Edition*, USA, 2021, *https://store.isaca.org/s/store#/store/browse/detail/a2S4w000004Ko8XEAS*

2.2.4 Control Relationship to Risk

There is a direct relationship between risk and control that demonstrates that risk is addressed through control and control is justified by the risk it addresses. **Figure 2.5** shows this relationship.

Figure 2.5—Control Relationship to Risk

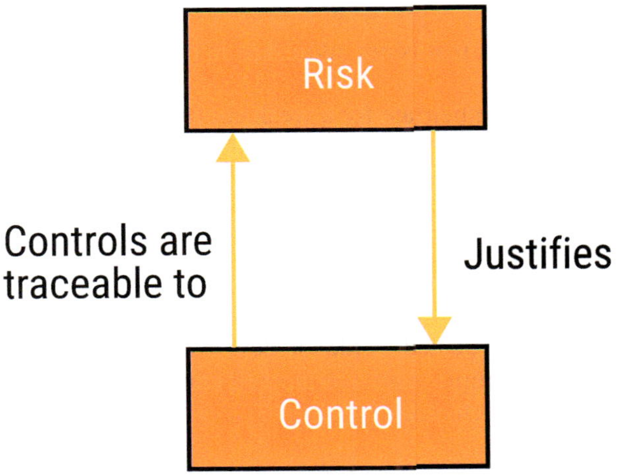

Source: ISACA, *IT Risk Fundamentals Study Guide*, USA, 2020, figure 1.6, *https://store.isaca.org/s/store#/store/browse/detail/a2S4w000004KoY1EAK*

ISACA. All Rights Reserved.

Prior to controls being implemented, the area being audited can be susceptible to error, assuming there are no related internal controls (inherent risk). Even after management has implemented a risk response, there may be remaining risk, which is called residual risk. In this case, the response is the mitigation or reduction of risk through the implementation of controls. The enterprise risk appetite (the amount of risk, on a broad level, that an entity is willing to accept in pursuit of its mission) determines the level of acceptable residual risk. Acceptable residual risk is typically expressed as risk tolerance, which is the acceptable level of variation that management is willing to allow for any particular risk as the enterprise pursues its objectives. There is a balance between the amount of risk that the enterprise is willing to mitigate, regarding cost, and the resulting impact on the overall residual risk levels. There may be circumstances in which the cost/business impact of risk mitigation options exceeds the capabilities/resources of an enterprise, thus forcing higher tolerance for one or more risk conditions.

Control weaknesses—deficiencies in the design or operation of a control procedure—can potentially result in risk relevant to the area of activity not being reduced to an acceptable level (i.e., relevant risk threatens achievement of the objectives pursuant to the area of activity being examined). Control weaknesses can be material when the design or operation of one or more control procedures does not reduce to a relatively low level the risk that misstatements caused by illegal acts or irregularities may occur and not be detected by the related control procedures.

Compensating Controls

If a control weakness exists, a compensating control may be considered when an enterprise cannot meet a stated requirement due to a legitimate technical or business constraint. However, the compensating control must achieve the same result as the control for which it is an alternative. Placing unsecured systems on isolated network segments with strong perimeter security and adding third-party challenge-response mechanisms to devices that do not support individual login accounts are examples of compensating controls. Although the following examples are IT-specific, it is possible for non-IT compensating controls to exist.

Compensating controls address weaknesses in the existing controls through concepts such as:

- Layered defense
- Increased supervision
- Procedural controls
- Increased audits and logging of system activity
- Administrative alerts
- Double-checking input data

These measures help to compensate for risk that is not addressed in other ways.

In some instances, a strong control may compensate for a weak control in another area. For example, if an IT auditor finds weaknesses in a system transaction error report, a detailed manual balancing process over all transactions may be put in place to compensate for the weaknesses in the error report. An IT auditor should be aware of compensating controls in areas where controls are identified as weak.

While a compensating control situation occurs when a stronger control supports a weaker one, an overlapping control situation occurs when there are two strong controls. For example, a data center employs a card key system to control physical access and a guard, who is posted inside the door and require employees to show their card key or badge, to control physical access. This example is an overlapping control—either control may be adequate to restrict access, but the two controls complement each other.

Normally, a control objective is not achieved by considering one control adequate. Rather, an IT auditor needs to perform a variety of testing procedures and evaluate how they relate to one another.

ISACA. All Rights Reserved.

Generally, a group of aggregated controls may act as compensating controls and thereby minimize the risk. An IT auditor should always look for compensating controls prior to reporting a control weakness.

2.2.5 Control Assessment

Assessing the control environment provides an opportunity to evaluate not only the risk culture (i.e., the shared values and beliefs that govern attitudes toward risk-taking, care and integrity, and determine how openly risk and losses are reported and discussed), but also the effectiveness of the current risk management program, which can help determine the level of risk currently facing the enterprise and the seriousness of that risk.

In general, risk is more severe when any of the following are true:

- Controls are inadequate.
- The wrong controls are being used.
- Controls are ignored or bypassed.
- Controls are poorly maintained.
- Logs or control data are not reviewed.
- Controls are not tested.
- Changes to the configuration of controls are not managed.
- Controls can be physically accessed and altered.
- Duties are inadequately segregated.
- Control objectives are not appropriately defined.

An IT auditor should be able to evaluate the strengths and weaknesses of controls and determine if they are effective in meeting the control objectives established as part of the IT audit planning process.

Controls should be regularly reviewed to:

- Determine and ensure their effectiveness and identify weaknesses.
- Verify the correct balance between technical, managerial and physical controls.

Control assessments may be in the form of:

- Control self-assessments.
- Control monitoring.
- Continuous auditing/monitoring.

Control Self-Assessments

A control self-assessment (CSA) is an assessment of controls made by the staff and management of the unit or units involved. It is a management technique that assures stakeholders, customers and other parties that the internal control system of the enterprise is reliable. CSA also ensures that employees are aware of the risk to the business and that they conduct periodic, proactive reviews of controls to evaluate the completeness and effectiveness of management control over processes, policies and contracts. CSA is a methodology to review:

- Key business objectives
- Risk involved in achieving the business objectives.
- Internal controls designed to manage business risk in a formal, documented and collaborative process.

ISACA. All Rights Reserved.

Benefits of a CSA include:

- Early detection of risk
- More effective and improved internal controls
- Development of a sense of ownership of the controls in the employees and process owners, and reduction of their resistance to control improvement initiatives
- Increased employee awareness of enterprise objectives and knowledge of risk and internal controls
- Reduction in control cost

A self-assessment of IT-related controls is often facilitated by an IT auditor and/or risk manager. An IT auditor should ensure that there is an explicit acknowledgment by management that all monitoring activities are recorded in the enterprise IT risk register. A risk register is a repository of the key attributes of potential risk, known risk and accepted risk (i.e., senior management decisions to assume risk and absorb any losses). Risk attributes may include name, description, owner, expected/actual frequency, potential/actual magnitude, potential/actual business impact and disposition.

Control Monitoring

It is important to have proven methods that can measure and ascertain the extent to which IT-related activities support business success. Such methods help identify where active monitoring may be useful and where corrective actions can be taken to reduce the risk that IT-related activities do not result in the expected business contributions.

Control monitoring ensures that:

- Control requirements are being met.
- Standards are being followed.
- Employees are complying with enterprise policies, practices and procedures.

The purpose of control monitoring is to verify whether the control is effectively addressing the risk, not to see whether the control itself is working. For example, a firewall that is configured in a way that does not regulate traffic between two networks may be ineffective even if the firewall is operational and processing traffic.

The monitoring and metrics of managing a control must be based on data that are relevant to the risk and overall performance.

The monitoring of controls may be conducted through self-assessment or independent assurance reviews. When risk action plans are required to address a risk, the plans should be monitored to ensure that appropriate risk management practices are in alignment with the enterprise risk appetite and tolerance. Assurance activities should be independent of the function, group or enterprise being monitored, and the reviewers should have the necessary skills and competence to perform assurance and adhere to codes of ethics and professional standards.

Continuous Auditing/Monitoring

IT-related controls should be continuously monitored, benchmarked and improved. When the results of monitoring indicate an area of noncompliance or unacceptable performance, mitigation activities should be employed, including:

- Implementation of new controls
- Adjustment or enforcement of existing controls
- Changes to a business process to address the risk environment

ISACA. All Rights Reserved.

Continuous auditing is an approach used by an IT auditor to monitor system reliability on a continuous basis and gather selective audit evidence. A distinctive characteristic of continuous auditing is the short time-lapse between the transactions to be audited, the collection of evidence and the audit reporting.

Continuous IT control monitoring is a process that includes:

- Developing a strategy to regularly evaluate selected IT-related controls/metrics
- Recording and evaluating IT-related events and the effectiveness of the enterprise in dealing with those events
- Recording changes to IT-related controls or changes that affect IT-related risk
- Communicating the current risk and control status to enable information-sharing decisions involving the enterprise

Continuous IT control monitoring involves the monitoring of controls by every manager and every department.

To properly understand the implications and requirements of continuous auditing, the following distinction is made between continuous auditing and continuous monitoring:

- **Continuous auditing**—Enables an IT auditor to perform tests and assessments in a real-time or near-real-time environment. Continuous auditing is designed to enable an IT auditor to report results on the subject matter being audited within a much shorter time frame than a traditional audit approach allows.
- **Continuous monitoring**—Used by an enterprise to observe the performance of one or many processes, systems or types of data. For example, a real-time antivirus or intrusion detection system (IDS) may operate in a continuous monitoring fashion.

An IT auditor is directly involved in the performance of continuous auditing, but continuous monitoring is performed by management.

Continuous auditing should be independent of continuous control or monitoring activities. When both continuous monitoring and auditing take place, continuous assurance can be established. In practice, continuous auditing is the precursor to management adopting continuous monitoring as a process on a day-to-day basis. Often, the audit function hands over the techniques used in continuous auditing to the business, which then runs the continuous monitoring. This collaboration can lead to increased appreciation among process owners of the value that the audit function brings to the enterprise, leading to greater confidence and trust between the business and the audit function. Nevertheless, the lack of independence and objectivity inherent in continuous monitoring performed exclusively by management should not be overlooked; continuous monitoring should never be considered an appropriate substitute for the audit function.

Continuous auditing efforts often incorporate new IT developments and standards; increased processing capabilities of hardware; specialized software; AI tools; and attempts to collect and analyze data at the moment of the transaction. Data must be gathered from different applications working within different environments, transactions must be screened, the transaction environment has to be analyzed to detect trends and exceptions, and atypical patterns (i.e., a transaction with significantly higher or lower value than typical for a given business partner) must be exposed. For all this to happen in real time, perhaps even before final sign-off of a transaction, it is mandatory to adopt and combine various top-level IT techniques. The IT environment is a natural enabler for the application of continuous auditing because of the intrinsic automated nature of its underlying processes.

Continuous auditing aims to provide a more secure platform to avoid fraud and a real-time process aimed at ensuring a high level of financial control. Continuous auditing and monitoring tools are often built into many enterprise resource planning (ERP) packages and most OS and network security packages. Within these environments, tools that are appropriately configured and populated with rules, parameters and formulas can output exception lists on request, while operating against actual data. Therefore, these systems represent an instance of continuous auditing. Despite the potential for significant added value, the difficulty of using these built-in features is that they postulate a

ISACA. All Rights Reserved.

definition of a dangerous or exception condition. For example, whether a set of granted IT system-access permissions is to be deemed risk-free depends on having well-defined segregation of duties. In contrast, it may be much harder to decide if a given sequence of steps to modify and maintain a database record points to a potential risk. It is important to validate the source of the data used for continuous auditing and note whether manual changes are possible.

Continuous Auditing Techniques

Continuous audit techniques are important IT audit tools, particularly when they are used in time-sharing environments that process many transactions, but leave a scarce paper trail. By permitting an IT auditor to evaluate operating controls on a continuous basis without disrupting the enterprise usual operations, continuous audit techniques improve the security of a system. For example, when a system is misused by someone withdrawing money from an inoperative account, a continuous audit technique reports this withdrawal in a timely manner to an IT auditor. Thus, the time lag between the misuse of the system and the detection of that misuse is reduced. The realization that failures, improper manipulation and lack of controls are detected on a timely basis by the use of continuous audit procedures gives an IT auditor and management greater confidence in the reliability of an IT system. Five types of automated evaluation techniques are applicable to continuous auditing:

1. **Systems control audit review file and embedded audit modules (SCARF/EAM)**—This technique embeds specially written audit software in the enterprise host application system to allow application systems monitoring on a selective basis.
2. **Snapshots**—This technique takes what might be termed pictures of the processing path that a transaction follows from the input to the output stages. Transactions are tagged by applying identifiers to input data and recording selected information for subsequent review by an IT auditor.
3. **Audit hooks**—This technique embeds hooks in application systems to function as red flags and alert IT auditors to act before an error or irregularity gets out of hand.
4. **Integrated test facility (ITF)**—In this technique, dummy entities are set up and included in an auditee's production files. An IT auditor can make the system either process live transactions or test transactions during regular processing runs and have these transactions update the records of the dummy entity. The operator enters the test transactions simultaneously with the live transactions that are entered for processing. An IT auditor then compares the output with the data that have been independently calculated to verify the correctness of the computer-processed data.
5. **Continuous and intermittent simulation (CIS)**—During a process run of a transaction, the computer system simulates the instruction execution of the application. As each transaction is entered, the simulator decides whether the transaction meets certain predetermined criteria and, if so, audits the transaction. If it does not meet the criteria, the simulator waits until it encounters the next transaction that meets the criteria.

Figure 2.6 presents the relative advantages and disadvantages of the various continuous audit tools.

Figure 2.6—Continuous Audit Tools Advantages and Disadvantages

	SCARF/EAM	Snapshots	Audit Hooks	ITF	CIS
Complexity:	Very high	Medium	Low	High	Medium
Useful when:	Regular processing cannot be interrupted.	An audit trail is required.	Only select transactions or processes need to be examined.	It is not beneficial to use text data.	Transactions meeting certain criteria need to be examined.

Source: ISACA, *CISA® Review Manual, 27th Edition*, USA, 2019, figure 1.13, *www.isaca.org/bookstore/cisa-exam-resources/crm27ed*

ISACA. All Rights Reserved.

The use of each of these continuous audit techniques has advantages and disadvantages. Their selection and implementation largely depend on the complexity of the enterprise IT systems and applications and an IT auditor's ability to understand and evaluate the system with and without the use of continuous audit techniques. In addition, an IT auditor must recognize that continuous audit techniques are not a cure for all control problems, and the use of these techniques provides only limited assurance that the information processing systems examined are operating as they are intended to function.

Techniques that are used to operate in a continuous auditing environment must work at all data levels—single input, transaction and databases. Techniques include:

- Transaction logging
- Query tools
- Statistics and data analysis
- Database management systems (DBMSs)
- Data warehouses, data marts, data mining
- Intelligent agents
- Embedded audit modules (EAMs)
- Neural network technologies
- Standards, such as Extensible Business Reporting Language (XBRL)

Continuous auditing has an intrinsic edge over point-in-time or periodic auditing because it captures internal control problems as they occur, preventing negative effects. Implementation can also reduce possible or intrinsic audit inefficiencies, such as delays, planning time, inefficiencies of the audit process, overhead due to work segmentation, multiple quality or supervisory reviews, or discussions concerning the validity of findings. Consideration should be given to the elimination of reporting of false negatives and false positives that may result from continuous auditing techniques.

2.3 Control and Risk-Related Frameworks, Standards and Guidance

An enterprise can either fail or succeed based on how it approaches and uses technology. To address this reality, IT-related frameworks, standards and guidelines have been developed to help enterprise management secure and protect the integrity of enterprise information assets and to deliver value to stakeholders.

- **Framework**—A framework is a basic conceptual structure used to solve or address complex issues. It is an enabler of governance. A framework is a set of concepts, assumptions and practices that define how something can be approached or understood, the relationships among the entities involved, the roles of those involved and the boundaries (what to include and to exclude in the governance system).
- **Standard**—A standard is a mandatory requirement, code of practice or specification approved by a recognized external standards organization, such as International Organization for Standardization (ISO).
- **Guideline**—A guideline is a description of a particular way of accomplishing something that is less prescriptive than a procedure.

These tools often include best practices that an enterprise can adopt to address business issues through the efficient and effective governance and management of information and technology. Many authoritative standards and guidance that pertain to risk and control are available as sources of good practice for the management of IT-related risk. These reference materials are managed and published by authoritative bodies and kept current. They help with the development of an enterprise risk management program, but these reference materials may require an enterprise to tailor its practices to meet specific enterprise goals.

ISACA. All Rights Reserved.

An IT auditor should be familiar with IT-related risk and control frameworks, standards and guidance being used within enterprises and how these tools are being used.

The following sections describe the frameworks and standards that are among the most recognized for their application to risk and control.

2.3.1 COBIT Framework

COBIT is a framework offered by ISACA for use in the governance and management of enterprise information and technology (I&T). To satisfy governance and management objectives, each enterprise needs to establish, tailor and sustain a governance system built from a number of components. These components include:[23]

- **Processes**—organized sets of practices and activities to achieve certain objectives and produce a set of outputs that support achievement of overall IT-related goals.
- **Organizational structures**—the key decision-making entities in an enterprise.
- **Principles, policies and frameworks**—tools for translating desired behavior into practical guidance for day-to-day management.
- **Information**—pervasive throughout any enterprise and includes all information produced and used by the enterprise.
- **Culture, ethics and behavior**—beliefs, values and conduct pertaining to individuals and the enterprise and often underestimated as factors in the success of governance and management activities.
- **People, skills and competencies**—elements required for good decisions, execution of corrective action and successful completion of all activities.
- **Services, infrastructure and applications**—the infrastructure, technologies and tools that provide the enterprise with the governance system for information and technology processing.

COBIT provides guidance on how to build and sustain a governance system that aligns with major related standards, frameworks and regulations. COBIT includes a comprehensive repository of guidance, tools, models and resources to help enterprises provide effective IT governance and to better understand and identify potential risk in the process of building a mature relationship between business units and IT.

Governance objectives are grouped in the *Evaluate, Direct and Monitor* (EDM) domain. In this domain, the governing body evaluates strategic options, directs senior management on the chosen strategic options and monitors achievement of the strategy.

Management objectives are grouped into four domains:[24]

- **Align, Plan and Organize** (APO)—addresses the overall organization, strategy and supporting activities for I&T.
- **Build, Acquire and Implement** (BAI)—treats the definition, acquisition and implementation of I&T solutions and their integration in business processes.
- **Deliver, Service and Support** (DSS)—addresses the operational delivery and support of I&T services, including security.
- **Monitor, Evaluate and Assess** (MEA)—addresses performance monitoring and conformance of I&T with internal performance targets, internal control objectives and external requirements.

The COBIT Core Model is shown in **figure 2.7**.

[23] ISACA, *COBIT® 2019 Framework: Governance and Management Objectives*, USA, 2018, *www.isaca.org/bookstore/bookstore-cobit_19-digital/wcb19fgm*
[24] ISACA, *COBIT® 2019 Framework: Introduction and Methodology*, USA, 2018, *www.isaca.org/bookstore/bookstore-cobit_19-digital/wcb19fim*

ISACA. All Rights Reserved.

Figure 2.7—COBIT Core Model

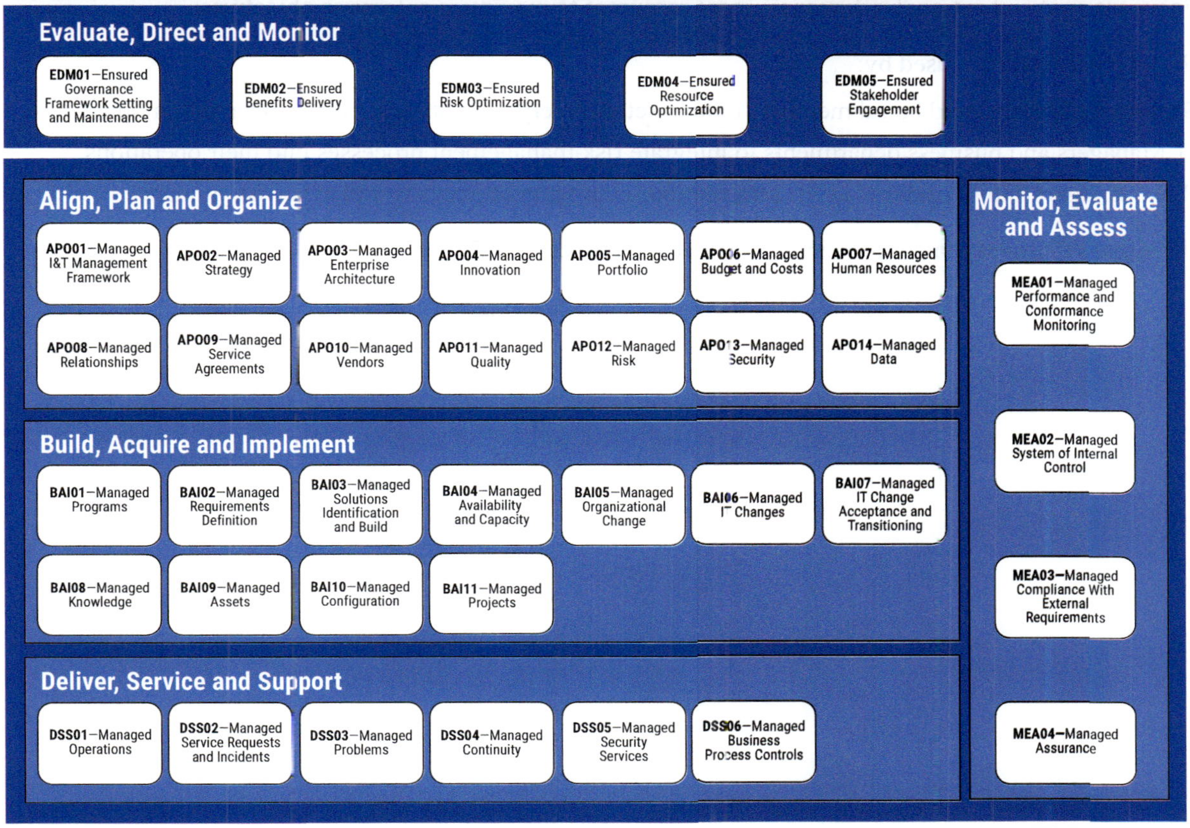

Source: ISACA, *COBIT 2019 Framework: Introduction and Methodology*, USA, 2018, figure 4.2, *https://www.isaca.org/bookstore/bookstore-cobit_19-digital/wcb19fim*

COBIT is a reference that many enterprises find useful and embrace for numerous purposes. With respect to IT audit, COBIT governance and management objectives are linked to ISACA standards and guidelines and used in the development of ISACA audit/assurance programs.

2.3.2 Risk IT Framework

ISACA Risk IT Framework is a useful reference for an IT auditor to gain a comprehensive view of IT-related risk and a useful tool in the conduct of focused risk-based audits. The Risk IT Framework helps to:

- Identify current and emerging risk throughout the extended enterprise.
- Develop appropriate operational capabilities to ensure that business processes continue operating through adverse events.
- Leverage investments in compliance or internal control systems already in place to optimize IT-related risk.
- Recognize IT-related risk that exceeds the scope of technical controls and IT-related tools and techniques to integrate into the risk management program.
- Raise awareness of the balance between the benefits of technology and external partners (on the one hand) and the potential impact of cyberthreats, internal control failures and risk introduced by vendors, suppliers and partners (on the other hand).
- Promote risk awareness, accountability and responsibility throughout the enterprise.

ISACA. All Rights Reserved.

- Frame IT-related risk within a business context to show aggregate exposure in terms of enterprise value.
- Focus internal and external risk management resources to maximize enterprise objectives.

The Risk IT framework is used by:

- Senior management and board members to help set an enterprise's strategic direction and to monitor risk.
- IT Managers and business departments to integrate risk management processes into their operations.
- Risk managers and IT auditors as IT, information security, cybersecurity and cyberrisk guidance.

COBIT aligns risk management principles with risk objectives. See **figure 2.8**.

ISACA. All Rights Reserved.

Figure 2.8—Alignment of I&T-Related Risk Management Principles with COBIT Risk Objectives EDM03 and APO12

Source: ISACA, *Risk IT Framework*, 2nd *Edition*, USA, 2020, figure 3.1, *https://www.isaca.org/bookstore/bookstore-risk-digital/ritf2*

ISACA. All Rights Reserved.

2.3.3 COSO Enterprise Risk Management – Integrated Framework

The Committee of Sponsoring Organizations of the Treadway Commission (COSO) developed its *Enterprise Risk Management – Integrated Framework* to enhance enterprise risk management (ERM) and governance through key principles and concepts and provide a common language around risk management.[25]

The framework assists with:

- Aligning risk appetite
- Enhancing risk response
- Reducing operational surprises
- Identifying and managing multiple and cross-enterprise risk
- Seizing opportunities
- Improving deployment of capital

The framework uses risk management objectives and components to demonstrate a direct relationship between enterprise objectives (what an enterprise strives to achieve) and ERM components (what is needed to achieve the objectives). The relationship is depicted in a three-dimensional matrix in the form of a cube, shown in **figure 2.9**.

Figure 2.9—COSO Framework Objectives, Components and Organizational Structural Model

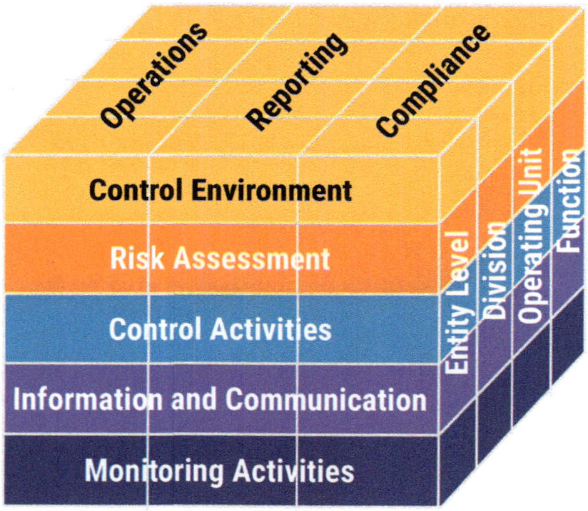

Source: COSO, "Internal Control – Integrated Framework, Executive Summary," USA, May 2013. Used with permission.

The four categories of objectives—strategic, operations, reporting and compliance—are represented by the vertical columns, the eight components by horizontal rows, and enterprise units by the third dimension. This depiction portrays the ability either to focus on the entirety of an enterprise ERM or to zero in on an objective category, component, enterprise unit or any subset of dimensions. The framework is useful to assist development of an enterprise design, implement an internal control, broaden the application of an internal control in addressing operations and achieving objectives, and clarify the requirements for determining what constitutes an effective internal control.

The framework is used to integrate the management of all types of risk and emphasizes that strategic plans to support the mission and vision of an enterprise must be accompanied by elements of governance, performance measurement

[25] *Op cit* COSO

ISACA. All Rights Reserved.

and internal control. The framework is often used to make decisions in support of technology risk management objectives and is a good resource for IT auditors when evaluating risk and developing risk-based audit plans.[26]

2.3.4 International Organization for Standardization (ISO)/International Electrotechnical Commission (IEC)

The International Organization for Standardization (ISO®) is an independent, nongovernmental organization that creates international standards covering many products and services, some specific to security and risk management. Compliance with its standards is voluntary.

ISO/IEC 20000

ISO/IEC 20000 is an international standard for IT service management. ISO/IEC 20000-1:2018 (part 1) includes "the design, transition, delivery and improvement of services that fulfill service requirements and provide value for both the customer and the service provider. This part of ISO/IEC 20000 requires an integrated process approach when the service provider plans, establishes, implements, operates, monitors, reviews, maintains and improves a service management system (SMS)."[27] Guidance includes:

- Service management system general requirements
- Design and transition of new or changed services
- Service delivery processes
- Relationship processes
- Resolution processes
- Control processes

ISO 27000 series

The ISO 27000 series is a set of best practices that provide guidance to enterprises implementing and maintaining information security programs. The series provides recommendations on information security management, risk and controls within the context of an overall information security management system (ISMS).[28] ISO 27002 is a standard that lists potential controls that may be used to mitigate risk that may adversely affect the implementation and maintenance of an effective security management program. ISO/IEC 27001 is a well-known standard in the industry that provides guidance for implementation of these controls.

ISO 27002 covers:

- Security policy
- Organization of information security
- Asset management
- Human resources security
- Physical and environmental security
- Communications and operations management

[26] Bayuk, J.; "Technology's Role in Enterprise Risk Management," *ISACA® Journal*, 1 March 2018, *www.isaca.org/resources/isaca-journal/issues/2018/volume-2/technologys-role-in-enterprise-risk-management*

[27] International Organization for Standardization (ISO®)/International Electrotechnical Commission® (IEC®), ISO/IEC-20000-1: 2018 *Information technology – Service management – Part 1: Service management system requirements*, Switzerland, September 2018, *www.iso.org/standard/70636.html*

[28] ISO/IEC 27000:2018 *Information technology – Security techniques – Information security management systems – Overview and vocabulary*, February 2018, *www.iso.org/standard/73906.html*

ISACA. All Rights Reserved.

- Access control Information systems acquisition, development and maintenance
- Information security incident management
- Business continuity management
- Compliance

ISO/IEC 27001 provides a useful framework to gauge the comprehensiveness of an enterprise cybersecurity strategy. Enterprise policies and standards can be designed to track directly to the standard. An IT auditor can use ISO 27001 to help in performing an evaluation of enterprise security controls.

ISO/IEC 31010

ISO/IEC 31010 focuses on risk assessment concepts and processes, and the selection and application of risk assessment techniques.[29] Risk assessment helps decision makers understand how risk can affect the achievement of objectives and gauge the adequacy of the controls already in place.

2.3.5 National Institute of Standards and Technology

The US National Institute of Standards and Technology (NIST) offers several publications that provide risk and control guidance to IT professionals.

NIST Framework for Improving Critical Infrastructure Cybersecurity

The NIST Cybersecurity Framework (**figure 2.10**) provides guidance to enterprise management to identify and manage cybersecurity risk. The framework defines five key functions for the protection of digital assets:[30]

- **Identify**—Use enterprise understanding to minimize risk to systems, assets, data and capabilities.
- **Protect**—Design safeguards to limit the impact of potential events on critical services and infrastructure.
- **Detect**—Implement activities to identify the occurrence of a cybersecurity event.
- **Respond**—Take appropriate action after learning of a security event.
- **Recover**—Plan for resilience and the timely repair of compromised capabilities and services.

Figure 2.10—NIST Cybersecurity Framework

Function Unique Identifier	Function	Category Unique Identifier	Category
ID	Identify	ID.AM	Asset Management
		ID.BE	Business Environment
		ID.GV	Governance
		ID.RA	Risk Assessment
		ID.RM	Risk Management Strategy
		ID.SC	Supply Chain Risk Management
PR	Protect	PR.AC	Identity Management and Access Control
		PR.AT	Awareness and Training
		PR.DS	Data Security
		PR.IP	Information Protection Processes and Procedures

[29] IEC 31010:2019 *Risk management – Risk assessment techniques*, June 2019, *www.iso.org/standard/72140.html*

[30] National Institute of Standards and Technology (NIST), *Framework for Improving Critical Infrastructure Cybersecurity*, Version 1.1, 16 April 2018, *https://nvlpubs.nist.gov/nistpubs/CSWP/NIST.CSWP.04162018.pdf*

ISACA. All Rights Reserved.

Figure 2.10—NIST Cybersecurity Framework *(cont.)*

Function Unique Identifier	Function	Category Unique Identifier	Category
		PR.MA	Maintenance
		PR.PT	Protective Technology
DE	Detect	DE.AE	Anomalies and Events
		DE.CM	Security Continuous Monitoring
		DE.DP	Detection Processes
RS	Respond	RS.RP	Response Planning
		RS.CO	Communications
		RS.AN	Analysis
		RS.MI	Mitigation
		RS.IM	Improvements
RC	Recover	RC.RP	Recovery Planning
		RC.IM	Improvements
		RC.CO	Communication

Source: National Institute of Standards and Technology (NIST), *Framework for Improving Critical Infrastructure Cybersecurity*, Version 1.1, USA, 16 April 2018, *https://nvlpubs.nist.gov/nistpubs/CSWP/NIST.CSWP.04162018.pdf*

Following are other NIST special publications that may be useful to IT auditing:[31]

- **NIST Special Publication 800-30 Revision 1**—Guide for Conducting Risk Assessments
- **NIST Special Publication 800-37 Revision 2**—Risk Management Framework for Information Systems and Organizations: A System Life Cycle Approach for Security and Privacy
- **NIST Special Publication 800-39**—Managing Information Security Risk

2.4 Risk-Based Audit Approach

An IT auditor is challenged with deciding what to audit and how to prioritize the order in which audits are performed. Resolution of this challenge ultimately results in an audit plan. But before getting to the audit plan, an IT auditor must decide what to audit and when.

Risk-based auditing is the deployment of audit resources to areas within an enterprise that represent the greatest risk. It requires an understanding of the enterprise and its environment, specifically:

- External and internal factors affecting the enterprise
- Enterprise selection and application of policies and procedures
- Enterprise business objectives and strategies
- Measurement and review of the enterprise performance

To be able to obtain the previous understanding, an IT auditor must gain an understanding of the key components of the enterprise:

- Business strategy
- Business products and services
- Governance process

[31] National Institute of Standards and Technology, "NIST Special Publication Subseries Descriptions," 23 August 2016, *www.nist.gov/nist-research-library/nist-special-publication-subseries-descriptions*

ISACA. All Rights Reserved.

- Transaction types, transaction partners and transaction flows within IT systems

A risk-based auditing approach provides the enterprise with feedback on whether its operational practices are aligned with its risk appetite. This is determined as an IT auditor assesses the controls that management has designed and put in place to mitigate risk that may hinder or prevent the enterprise from achieving its strategic goals.

2.4.1 Business Risk

Business risk is a probable situation with uncertain frequency and magnitude of loss (or gain). Business risk includes concerns about the probable effects of an uncertain event on achieving established business objectives. The nature of business risk may be financial, regulatory, operational, strategic or reputational. Business risk may also include risk derived from specific technology. For example, an airline company is subject to extensive safety regulations and economic changes, both of which impact the continuing operations of the enterprise. In this context, the availability of IT service and its reliability are critical. Business risk includes the measures an enterprise is willing to take to achieve or advance its objectives even though the results may be unproven or uncertain.

Business risk may negatively impact the assets, processes or objectives of a specific business or enterprise. An IT auditor is often focused on high-risk issues associated with the confidentiality, integrity or availability of sensitive and critical information and the underlying IT systems and processes that generate, store and manipulate such information. In reviewing these types of IT-related business risk, an IT auditor often assesses the effectiveness of the risk management process that an enterprise uses.

In analyzing the business risk arising from the use of IT, it is important for an IT auditor to have a clear understanding of the following:

- Industry and/or internationally accepted risk management processes
- Purpose and nature of business, the environment in which the business operates and related business risk
- Dependence on technology in the achievement of business goals and objectives
- Business risk of using IT and how it impacts the achievement of the business goals and objectives
- A good overview of the business processes and the impact of IT and related risk on the business process objectives

By understanding the nature of the business, an IT auditor can identify and categorize the types of risk that will better determine the risk approach used in conducting an IT audit. This approach should ensure the complete and accurate coverage of the audit plan.[32]

2.4.2 Enterprise Risk Assessment

A risk assessment is a process used to identify and evaluate risk and its potential effects. An IT auditor should understand how the enterprise approaches risk assessment. Enterprise risk assessments should identify, quantify and prioritize risk against criteria for risk acceptance and objectives relevant to the enterprise. The results should guide and determine the appropriate management action, priorities for managing risk and priorities for implementing controls selected to protect against risk.

Enterprise risk assessments should be performed periodically and when significant changes occur in the environment, business requirements and risk situation (e.g., in the assets, threats, vulnerabilities and impacts). These assessments should be performed methodically and be capable of producing comparable and reproducible results.

[32] ITAF 2201.3.1

ISACA. All Rights Reserved.

The scope of a risk assessment can be:

- Entire enterprise
- Parts of the enterprise
- An individual IT system
- Specific IT components
- Specific IT services

To address risk, an enterprise should establish the criteria for determining whether risk can be managed within its risk appetite. Risk may be accepted if, for example, the risk is assessed as low or the cost of treatment is not cost-effective for the enterprise. Such decisions should be recorded.

In evaluating IT-related business processes applied by an enterprise, it is important for an IT auditor to understand the relationship between risk and control. IT auditors must be able to identify and differentiate risk types and the controls used to mitigate each type of risk. They should have knowledge of common business risk areas, related IT risk and relevant controls. They should also be able to evaluate the risk assessment and management processes and techniques used by business managers, and to make assessments of risk to help focus and plan audit work.

From an IT auditor's perspective, an enterprise risk assessment serves several purposes:

- It assists an IT auditor in identifying risk and threats to an IT environment and IT system—risk and threats that would need to be addressed by management—and in identifying system specific internal controls. Depending on the level of risk, the assessment assists an IT auditor in selecting certain areas to select and include in an audit plan.
- It helps an IT auditor in the evaluation of controls in audit planning.
- It assists an IT auditor in determining audit objectives.
- It supports risk-based audit decision making.

2.4.3 IT-Related Risk Assessment

The purpose of an IT-related risk assessment is to build an initial view of the overall IT-related risk for the enterprise by looking at the components of the risk at a high level. The assessment is performed by those responsible for risk governance to:

- Identify potential high-risk areas.
- Gain an overview of major risk factors.
- Detect the most critical risk scenarios that should be examined in greater detail at a later stage.

Meaningful IT-related risk assessments and risk-based decisions require IT-related risk to be expressed in unambiguous and clear, business or mission-relevant terms, such as achieving financial, revenue or desired strategic outcomes. An IT-related risk assessment should involve all major stakeholders of the enterprise who possess the ability to understand and express how adverse events may affect business or mission objectives. This means that:

- A shared understanding of IT-related failures, compromises, mistakes or events can impact enterprise objectives and result in direct costs, e.g., financial loss, or indirect costs, e.g., exposure of customer-sensitive information resulting in reputational damage.
- Losses to the enterprise from IT-related events can compromise an enterprise's ability to deliver its key services and products. This is true even when the enterprise relies on IT suppliers to provide goods and resources that are integral to its strategic objectives.

To remain relevant, an IT-related risk assessment must be regularly repeated. If no major changes have occurred in any of the risk factors, a simple annual confirmation of earlier results is sufficient. Major changes in an enterprise

ISACA. All Rights Reserved.

environment, such as mergers and new markets, necessitate a new assessment. An annual update or confirmation of the assessment is recommended for stable environments.

2.4.4 Risk Assessment Approach—IT Audit

To assess the risk that is related to the complete scope of the IT audit area, an IT auditor should consider the following elements when developing the IT audit plan:

- Full coverage of all areas within the scope of the IT audit universe, which represents the range of all possible audit activities[33]
- Reliability and suitability of the risk assessment provided by enterprise management
- Processes followed by enterprise management to supervise, examine and report possible risk or issues
- Coverage of risk in related activities relevant to the activities under review

When developing the overall IT audit plan, an IT auditor should use a suitable risk assessment approach to identify areas that should receive more audit focus.[34]

The risk assessment approach can be as simple as using classifications of high, medium and low, based on an IT auditor's judgment, or creating weights for the types of risk associated with the business and identifying the risk in an equation.[35] On the other hand, risk assessment can use a scheme in which risk has been assessed quantitatively based on business significance and scientific calculations that provide a numeric risk rating.[36]

To determine the most appropriate risk assessment approach, an IT auditor should consider the:

- Type of information required to be collected
- Extent to which the information required is available
- Time and cost to collect information
- Likelihood of acceptance by those charged with governance of the IT audit function

ADDITIONAL GUIDANCE

For additional guidance, see ISACA Standard 1201 Risk Assessment in Planning and Guideline 2201 Risk Assessment in Planning.

2.5 Agile Audit Approach

The Agile methodology comes from the software development field. Agile provides an approach and expectations for managing a process but not formal prescriptions for performing work.

An Agile approach to auditing is adaptable to changing audit expectations and provides flexibility in the execution of an audit plan. The genesis of applying an Agile audit approach is the intent to shift away from a static plan. Key strategies in applying an Agile approach to audit planning include:

- **Prioritization**—Regularly evaluating and prioritizing audit areas based on risk. Instead of requiring a rigid audit plan, this approach allows for timely inclusion of new risk or auditable areas throughout the year. The

[33] ITAF 2201.2.2
[34] ITAF 2201.2.7
[35] ITAF 2201.3.3
[36] ITAF 2201.3.5

ISACA. All Rights Reserved.

importance of collaboration with stakeholders during the planning and prioritization process cannot be overstated.[37]

- **Segmentation**—Breaking an IT audit into fixed-length activities that support meeting a tight deadline without stressing available audit resources. The goal is to be quick and iterative, versus confined to a predetermined plan, eliminating unnecessary resources and efforts.
- **Communication**—Embedding quality reviews and opportunities for staff questions or issues as they come up in fieldwork.[38]

An Agile audit approach is intended to provide results throughout the audit rather than delivering them only at the end of an audit. Early and frequent communication with the auditee allows the final report or presentation to reflect a summary of issues that have already been identified.

An objective of an Agile audit approach is the timely completion of audits. This depends on a number of factors, including the availability of key personnel and information. A rigid separation between audit phases—such as planning, fieldwork and reporting—often results in failure to keep up with changing requirements, staffing priorities and availability. The need for timely meetings with key personnel can create bottlenecks and cause delays in moving from one phase to the next phase.[39]

With an Agile approach, an IT auditor considers the expected and the unexpected. **Figure 2.11** shows some issues that can arise during the audit planning, fieldwork and reporting stages, potentially resulting in delays in the execution of an audit.

Figure 2.11—Possible Audit Execution Delays

Audit Planning	Fieldwork	Reporting
Additional resources needed to address lack of audit staff resources or lack of expertise for specialized audits are not recruited.	Audit material requested is not the material received.	Rewrites/edits of the audit report as it progresses through different review phases of the audit department takes longer than planned.
Audit staff and IT department staff are unavailable during fieldwork. This is particularly applicable to key personnel in IT departments.	The process as understood during planning varies from the organization's actual practices.	Determination of target dates for remediation takes longer than planned.

Source: ISACA, *Fundamentals of IS Audit and Assurance Facilitator Guide*, USA, 2018

The use of an Agile audit approach entails:[40]

- **No strict separation between phases**—IT audit planning and fieldwork can occur at the same time. Fieldwork can begin on steps that have already been planned. In this case, if key resources or stakeholders are unavailable only certain audit steps are delayed and other work can continue.
- **Requesting data at the start of the audit**—An IT auditor requests data early during the planning process to reduce any potential delay in actually having the data when it is needed for the audit. In addition, an IT auditor can continue audit planning activities while the data request is being fulfilled.
- **Reporting formally at the end of the audit**—An IT auditor develops formal documents and reports at the end of the audit documenting audit results. This greatly improves efficiency by reporting the results of material tests that were performed during the audit rather than all tests that were planned or performed.

37 Yonker, M.; "An Agile Approach to Internal Auditing," *ISACA Now Blog*, 12 April 2018, *www.isaca.org/resources/news-and-trends/isaca-now-blog/2018/an-agile-approach-to-internal-auditing*

38 *Ibid.*

39 Alexiou, S.; "Agile Audit," *ISACA® Journal*, 1 March 2017, *www.isaca.org/resources/isaca-journal/issues/2017/volume-2/agile-audit*

40 *Ibid.*

ISACA. All Rights Reserved.

- **Focusing on material issues**—An IT auditor can give attention at the start of the audit to potential material issues that may be discovered during the audit.
- **Using downtime effectively**—An IT auditor uses any downtime that occurs during an audit—due to staffing issues, unavailability of data or other delays—to document and write up audit findings.
- **Shifting resources**—If necessary, an IT auditor can shift audit resources to areas where there is the greatest need.

An Agile audit approach requires proper risk identification and planning. Identifying and prioritizing risk areas are key components in any audit program.[41] However, with an Agile audit approach, an audit program or a framework for discussion is established at the start of an audit and then built on by the audit team. [42] The audit team and leader also decide if performing audit tasks in parallel adds any efficiency. If not, there may be little deviation from a non-Agile audit approach. **Figure 2.12** compares Agile and non-Agile audits.

Figure 2.12—Agile and Non-Agile Audit Comparison

Audit Aspect	Agile	Non-Agile
Audit duration	Fast	Slow
Audit quality	Generally better, as more time can be devoted to material issues	More challenging, especially for complex audits
Audit complexity	Generally needs more highly qualified auditors	Can be executed by less qualified auditors who get a list of detailed steps
Audit flexibility	Easier to adapt to changes in risk evaluation	Needs a formal audit program revision
Leadership	Generally more important, at least during the initial changes	More democratic, as all team members participate more or less equally (in principle) to planning
Interference with auditees' time	In principle, may involve more short meetings with auditees	In principle, fewer, but longer meetings assuming all goes well

Source: "Agile Audit," *ISACA Journal*, 1 March 2017, *www.isaca.org/resources/isaca-journal/issues/2017/volume-2/agile-audit*

2.6 Audit Risk

Audit risk is the risk of reaching an incorrect conclusion based on audit findings. This is the risk that information collected may contain a material error that may go undetected during the course of the audit.

Audit risk is influenced by:

- **Inherent risk**—Inherent risk is the susceptibility of an audit area to an error that can be material (individually or in combination with other errors), assuming there are no related internal controls. For example, the inherent risk associated with operating systems without appropriate controls is ordinarily high, because changes to, or even disclosure of, data or programs through operating system security weaknesses can result in false management information or competitive disadvantage. By contrast, the inherent risk associated with security for a standalone PC without controls, when a proper analysis demonstrates it is not used for business-critical purposes, ordinarily is low.
- **Control risk**—Control risk is the risk of a material error not being prevented or detected on a timely basis by the system of internal controls. For example, the control risk associated with manual reviews of computer logs can be high because activities requiring investigation are often easily missed due to the volume of logged information. The control risk associated with computerized data validation procedures is ordinarily low if the

[41] *Ibid.*
[42] *Ibid.*

ISACA. All Rights Reserved.

processes are consistently applied.[43] Control risk varies inversely with the level of effectiveness of the internal control structure.

- **Detection risk**—Detection risk is the risk that the IT audit or assurance professional's substantive procedures do not detect an error that could be material, individually or in combination with other errors.[44] For example, the detection risk associated with identifying security breaches in an application system is often high because logs for the whole period of the audit may not be available at the time of the audit. The detection risk associated with identifying the lack of disaster recovery plans tends to be low since their existence is easily verified.

  Detection risk is a function of the effectiveness of an IT auditor's audit procedures and how well the IT auditor applies them. It can be affected by:

  - Sampling risk
  - Inadequate or inappropriate audit procedures
  - Wrongly applied procedures
  - Misinterpreted results of procedures

Overall audit risk represents the probability that information or financial reports may contain material errors and that the IT auditor may not detect an error that has occurred. An objective in formulating the IT audit approach is to limit the audit risk in the area under scrutiny so the overall audit risk is at a sufficiently low level at the completion of the audit.

An IT auditor should have a good understanding of audit risk when planning an audit. When evaluating internal controls, an IT auditor should realize that a given system may not detect a minor error. However, that specific error, combined with others, can become material to the overall system.

When planning an individual engagement, an IT auditor should:

- Attempt to reduce audit risk to an acceptable level and meet audit objectives by conducting an appropriate assessment of the IT subject matter and related controls, while planning and performing the IT audit.
- Extend the test of controls (reduce control risk) and/or extend substantive testing procedures (reduce detection risk) to gain additional assurance to reduce audit risk where higher materiality exists

ADDITIONAL GUIDANCE

For additional guidance, see ISACA Standard 1201 Risk Assessment in Planning and Guideline 2201 Risk Assessment in Planning.

[43] ITAF 2201.7.1
[44] ITAF 2201.8.1

ISACA. All Rights Reserved.

Page intentionally left blank

ISACA. All Rights Reserved.

2.7 Chapter Two Knowledge Check

Review Questions

1. Which of the following is an example of a preventive control?

   A. Use of hash totals
   B. Programmed edit checks
   C. System backup procedures

2. When using authoritative governance and risk management frameworks, standards and guidelines to develop enterprise practices, an IT auditor would advise that the enterprise:

   A. Tailor the practices from authoritative sources to meet enterprise goals.
   B. Build practices directly from authoritative sources without alteration.
   C. Only choose practices from authoritative sources that are used by its peers.

3. An objective of a risk-based auditing approach is to provide an enterprise with feedback on whether:

   A. All enterprise risk is being properly managed.
   B. An enterprise risk assessment needs to be updated.
   C. Its operational practices and controls are aligned with its risk appetite.

4. Which of the following is a characteristic of an Agile auditing approach?

   A. Audit resources are selected and assigned to perform specific functions.
   B. IT audit planning and fieldwork can occur at the same time.
   C. Audit results are reported at the end of the audit.

5. The probability that information or financial reports may contain material errors and that the IT auditor may not detect an error that has occurred is known as:

   A. Audit risk
   B. Inherent risk
   C. Control risk

Answers on page 62

ISACA. All Rights Reserved.

Chapter 2 ANSWER KEY

Review Questions

1. A. A hash total is the total of any numeric data field in a document or computer file. This total is checked against a control total of the same field to facilitate accuracy of processing. Hash totals are a detective control used to detect and report the occurrence of an error, omission or malicious act.
   B. Edit checks are used to identify erroneous, unusual or invalid transactions prior to updating an application. They are a preventive control used to prevent an error, omission or malicious act from occurring.
   C. Backup procedures are used to ensure that files, equipment and data are available for use in the event of a failure or loss. Backup procedures are a corrective control used to minimize the impact of a threat.

2. **A. An IT auditor should be familiar with IT-related risk and control frameworks, standards and guidance being used within the enterprise and how they are being used. These authoritative sources are useful for the development of an enterprise risk management program, but they do require an enterprise to tailor the practices to meet its specific enterprise goals.**
   B. Many authoritative standards and guidance that pertain to risk and control are available as sources of good practice for the management of IT-related risk. As mentioned in choice A, these authoritative sources are useful for the development of an enterprise risk management program, but they do require an enterprise to tailor the practices to meet its specific enterprise goals.
   C. Having an awareness of practices used by other enterprises within a peer group is useful. However, an enterprise should not simply adopt practices used by others, but instead should tailor its practices to meet its specific enterprise goals.

3. A. A risk-based audit approach is not focused on all enterprise risk but involves the deployment of audit resources to areas within an enterprise that represent the greatest risk.
   B. A risk-based auditing approach is typically based on a risk assessment provided by the enterprise. When developing an IT audit plan, an IT auditor considers the reliability and suitability of the risk assessment provided by enterprise management. Although it is possible with a risk-based audit approach that the discovery of additional risk may require an assessment update, that is not an objective. To remain relevant, a risk assessment should be regularly repeated. If no major changes have occurred in any of the risk factors, a simple annual confirmation of earlier results is sufficient. Major changes in an enterprise environment may necessitate a new assessment.
   C. A risk-based auditing approach provides the enterprise with feedback on whether its operational practices are aligned with its risk appetite. This is determined as an IT auditor assesses the controls that management has designed and put in place to mitigate risk that may hinder or prevent the enterprise from achieving its strategic goals.

4. A. In an Agile auditing approach, if necessary, an IT auditor can shift audit resources to areas of greatest need.
   B. In an Agile audit approach, IT audit planning and fieldwork can occur at the same time. Fieldwork can begin on steps that have already been planned. In this case, if key resources or stakeholders are unavailable, only certain audit steps are delayed and other work can continue.
   C. An Agile audit approach is intended to provide results throughout the audit rather than only at the end of an audit. Early and frequent communication with the auditee allows the final report or presentation to reflect a summary of the issues that have already been identified.

5. **A. Audit risk is the risk of reaching an incorrect conclusion based on audit findings. Essentially, this is the risk that information collected may contain a material error that may go undetected during the course of the audit.**
   B. Inherent risk is the risk identified without taking into account the actions that management has taken or might take (e.g., implementing controls). Inherent risk exists independently of an audit and can occur because of the nature of the business.
   C. Control risk is the risk that a material error would not be prevented or detected on a timely basis by the system of internal controls. Control risk will vary inversely with the level of effectiveness of the internal control structure.

ISACA. All Rights Reserved.

IT AUDIT
FUNDAMENTALS
An ISACA® Certificate

Chapter 3:
Performing an Audit

Performing an Audit

ISACA. All Rights Reserved.

Performing an Audit

3.1 Learning Objectives

After completing this chapter, learners will be able to:

- Evaluate senior management responsibilities and the purpose and achievement of management assertions.
- Perform IT audits with objectivity and due professional care.
- Summarize different types of audits and related audit procedures.
- Explain specialized assessments (e.g., vulnerability) and related scanning and testing (e.g., penetration) activities.
- Articulate audit advisory and consulting roles and services that provide value and improve the quality and control of IT systems.
- Describe the purpose of independent third-party assurance or attestation assessments and how they are used (e.g., ISAE 3402 and SOC reviews and reports).
- Plan an IT audit to determine whether IT systems are protected and controlled, and whether they provide value to the enterprise.
- Conduct an IT audit in accordance with professional IT audit standards.
- Explain how to collect and evaluate different types of audit evidence.
- Use data analytics tools to streamline the audit processes.
- Report audit findings, results and recommendations to stakeholders.
- Conduct audit follow-up procedures to evaluate whether risk has been sufficiently addressed.

3.2 Audit Expectations

This chapter covers the process of performing an audit. The audit process involves planning activities, gathering evidence, evaluating the strengths and weaknesses of internal controls based on the evidence gathered through audit tests, and preparing an audit report that presents weaknesses and recommendations for remediation to stakeholders in an objective manner. In general terms, the typical audit process consists of three major phases: planning, fieldwork and reporting, as shown in **figure 3.1**.

This chapter also covers types of audits and assessments that an IT auditor may perform or that an IT auditor may rely on as part of the audit process.

An IT audit function ensures value-added contributions to senior management in the efficient management of IT and the achievement of business objectives. An IT audit function also ensures that the diverse tasks it performs fulfill audit function objectives, while preserving audit independence and competence.

ISACA. All Rights Reserved.

Figure 3.1—Typical Audit Process Phases

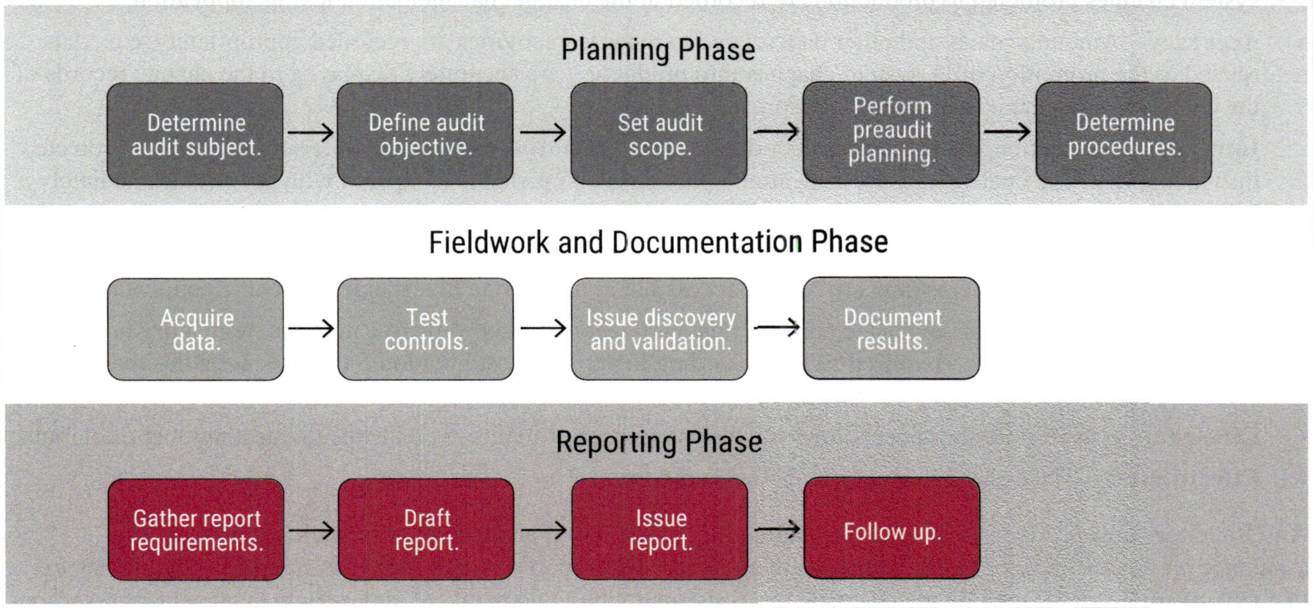

Source: Sweet, E.; "Information Systems Auditing: Tools and Techniques—Creating Audit Programs," ISACA, 31 March 2016, *https://store.isaca.org/s/store#/store/browse/detail/a2S4w000004KoDbEAK*

During the audit, there are expectations of management and of auditors. These expectations include, but are not limited to, the assertions (or statements) made by management that auditors rely on and the expectations others have of auditors as they plan, perform and report their work.

3.2.1 Management Assertions

As discussed in chapters 1 and 2, a board of directors and senior management are responsible for:

- Making sure the enterprise has the appropriate IT resources.
- Implementing IT systems and controls.
- Ensuring that the enterprise IT sustains and extends the enterprise strategies and objectives.
- Protecting the enterprise and ensuring the accuracy of information.
- Complying with applicable regulations.

In meeting these responsibilities, senior management makes assertions, i.e., formal declarations or sets of declarations about the subject matter. These declarations are statements that management makes regarding the business. Assertions are usually made in writing and commonly contain a list of specific attributes about the subject matter or about a process involving the subject matter. The subject matter, which comprises the specific information relevant to an IT auditor's report and related procedures, can include the design or operation of internal controls; and compliance with privacy practices, standards or specific laws and regulations based on area of activity, among other things.

Common assertions include:

- **Confidentiality**—Authorized restrictions on access and disclosure, including means for protecting privacy and proprietary information, are preserved.

ISACA. All Rights Reserved.

- **Completeness**—All activities, information and other data that should be recorded are recorded, e.g., all IT system changes promoted to production are recorded in the change management tracking application.
- **Accuracy**—Amounts, dates and other data related to recorded activities are recorded appropriately, e.g., data related to the promotion of IT system changes into production are accurately displayed in the change records of the change management tracking application.
- **Integrity**—Information, evidence and other data come from trustworthy and reliable sources and are protected throughout their life cycles, e.g., the hash after a backup is completed is compared with the hash immediately before a backup is restored to check for indications of tampering.
- **Availability**—Information, evidence and other data required for an audit exist and are accessible, e.g., the requested change records exist and are readily accessible in the change management tracking application.
- **Compliance**—Information, evidence and other data are recorded according to enterprise, regulatory or other applicable stipulations, e.g., required fields, according to applicable stipulations, are present on the change records of the change management tracking application.
- **Efficiency**—Level of performance allows the lowest number of inputs to create the greatest number of outputs.
- **Effectiveness**—The desired output or objective is produced.[45]

An IT auditor considers these assertions throughout the execution of an IT audit, tests their validity, obtains assurance on their achievement and addresses them in the audit report.[46] Additionally, an IT auditor should ensure that any assertions developed by management are consistent with good practice[47] and review management assertions for an IT audit to ensure that they are:

- **Sufficient**—Enough to meet the purpose of the IT audit
- **Valid**—Able to be tested
- **Relevant**—Directly connected to the IT audit[48]

Before beginning an audit, an IT auditor should ensure that management fully understands its responsibility to provide all required information regarding the subject matter and the assertions. An IT auditor who feels that management will not be able to fulfill this responsibility should:

- Inform IT audit management and those charged with governance of the audit function of the identified issue.
- Not perform the IT audit or determine an appropriate course of action based on the level of risk if the IT audit is performed.[49]

The scope of an IT audit should be sufficient to permit a conclusion to be drawn on the subject matter and restrictions to be addressed. An IT auditor should have a reasonable expectation that the audit can be completed in accordance with appropriate professional, regulatory or industry standards, with the end result being a professional audit opinion or statement.

ADDITIONAL GUIDANCE

For additional guidance, see ISACA Standard 1007 Assertions and Guideline 2007 Assertions.

45 ITAF 2007.2.2
46 ITAF 2007.2.1
47 ITAF 2007.2.3
48 ITAF 2007.2.5
49 ITAF 2007.2.4

ISACA. All Rights Reserved.

3.2.2 Auditor Expectations

IT auditors are expected to conduct audits proficiently and to conduct themselves in a professional manner. This includes abiding by a code of professional ethics and performing IT audits with objectivity and due care while having the appropriate knowledge, competency and skill to perform each IT audit.

Code of Professional Ethics

In the IT audit profession, a code of professional ethics is used to define and guide professional and personal conduct. A code of ethics is a document designed to influence individual and organizational behavior of employees by defining organizational values and the rules to be applied in certain situations. A code of ethics is adopted to assist enterprise decision-makers to understand the difference between right and wrong and to apply that understanding to their decisions. ISACA's "Code of Professional Ethics"[50] is shown in **figure 3.2**.

Figure 3.2—ISACA Code of Professional Ethics
• Support the implementation of, and encourage compliance with, appropriate standards and procedures for the effective governance and management of enterprise information systems and technology, including audit, control, security and risk management.
• Perform their duties with objectivity, due diligence and professional care, in accordance with professional standards.
• Serve in the interest of stakeholders in a lawful manner, while maintaining high standards of conduct and character, and not discrediting their profession or the Association.
• Maintain the privacy and confidentiality of information obtained in the course of their activities unless disclosure is required by legal authority. Such information shall not be used for personal benefit or released to inappropriate parties.
• Maintain competency in their respective fields and agree to undertake only those activities they can reasonably expect to complete with the necessary skills, knowledge and competence.
• Inform appropriate parties of the results of work performed including the disclosure of all significant facts known to them that, if not disclosed, may distort the reporting of the results.
• Support the professional education of stakeholders in enhancing their understanding of the governance and management of enterprise information systems and technology, including: audit, control, security and risk management.
Source: ISACA, "Code of Professional Ethics," *www.isaca.org/credentialing/code-of-professional-ethics*

ISACA requires its members and certification holders to comply with its Code of Professional Ethics. Failure to do so can result in an investigation into the conduct of a member or certification holder and, ultimately, in disciplinary measures. The content in this chapter provides guidance on how the ISACA Code of Professional Ethics applies to the work performed by an IT auditor.

Due Professional Care

An IT auditor and others providing assistance during an audit should collectively possess adequate skills and proficiency in conducting an IT audit and adequate knowledge of the subject matter.

An IT auditor should exercise due care in planning, performing and reporting on the results of the IT audit, possess the necessary skill and competence, and be able to comply with professional standards in order to achieve audit objectives. Due professional care is the diligence exercised by a person with a special skill under a given set of circumstances.

[50] ISACA, "Code of Professional Ethics," *www.isaca.org/credentialing/code-of-professional-ethics*

ISACA. All Rights Reserved.

An IT auditor must maintain high standards of conduct and character and refrain from engaging in acts that may discredit the auditor or the profession. Privacy and confidentiality of information obtained in the course of carrying out an IT auditor's duties should be maintained. Further, such information should not be used for personal benefit, and it should not be disclosed unless required by legal authority.[51]

An IT auditor should approach matters requiring professional judgment with professional skepticism, diligence, integrity and care, and should maintain this attitude throughout an IT audit.[52] Exercising due professional care requires that an IT auditor consider conditions or activities that might give rise to any of the following issues:

- Inefficiencies
- Misuses
- Errors
- Scope limitations
- Incompetence
- Conflicts of interest
- Fraud[53]

The technology landscape is constantly changing. Therefore, it is important that IT auditors maintain their competencies through updates of existing skills and obtain training directed toward new audit techniques and technologies. An IT auditor must be technically competent, having the skills and knowledge necessary to perform audit work. Further, an IT auditor must maintain technical competence through appropriate continuing professional education. Skills and knowledge should be taken into consideration when planning audits and assigning IT audit staff to specific IT audits.

In summary, an IT auditor should:

- Perform IT audits with integrity and care.
- Demonstrate sufficient understanding and competency to achieve IT audit objectives.
- Maintain professional skepticism throughout an IT audit.
- Maintain professional competency by keeping informed of and complying with developments in professional standards.
- Communicate roles and responsibilities to team members and ensure the team's adherence to the appropriate standards in conducting IT audits.
- Address all concerns regarding the application of standards during the conduct of the audit.
- Maintain effective communication with relevant stakeholders throughout an IT audit.
- Take reasonable measures to protect information obtained or derived during an IT audit from inadvertent release or disclosure to unauthorized parties.
- Conduct all IT audits with the aim of reasonable assurance. The level of testing will vary with the type of audit.
- Have the competency to use relevant technology and data analysis techniques.
- Be mindful of the cost of performing an IT audit relative to the potential benefits that may be derived.[54]

ADDITIONAL GUIDANCE

For additional guidance, see ISACA Standard 1005 Due Professional Care and Guideline 2005 Due Professional Care.

[51] ITAF 1005.1
[52] ITAF 2005.2.1
[53] ITAF 2005.2.3
[54] ITAF 2005.7.1

ISACA. All Rights Reserved.

Objectivity

One of the audit concepts addressed in the Code of Professional Ethics is objectivity—the ability to exercise judgment, express opinions and present recommendations with impartiality. An IT auditor should be objective in all matters related to IT audits.[55]

Threats to objectivity may be created by a broad range of relationships and circumstances. These include:

- **Self-interest**—The threat that a financial or other interest will influence professional judgment or behavior inappropriately.
- **Self-review**—The threat that an IT auditor will not appropriately evaluate the results of previous judgments made or services performed, which will be relied upon when forming judgments during the current audit.
- **Advocacy**—The threat that an IT auditor will promote an auditee's position to the point that professional objectivity is compromised.
- **Familiarity**—The threat that due to a long or close relationship with the auditee, an IT auditor will be too sympathetic to the interests of the auditee, or will be too accepting of the auditee's work, views or arguments.
- **Intimidation**—The threat that an IT auditor will be deterred from acting with integrity and objectivity because of actual or perceived pressures.
- **Bias**—The threat that political, ideological, social, psychological or other convictions will influence an IT auditor to take positions that are not objective.
- **Management Participation**—The threat of impairments to objectivity resulting from an IT auditor taking on the role of management, or otherwise performing management functions on behalf of the entity undergoing an audit.[56]

When an IT auditor determines that objectivity is threatened, the auditor should attempt to eliminate or reduce any impairment to an acceptable level or decline or terminate the audit.

If an IT auditor cannot decline or terminate the audit, an appropriate disclosure of the impairment to objectivity or independence must be made to those charged with governance and must be included in the audit report.[57]

ADDITIONAL GUIDANCE

For additional guidance, see ISACA Standard 1003 Auditor Objectivity and Guideline 2003 Auditor Objectivity

An IT auditor should not perform nonaudit services or roles in areas where it is likely that a current or future audit is planned and would likely be performed by the same IT auditor. If the enterprise has no other recourse (i.e., engaging an alternative internal or external resource), an IT auditor's involvement in the nonaudit service should be approved by the chief audit executive (or VP/director of audit) and by those formally charged with governance and oversight of the audit function (e.g., the board of directors and/or the audit committee).[58] Activities that are routine and administrative or involve matters that are insignificant generally are deemed not to be management responsibilities and therefore would not impair objectivity.[59]

[55] ITAF 1003.1
[56] ITAF 2003.3.1
[57] ITAF 2003.2.3
[58] ITAF 2003.2.5
[59] ITAF 2003.6.1

ISACA. All Rights Reserved.

Organizational Independence

An additional audit concept that supports objectivity is organizational independence. Organizational independence ensures that the IT auditor has autonomy and is not subject to conflicts of interest and undue influence exerted by the enterprise being audited (management and employees).

Impairment

Impairment exists when either objectivity or independence is absent. IT auditor impairment is a condition that causes a weakness or diminished ability to execute audit objectives. Impairment of objectivity may include:

- Personal conflict of interest
- Scope limitations
- Restrictions on access to records, personnel, equipment or facilities
- Limitations on resources (such as funding or staffing)

3.2.3 Fraud, Irregularities and Illegal Acts

Fraud is the crime of using dishonest methods to take something valuable from a person or enterprise. There can be many reasons a person commits fraud. One accepted model for analyzing these reasons is the fraud triangle (**figure 3.3**), based on a theory developed by criminologist Donald R. Cressey in the 1950s.[60]

Figure 3.3—The Fraud Triangle

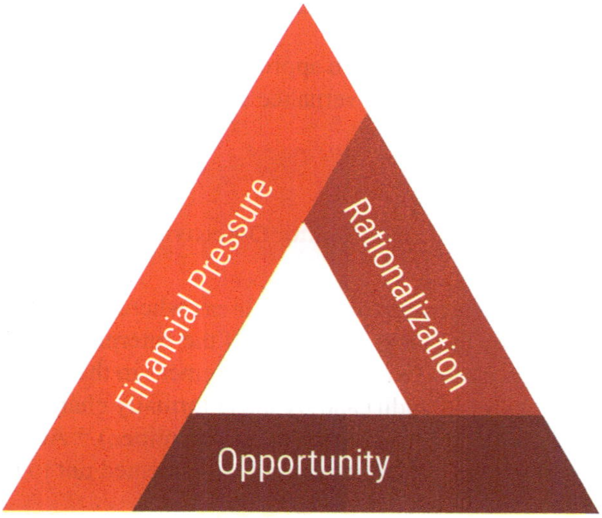

Source: Association of Certified Fraud Examiners® (ACFE®), "The Fraud Triangle," *www.acfe.com/triangle/*

Cressey identified the three key elements in the fraud triangle as opportunity, motivation and rationalization:[61]

[60] Cressey, D.R.; *Other People's Money: A Study in the Social Psychology of Embezzlement*, Free Press, USA, 1953
[61] *Ibid.*

ISACA. All Rights Reserved.

- Motivation refers to a perceived financial or other need. The fraudster may be in debt, hold a personal grudge, have a problem with drugs or gambling, or want to enjoy status symbols such as a bigger house or car.
- Rationalization refers to the way the fraudster internally justifies the crime. Rationalization may include thoughts such as, "I deserved the money," "I was only borrowing the money," "my family needs the money," "my employer has loads of money anyway," or "my employer treats me unfairly." [62]
- Opportunity refers to the method of committing the crime. Opportunity is created by abuse of position and authority, poor internal controls, poor management oversight, etc. Failure to establish procedures to detect fraud increases the likelihood of fraud occurring. Opportunity is the element over which an enterprise—and, by extension, an IT auditor— has the most control. When considering IT assets, opportunities to commit fraud can be limited by security-related controls. These controls typically include logical access (including those for third parties), segregation of duties (SoD), human resources security, etc.

Management is responsible for establishing, implementing and maintaining an internal control system that leads to the deterrence and/or timely detection of fraud. Management typically does this through:

- Internal control systems that include transaction review and approval and management review procedures
- Policies and procedures governing employee conduct
- Policies and procedures that establish governing compliance and regulatory requirements and monitor and validate compliance activities
- Systems that report, record and manage incidents relating to fraud and irregularities or illegal acts.[63]

In addition to designing internal controls, it is management's responsibility to disclose to an IT auditor any irregularities or illegal acts, the areas affected and any action taken. It an act is alleged, suspected or detected, management should participate in the investigation process.[64]

Internal controls may fail if controls are circumvented by exploiting vulnerabilities or through management-perpetrated weakness in controls or collusion among people. Thus, the presence of internal controls does not altogether eliminate fraud. IT auditors should observe and exercise due professional care in all aspects of their work and be alert to the possible opportunities that allow fraud to materialize. They should be aware of the possibility and means of perpetrating fraud, especially by exploiting the vulnerabilities and overriding controls in the IT-enabled environment. They should have knowledge of fraud and fraud indicators and be alert to the possibility of fraud and errors while performing an IT audit.

An irregularity is a violation of an established management policy or regulatory requirement, and illegal acts are violations of laws or governmental regulations.[65] Irregularities and illegal acts can directly impact an enterprise in many negative ways. They can harm finances and reputation and indirectly affect productivity and the retention of employees. It is important that enterprises have awareness, prevention and detection mechanisms in place to identify irregularities and illegal acts quickly. Irregularities and illegal acts are more likely to occur if controls are nonexistent, poorly designed or malfunctioning.[66]

Irregularities and illegal acts can be committed by an employee at any level within the enterprise. Following are some examples:

- Deliberate misstatements or the omission of information concerning the area under audit or the enterprise as a whole, including:
  - Manipulation, falsification, forgery or alteration of records or documents.
  - Suppression or omission of the effects of transactions from records or documents.

[62] ISACA, *CISA® Review Manual, 27th Edition*, USA, 2019, *https://www.isaca.org/bookstore/cisa-exam-resources/crm27ed*
[63] ITAF 2207.3
[64] ITAF 2007.3.3 and 3.4
[65] PCAOB, AS 2405: *Illegal Acts by Clients, https://pcaobus.org/oversight/standards/auditing-standards/details/AS2405*
[66] ITAF 2207.2.1

ISACA. All Rights Reserved.

    - Recording transactions that lack substance and are known to be false—e.g., false disbursements, payroll fraud, tax evasion.
- Acts that involve noncompliance with laws and regulations, including:
    - Failure to ensure that IT systems or processes meet applicable laws and regulations
    - Unauthorized disclosure of data subject to privacy laws
    - Data retention practices that violate applicable privacy laws and regulations
- Acts that involve noncompliance with enterprise agreements and contracts entered with third parties
- Inappropriate or deliberate disclosure of confidential information
- Misappropriation and misuse of assets
- Skimming or defalcation, which is the misappropriation of cash before it is recorded in the financial records of an enterprise
- Acts that violate intellectual property (IP) rights, such as copyrights, trademarks and patents, whether intentional or unintentional
- Acts that permit unauthorized access to information and systems
- Errors in financial or other records that arise due to unauthorized access to data and systems[67]

Although an IT auditor should consider the risk of irregularities, illegal acts and fraud during an IT audit,[68] the auditor is not responsible for the prevention or detection of irregularities or illegal acts. The audit itself cannot guarantee that irregularities will be detected; however, an IT auditor is responsible for:

- Assessing the risk of irregularities or illegal acts
- Evaluating the impact of identified irregularities
- Designing and performing tests based on the nature of the IT audit[69]

When performing an audit, an IT auditor should be aware of the following red flags that may be an indication of persons committing irregularities or illegal acts:

- Overrides of controls by management
- Irregular or poorly explained management behavior
- Consistent overperformance compared to set targets
- Problems with or delays in receiving requested information or evidence
- Transactions not following the normal approval cycles
- Increase in activity of a certain customer
- Increase in complaints from customers
- Deviation from access controls for some applications or users[70]

During the course of regular assurance work, an IT auditor may discover instances or indicators of fraud. These discoveries may result in a need for further investigation and analysis. An IT auditor may communicate the need for a detailed investigation to appropriate authorities. If a major fraud is identified by an IT auditor, or if the risk associated with the detection of indicators is high, audit management should communicate this in a timely manner to the audit committee.

Irregularities or illegal acts discovered by an IT auditor should first be reported to and discussed with audit management to determine subsequent actions, such as reporting to enterprise management or internal fraud

[67] ITAF 2207.2.2
[68] ITAF 1207.1
[69] ITAF 2207.4.2 and 4.3
[70] ITAF 2207.7.2

ISACA. All Rights Reserved.

investigators, and/or reporting to law enforcement or regulators.[71] After receiving direction from the appropriate informed parties an IT auditor should:

- Obtain an understanding of the nature of the act.
- Understand the circumstances in which the act occurred.
- Gather evidence of the act (e.g., letters, system records, computer files, security logs and customer or vendor information).
- Identify all persons involved in committing the act.
- Obtain sufficient supportive information to evaluate the effect of the act.
- Perform limited additional procedures to determine the effect of the act and whether additional acts took place.
- Document and preserve all evidence and work performed.[72]

3.3 Types of Audits

An IT auditor should understand the various types of audits that can be performed internally or externally and the basic audit procedures associated with each. Different types of audits performed by the audit function may include:

- IT audits
- Financial audits
- Operational audits
- Integrated audits
- Compliance audits
- Administrative audits
- Specialized audits (third-party service audits, fraud audits or forensic audits)
- Computer forensic audits
- Functional audits[73]

3.3.1 IT Audit

An IT audit is the formal examination and/or testing of information systems to determine whether:

- IT systems comply with applicable laws, regulations, contracts and/or industry guidelines.
- IT systems and related processes comply with governance criteria and related and relevant policies and procedures.
- Data and information have appropriate levels of confidentiality, integrity and availability.
- IT operations are being accomplished efficiently and effectiveness targets are being met.

An IT audit is designed to collect and evaluate evidence to determine whether an IT system and related resources are:

- Adequately safeguarded and protected
- Maintaining the integrity and availability of data and systems
- Providing relevant and reliable information
- Achieving enterprise goals effectively
- Consuming IT resources efficiently

[71] ITAF 2207.4.4, 4.5 and 2207.7.4
[72] ITAF 2207.7.3
[73] ITAF 2001.2.3

ISACA. All Rights Reserved.

In addition, an IT audit is designed to evaluate if internal controls that have been implemented by management provide reasonable assurance that business, operational and control objectives will be met, and undesired events will be prevented or detected and corrected in a timely manner.

Examples of audits that may be subject to an IT audit function evaluation of internal controls are:

- IT general controls audits
- Application audits
- IT process audits
- Cybersecurity audits
- IT governance audits
- IT infrastructure audits
- Physical security audits
- IT compliance audits
- Pre- and postimplementation audits and testing
- Business continuity/disaster recovery audits and testing[74]

3.3.2 Financial Audit

A financial audit is an audit designed to determine the accuracy of financial records and information. A financial audit relates to financial information integrity and reliability and often involves detailed, substantive testing.

3.3.3 Operational Audit

An operational audit is designed to evaluate the various internal controls, economy and efficiency of a function or department. An IT audit of application controls or an audit of logical security systems are examples of an operational audit.

3.3.4 Integrated Audit

There are many types of integrated audits, but typically an integrated audit combines financial, operational and IT audit procedures and professionals. An integrated audit can be performed by external or internal auditors.

Due to the dependence of business processes on IT, all auditors must develop an understanding of IT control structures. In addition, an IT auditor must develop an understanding of business control structures. This type of integrated audit can be defined as a process focused on risk, whereby appropriate audit disciplines are combined to assess key internal controls over an operation, process or entity. An integrated audit is a team effort by audit professionals with complementary knowledge and skill sets.

Figure 3.4 shows an integrated auditing approach.

[74] Protiviti and ISACA, *Today's Toughest Challenges in IT Audit: Tech Partnerships, Talent, Transformation*, 2019, *www.protiviti.com/sites/default/files/united_states/insights/8th-annual-it-audit-benchmarking-survey_isaca_protiviti.pdf*

ISACA. All Rights Reserved.

Figure 3.4—Integrated Audit Approach

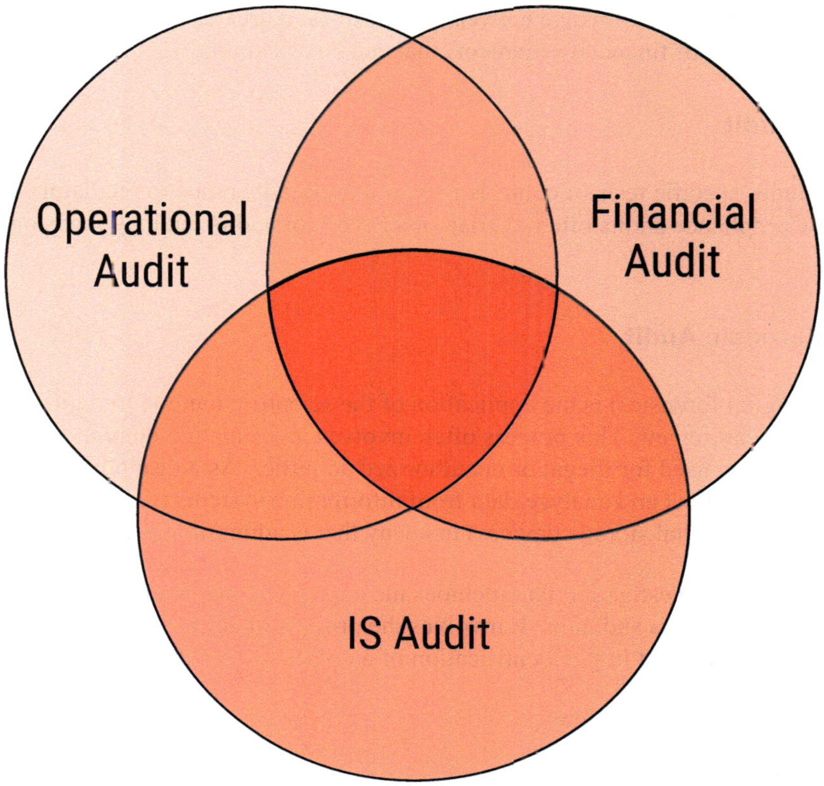

Source: ISACA, *CISA Review Manual, 27th Edition*, USA, 2019, figure 1.14, *https://www.isaca.org/bookstore/cisa-exam-resources/crm27ed*

The role of an IT auditor is typically to understand and identify risk under topical areas, such as IT management, IT infrastructure, IT governance and IT operations. Non-IT auditors typically seek to understand the enterprise environment, business risk and business controls. A key element of the integrated approach is a discussion among the whole audit team of emerging risk, with consideration of risk impact and likelihood.

An integrated audit process typically involves the following elements:

- Identification of risk faced by the enterprise for the area being audited
- Identification of relevant key controls
- Review and understanding of the design of key controls
- Test of key controls to determine if they are supported by the IT system
- Test of management controls to determine if they are operating effectively
- Combined report or opinion on control risk, design and weaknesses

An integrated audit provides the following advantages:

ISACA. All Rights Reserved.

- Employees or process owners better understand the objectives of an audit because they can see the linkage between controls and audit procedures.
- Senior management better understands the linkage between increased control effectiveness and corresponding improvements in the allocation and utilization of IT resources.
- Shareholders better understand the linkage between the push for a greater degree of enterprise governance and its impact on the generation of financial statements that can be relied on.

3.3.5 Compliance Audit

A compliance audit includes specific tests of controls to demonstrate adherence to regulatory or industry-specific standards or practices. Compliance audits often overlap other types of audits but may focus on a particular IT system or particular data.

3.3.6 Computer Forensic Audit

Computer forensics (or digital forensics) is the application of the scientific method to digital media to establish factual information for judicial review. This process often involves investigating computer systems to determine whether they are or were being used for illegal or unauthorized activities. As a discipline, it combines elements of law and computer science to collect and analyze data from information systems (e.g., personal computers, networks, wireless communications and digital storage devices) in a way that is admissible as evidence in a court of law.

A computer forensic audit is an investigation that includes the analysis of electronic devices such as computers, smartphones, disks, switches, routers and hubs. It involves the process of collecting, assessing, classifying and documenting digital evidence to assist in the identification of an offender and the method of compromise.

Examples of computer forensic areas include:

- Email forensics
- Malware forensics
- Memory forensics
- Mobile forensics
- Network forensics

An IT auditor possessing the necessary skills can assist an information security manager or forensic specialist in performing forensic investigations and conduct an audit of the system to ensure compliance with the evidence collection procedures for forensic investigation. An IT auditor may be required or asked to participate in a forensic analysis in progress to provide an expert opinion or to ensure the correct interpretation of information gathered.

It is important that an IT auditor use industry-specified best practices, proven tools and due diligence to provide reasonable assurance of the quality of computer forensic evidence. It is also important to demonstrate the integrity and reliability of evidence so that it will be acceptable to law enforcement authorities.

The information obtained from a computer forensics audit must include why the system was reviewed, how the computer data were reviewed and what conclusions were made from the analysis. A report should also identify the enterprise, sample reports and any restrictions on circulation and include any reservations or qualifications that the IT auditor had with respect to the audit.

Challenges associated with forensic audits are:

- Digital evidence is latent (i.e., evidence needs to be interpreted using a machine or process). Therefore, great care must be taken to ensure the admissibility of digital evidence.

ISACA. All Rights Reserved.

- Chain of custody over documentation is critical to collecting, preserving and presenting valid digital proofs.
- The order in which volatile data should be recovered from various storage locations and devices after a security incident occurs (order of volatility) should be from more volatile to less volatile.

3.3.7 Fraud Audit

A fraud audit is a specialized audit designed to discover fraudulent activity. Auditors often use specific tools and data analysis techniques to discover fraud schemes and business irregularities. Section 3.2.3 discusses the IT auditors role in fraud detection, assessment and investigation.

3.4 Specialized Assessments, Tests and Services

An IT auditor is often involved in performing or assisting in specialized assessments, tests and services, or in reviewing specialized assessments performed by experts.

Effective control monitoring relies on the accuracy and completeness of the data provided for monitoring and evaluation. Data must be genuine and free from errors or misstatements. There are many types of control assessment and testing activities, including:

- Penetration testing
- Vulnerability scanning and assessment

3.4.1 Penetration Testing

A penetration test is a live test of the effectiveness of security defenses through mimicking the actions of real-life attackers. It involves a combination of procedures whereby an IT auditor uses the same techniques as a hacker. Penetration tests are also referred to as intrusion tests or ethical hacking and are an effective method of identifying the real-time risk to an information processing environment. Penetration testing includes identifying existing vulnerabilities and then using known exploit methods to:

- Confirm exposures.
- Assess the level of effectiveness and quality of existing security controls.
- Identify how specific vulnerabilities expose IT resources and assets.
- Ensure compliance.

Penetration testing requires specialized knowledge of vulnerabilities, exploits, IT technology and the use of testing tools. Any penetration test should be carefully planned to mitigate the risk of causing a service outage. The results require careful interpretation and elimination of false positives.

Because penetration testing uses the same type of tools that a real adversary uses, penetration testing can help to establish the extent to which an identified vulnerability is a true weakness. Penetration tests may be conducted by internal or external teams. Rules can range from full knowledge of the infrastructure to zero-knowledge tests in which the testing team has no knowledge of the infrastructure being attacked. An expert penetration testing team is creative and attempts several types of tests to ensure that as many attack vectors as possible are tested, and then generates a report that can be used in the process of risk identification.

ISACA. All Rights Reserved.

Figure 3.5 shows the phases of penetration testing.

Figure 3.5—Penetration Testing Phases

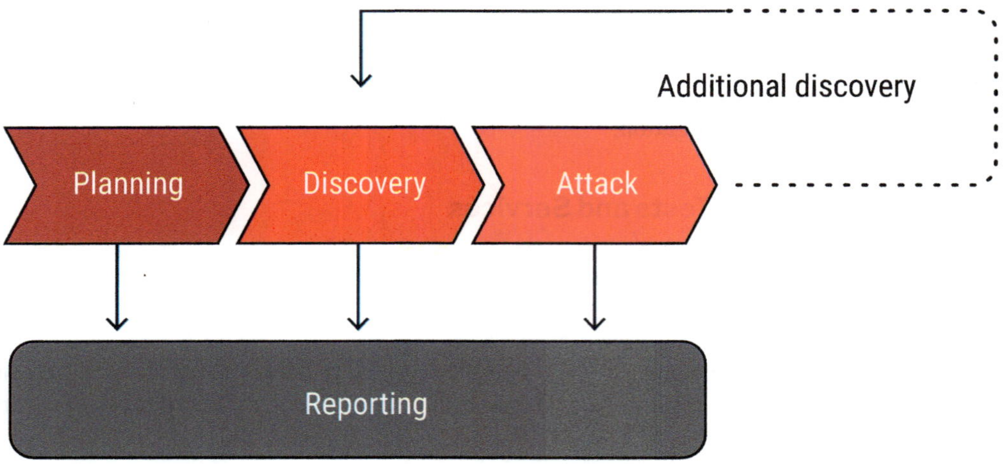

Source: ISACA, *CISA Review Manual, 27th Edition*, USA, 2019, figure 5.35, *https://www.isaca.org/bookstore/cisa-exam-resources/crm27ed*

Penetration testing should only be performed by experienced and qualified professionals who are aware of the legal considerations and the risk of undertaking such work, and can limit the damage resulting from a successful break in to a live site (e.g., avoidance of DoS attacks). It is a simulation of a real attack and may be restricted by the law, enterprise policy and federal regulations. It is therefore imperative to obtain senior management's consent in writing before finalization of any penetration test.

There are several types of penetration tests that may be employed, depending on the scope, objective and nature of the test. Generally accepted and common types of penetration tests are:

- **External testing**—Refers to attacks and control circumvention attempts on the network perimeter of the target, from outside the target system (i.e., usually the Internet).
- **Internal testing**—Refers to attacks and control circumvention attempts on the target from within the perimeter. The objective is to identify what occurs if the external network perimeter is successfully compromised and/or an authorized user from within the network wants to compromise security of a specific resource on the network.
- **Blind testing**—Refers to the condition of testing when the penetration tester is provided with limited or no knowledge of the target information systems. Such testing is expensive, because penetration testers must research the target and profile it based on publicly available information only.
- **Double blind testing**—Refers to an extension of blind testing because the administrator and security staff at the target are also not aware of the test. Such testing can effectively evaluate the incident handling and response capability of the target.
- **Targeted testing**—Refers to attacks and control circumvention attempts on the target, while the target IT team and penetration testers are aware of the testing activities. Penetration testers are provided with information related to target and network design. Additionally, they may be provided with a limited-privilege user account to be used as a starting point to identify privilege-escalation possibilities in the system.

ISACA. All Rights Reserved.

Risk associated with penetration testing includes the following:

- Penetration testing does not provide assurance that all vulnerabilities are discovered and may fail to discover significant vulnerabilities.
- Miscommunication may result in the test objectives not being achieved.
- Testing activities may inadvertently trigger escalation procedures that may not have been appropriately planned.
- Sensitive information may be disclosed, heightening the target exposure level.
- Without proper background and qualification checks of penetration testers, the penetration tester may damage the information assets or misuse the information gained for personal benefits.

Additionally, penetration testing can be used for testing the reliability of firewall access controls. An IT auditor should be extremely careful if attempting to break into a live production system, because, if successful, an IT auditor may cause the system to fail. Permission for the use of such techniques should always be obtained from top-level senior management. Permission from top-level senior management is also required to determine what other tests can be performed without informing the staff who are responsible for the monitoring and reporting of security violations (if any are aware that the attack will take place, they are likely to be more vigilant than usual).

3.4.2 Vulnerability Assessment and Scanning

A vulnerability is a weakness in the design, implementation, operation or internal control of a process that could expose the system to adverse threats from threat events.

A vulnerability assessment/analysis is a process of identifying and classifying vulnerabilities. A vulnerability assessment provides a careful examination of a target environment to discover any potential points of compromise or weakness. Vulnerabilities that may be identified by an assessment include:

- Network vulnerabilities
- Poor physical access controls (e.g., buildings, offices)
- Insecure applications
- Poorly designed or implemented web-facing services
- Disruption of utilities (e.g., power, telecommunications)
- Unreliable supply chain
- Untrained personnel (human resources)
- Inefficient processes (e.g., change control, incident handling)
- Poorly maintained or old equipment

A vulnerability assessment may be a manual process or may use automated tools. Automated tools have the ability to filter large amounts of data and can be used to:

- Examine logs.
- Compile and analyze data from multiple sources (e.g., a security incident and event management [SIEM] tool).
- Examine the functions of a program and run test files or data against a tool such as a firewall or application.

Where content is not easily quantified and requires judgment—including reviews of business processes, physical security and source code—a manual test is better (although automated tools for reviewing code continue to improve). Vulnerability assessments may contain data that is not accurate, particularly false positives that indicate a vulnerability where none exists.

In most enterprises, technical vulnerability assessments use automated scans. Comprehensive vulnerability assessments that include physical elements—such as procedures, practices, technologies, facilities, service level agreements (SLAs), and legal and contractual requirements—are essential.

ISACA. All Rights Reserved.

Vulnerability scanning is an automated process to proactively identify security weaknesses in a network or individual system. Vulnerability scanning is performed by security experts; an IT auditor generally is not involved. However, an IT auditor may be involved in a security audit that reviews alignment with set security criteria and the enterprise's security policy.

Vulnerability scanning uses tools to search for known vulnerabilities. Often the same tools used by adversaries to identify vulnerabilities are also used by enterprises to locate vulnerabilities proactively. Vulnerability scans should be conducted regularly to identify new vulnerabilities and ensure that previously identified vulnerabilities have been properly corrected.

3.4.3 Audit Consultative and Advisory Services

In addition to performing audits and assessments, an IT auditor may perform nonaudit-related consultative and advisory services for the enterprise or on behalf of clients. These consultative and advisory services usually involve a review and analysis of a particular area and typically conclude with an opinion on current performance and suggestions for improvement.[75]

The IT audit charter should establish whether an IT auditor is permitted to perform nonaudit services, and the broad nature, timing and extent of such services, to ensure that neither objectivity nor independence is impaired with respect to the technologies or IT areas that the IT audit function may audit.[76]

An IT auditor may be involved in nonaudit services or roles, such as:

- Advising on IT strategies relating to areas such as technology, applications and resources
- Evaluating, selecting and implementing technologies
- Evaluating, selecting, customizing and implementing third-party IT applications and solutions
- Designing, developing and implementing custom-built IT applications and solutions
- Establishing good practices, policies and procedures relating to various IT functions
- Designing, developing, testing and implementing IT security and IT controls
- Advising on IT projects[77]

Following are a few specific areas in which an IT auditor may provide advisory/consultative services:

- Business continuity plan:
  - Provide management with an evaluation of the enterprise preparedness in the event of a major business disruption.
  - Identify issues that may limit interim business processing and restoration of processes.
  - Provide management with an independent assessment of the effectiveness of the business continuity plan and its alignment with subordinate continuity plans.
- Disaster recovery:
  - Provide management with an evaluation of the enterprise disaster recovery plan.
  - Assess various components of a disaster recovery plan, including proprietary data centers and colocation (colo) sites.
- Third-party risk management:
  - Assess whether the third party is compliant with the terms of the agreement with the enterprise
  - Provide management with an evaluation of if and how the third-party exercises care over the enterprise's data.

[75] *Op cit* ISACA, *IT Audit Framework (ITAF™): A Professional Practices Framework for IT Audit*
[76] ITAF 2003.8.1
[77] ITAF 2003.5.1

ISACA. All Rights Reserved.

- Incident security management:
  - Assess the effectiveness of the incident response program, including (but not limited to) supporting infrastructure, policy and procedures, implementation and maturity.

Providing nonaudit services may threaten or create a potential impairment to an IT auditor's professional objectivity or independence.[78] If there is potential for impaired objectivity or independence in attitude or appearance, the nonaudit service should be closely monitored by audit management and evaluated for any significant indications of impairment of objectivity or independence. Any such impairments and any safeguards that have been implemented should be reported to those charged with governance.[79]

ADDITIONAL GUIDANCE

For additional guidance, see ISACA Standard 1003 Auditor Objectivity and Guideline 2003.5 through 2003.8 Nonaudit Services and Roles.

3.5 Independent Third-Party Assessments

An enterprise can earn customer and shareholder confidence by having a third party provide assurance or attestation of the validity of specific activities or functions. Third-party attestation may be based on an external IT audit or a certification of compliance with an internationally recognized standard. The third party is responsible for evaluating the processes of the subject enterprise and validating compliance with the requirements of the standard.

One source for attestation is the international service organization reporting standard International Standards for Assurance Engagements Number 3402 (ISAE 3402), Assurance Reports on Controls at a Service Organization. This form of third-party assurance is used by many enterprises when relying on cloud or other third-party suppliers that are delivering services outside the control of the enterprise.

In some industries, third-party audits may fall under regulatory oversight and control, e.g., the Statement on Standards for Attestation Engagements (SSAE) 18. It provides rules for conducting an attestation of the internal controls of a service organization, including IT controls and an audit guide by the American Institute of Certified Public Accountants (AICPA®), which provides a framework for three System and Organization Controls (SOC) reporting options (SOC 1, SOC 2 and SOC 3 reports).[80]

An IT auditor may place reliance on SOC reporting as part of the review process.[81] Under a SOC report, a Certified Public Accountant (CPA) firm performs an independent examination of a service organization's system of controls to provide assurance regarding the understanding and reliance on controls that support enterprise processes and systems. There are three SOC report forms available:[82]

- **SOC 1**—Report on the service organization system controls likely to be relevant to the user enterprise's internal control over financial reporting
- **SOC 2**—Report on the service organization system controls relevant to security, availability, processing integrity, confidentiality or privacy, including the enterprise compliance with its privacy practices

[78] ITAF 2003.5.3
[79] ITAF 2003.5.6
[80] AICPA®, "System and Organization Controls: SOC Suite of Services," *https://us.aicpa.org/interestareas/frc/assuranceadvisoryservices/sorhome*
[81] ITAF 2206.2.8
[82] ISACA, *CISM® Review Manual, 15th Edition*, USA, 2019, *https://www.isaca.org/bookstore/cism-exam-resources/cm15ed*

ISACA. All Rights Reserved.

- **SOC 3**—Similar to a SOC 2 report but does not include the detailed understanding of the design of controls and the tests performed by the service auditor

Each SOC report follows a basic outline and contains:[83]

- Service organization management assertion
- Independent service auditor's report
- Service organization description of its system
- Listing of controls tested, their results and any exceptions noted.

The independent service auditor's report documents the overall opinion regarding the service organization system, including whether the system description is presented fairly and whether the service organization controls are suitably designed and functioning as expected. An opinion is presented as follows:[84]

- **Unqualified**—The auditor fully supports the findings with no modifications.
- **Qualified**—The auditor cannot express an unqualified opinion; however, the issues are not pervasive.
- **Adverse**—The auditor believes that there are material and pervasive issues. Report readers should not rely on the service organization's system.
- **Disclaimer**—The auditor is unable to express an opinion due to insufficient evidence, and the possible effects could be both material and pervasive.[85]

  When other than an unqualified opinion is presented, a separate paragraph describing the reasons for the opinion are provided in the report.[86]

When an opinion that is not unqualified is presented, a separate paragraph describing the reasons for the opinion are provided in the report.

In the SOC report, the service organization provides a description of the system in scope. It also provides background information and a description of the infrastructure, software, people, procedures and data covered in the system description. Each type of SOC report includes any relevant exceptions noted during testing.

When relying on a SOC report, it is important that an IT auditor reviews the system description closely to determine what may have been excluded from the audit and determine if anything that was excluded is important to the security of the enterprise system and/or data.[87]

3.6 Audit Planning

IT auditors are challenged with the decision of what to audit and how to prioritize the order in which audits are performed. To meet this challenge, an IT audit function establishes an overall strategic plan resulting in short-term and long-term audit schedules.[88] Audit scheduling helps to ensure that appropriate attention is devoted to the audit function responsibilities as identified in the audit charter.[89]

Short-term schedules consist of audits to be performed within the year, while long-term schedules comprise audits based on risk-related matters within the enterprise information and technology (I&T) environment that may be

[83] Gardner, B.; "How to Properly Review an SOC Report," *ISACA Now Blog*, 19 June 2019, *www.isaca.org/resources/news-and-trends/isaca-now-blog/2019/how-to-properly-review-an-soc-report*
[84] *Ibid.*
[85] *Ibid.*
[86] *Ibid.*
[87] *Ibid.*
[88] ITAF 1202.1
[89] ITAF 2202.2.1

ISACA. All Rights Reserved.

performed in the future.[90] Short-term and long-term audit schedules should be agreed on with those charged with governance and oversight (e.g., audit committee) and communicated within the enterprise.[91]

To effectively develop long- and short-term audit schedules, an IT auditor should:

- Gain an understanding of the enterprise mission, objectives, purpose and processes, including IT requirements, such as availability, integrity, security and business technology, and information confidentiality. An IT auditor should also identify and understand any recent changes that have occurred in the enterprise business environment.
- Perform a risk assessment of areas subject to audit within the audit universe. Risk assessment helps an IT auditor in identifying risk and threats to an IT environment and IT system. Depending on the level of risk, this assists an IT auditor in selecting certain areas to examine and in evaluating IT controls. It also assists an IT auditor in determining audit objectives and in making risk-based audit decisions. (Section 2.3 provides additional detail on risk-based auditing.)
- Evaluate and consider available audit resources and capabilities.

The audit universe is an inventory that is compiled and maintained to identify areas for audit during the audit planning and scheduling process. All the relevant processes that represent the blueprint of the enterprise business should be included in the audit universe. Traditionally, the audit universe includes all financial and key operational and IT systems, and other units that are audited as part of an overall cycle of planned work. The audit universe serves as the source from which an annual audit schedule is prepared. The universe is periodically revised to reflect changes in the overall risk profile.

The structure of the audit universe is driven by how the enterprise manages its operations and the underlying assets that support those operations. For example, an enterprise may manage its operations by business process (e.g., procurement, billing or customer relationship management), by services (email, networking, software, data storage, web) or by any other means the enterprise uses to manage its operations. The audit universe ideally lists all processes that may be considered for audit.

Once the elements of the audit universe have been identified, the IT auditor can rank them. Typically, this ranking is risk-based.

An IT audit function should use an appropriate data-driven risk assessment approach—i.e., a qualitative or quantitative risk assessment performed by evaluating the risk with respect to the defined, relevant risk factors that influence the frequency and/or business impact of risk scenarios.

Many risk assessment methodologies are available to support the risk assessment. These range from simple classifications of high, medium or low, based on an IT auditor's judgment, to more quantitative and scientific calculations that provide a numeric risk rating. There are other methodologies that are a combination of the two. In the end, an IT auditor should consider the level of complexity and detail appropriate for the enterprise.[92]

The audit universe and risk assessment facilitate the creation of the audit schedule and help to determine priorities for the effective allocation of IT audit resources.[93] **Figure 3.6** shows an example of an audit schedule based on IT processes and functions.

[90] ITAF 1202.1
[91] ITAF 1202.2
[92] ITAF 2201.3.3
[93] ITAF 1201.1

ISACA. All Rights Reserved.

Figure 3.6—Sample Audit Schedule

	Sample Audit Schedule	Jan				Feb				Mar				Apr				May				Jun			
Audit Ref. Num	Title	1	2	3	4	1	2	3	4	1	2	3	4	1	2	3	4	1	2	3	4	1	2	3	4
	Business Processes																								
	Human Resource Hiriing/Termination																								
	Electronic Funds Transfer																								
	Governance and Management of IT																								
	Enterprise architecture																								
	HIPAA																								
	Information Systems Acquistion, Development and Implementation																								
	System Development																								
	System mitigation, infrastructure deployment, data conversion																								
	Information Systems Operations and Business Resilience																								
	IT Asset Management																								
	End-User Computing																								
	Change, configuration, release and patch management																								
	Protection of Information Assets																								
	Identity and access management																								
	Network and end-point security																								
	Data classification																								
	Encryption																								
	Virtualization environments																								
	Mobile, Wireless and IoT																								
	Security Event Management																								

Source: ISACA, *Fundamentals of Information Systems Audit and Assurance* (Facilitator Guide), USA, 2018

Audit schedules are typically and ideally constructed to include at a minimum all the processes that have high risk ratings.

An IT audit function should periodically review and modify its short-term and/or long-term audit schedules to be responsive to enterprise needs (i.e., unexpected events or unplanned initiatives).[94] This is necessary to consider new control issues; changes in the risk environment, technologies and business processes; and enhanced evaluation techniques. The results of this analysis for planning future audit activities should be reviewed by IT audit management, approved by the audit committee (if available, or alternatively by the board of directors), and communicated to relevant levels of senior management. After review, any audit that is displaced to accommodate an audit of an unexpected event or unplanned initiative should be reassigned to a future period.[95]

ADDITIONAL GUIDANCE

For additional guidance, see ISACA Standard 1201 Risk Assessment in Planning and 1202 Audit Scheduling and Guideline 2201 Risk Assessment in Planning and 2202 Audit Scheduling.

3.6.1 Individual Audit Planning

In addition to overall annual planning and scheduling, audits require adequate individual planning. A typical audit planning process consists of several steps, as shown in **figure 3.7**.

[94] ITAF 1202.3
[95] ITAF 1202.3

ISACA. All Rights Reserved.

Figure 3.7—Audit Planning Steps

Source: Sweet, E.; "Information Systems Auditing: Tools and Techniques – Creating Audit Programs," ISACA, 31 March 2016, *https://store.isaca.org/s/store#/store/browse/detail/a2S4w000004KoDbEAK*

Determine Audit Subject

The audit subject is the area to be audited. During planning, an IT auditor must identify and understand the overall environment for the audit subject. This should include a general understanding of the various business practices and functions relating to the audit subject, the IT systems that provide support, and any recent significant changes. In addition, an IT auditor should be familiar with the regulatory environment in which the business operates and how it relates to the audit subject.

Define Audit Objective

The audit objective consists of the specific goal(s) of an audit. An audit generally incorporates several audit objectives.

Audit objectives often focus on confirming that internal controls exist to minimize business risk and function as expected. Audit objectives include ensuring compliance with legal and regulatory requirements and ensuring the confidentiality, integrity, reliability and availability of information and IT resources. Audit management may give an IT auditor a general control objective to review and evaluate when performing an IT audit.

A key element in planning an IT audit is to translate basic and wide ranging audit objectives into specific IT audit objectives. For example, in a financial/operational audit, a control objective may be to ensure that transactions are properly posted to the general ledger accounts. However, in an IT audit, the objective can be extended to ensure that editing features are in place to detect errors in the coding of transactions that may impact the account-posting activities.

One of the primary purposes of an IT audit is to identify control objectives and related controls that address the audit objective. The IT auditor should conduct an initial review of the IT system to develop an understanding of the business processes and the applications/functions that support the processes and general support systems, and document them accordingly. Based on that understanding, an IT auditor should identify the key control points—key general controls and key application controls. The audit function should then determine whether to test the key controls for compliance.

Set Audit Scope

An IT auditor should establish the scope of the audit work based on the audit objectives.[96] Audit scope is the specific system, function or unit of the enterprise to be included in an audit. An IT auditor should understand the IT environment and its components to identify the resources required to conduct a comprehensive evaluation. A clear audit scope will help an IT auditor define what specifically will need to be tested and determine the technical skills and resources necessary to perform the audit.

[96] ITAF 2203.3.1

ISACA. All Rights Reserved.

Perform Preaudit Planning

Before beginning an audit, an IT auditor should gain an understanding of the types of personnel, events, transactions and practices that can have a significant effect on the specific enterprise, function, process or data subject to the audit.[97]

A risk assessment should be performed to enable an IT auditor to identify areas and activities for review.[98] A risk assessment is critical in setting the final scope of a risk-based audit. For other types of audits (e.g., compliance), conducting a risk assessment is a good practice because the results can help the IT audit team to justify the audit and further refine the scope and preplanning focus. As part of identifying risk relevant to the area under review, an IT auditor should also consider the results of prior audits, reviews and findings, including any remedial activities.

During the preaudit planning process, an IT auditor should establish levels of planning materiality to ensure that the audit work will be sufficient to meet the audit objectives and will use audit resources efficiently. For example, during the review of an existing system, an IT auditor should evaluate the materiality of the various components of the system with respect to planning the audit work to be performed. Both qualitative and quantitative aspects should be considered in determining materiality.

Preaudit planning may typically include:

- Interviewing the auditee to inquire about activities or areas of concern that should be included in the scope of the audit.
- Identifying regulatory compliance requirements.
- Identifying the resources that will be needed to perform the audit work. These may include:
    - Technical skills and resources needed
    - Budget and effort needed to complete the audit
    - Locations or facilities to be audited
    - Roles and responsibilities among the audit team
    - Time frame for the various stages of the audit
    - Sources of information for test or review, such as functional flowcharts, policies, standards, procedures and prior audit workpapers
    - Points of contact for administrative and logistics arrangements
    - A communication plan that specifies to whom communications should be made, when, how often and for what purposes

Determine Procedures

An IT audit involves the performance of specific procedures to provide reasonable assurance about the subject matter,[99] i.e., the specific information subject to an IT auditor's report and related procedures. Examples of subject matter include the design or operation of internal controls, compliance with privacy practices or standards, or compliance with specific laws and regulations (area of activity). An IT auditor selects and applies criteria against which the subject matter will be assessed.[100] Criteria are the standards and benchmarks used to measure and present the subject matter and against which an IT auditor evaluates it.

[97] ITAF 2203.3.2
[98] ITAF 2003.4.1
[99] *Op cit* ISACA, *IT Audit Framework (ITAF™): A Professional Practices Framework for IT Audit*
[100] ITAF 1008

ISACA. All Rights Reserved.

Suitable criteria include:[101]

- **Objectivity**—Free from bias that may adversely impact an IT auditor's findings and conclusions and thus may mislead the user of the audit report, e.g., the criterion is objective because it was ratified by local law.
- **Completeness**—Sufficiently complete so that all criteria that could affect an IT auditor's conclusions about the subject matter are identified and used in the conduct of an IT audit. Thus, completeness of all criteria used should be achieved, given the IT audit objectives.
- **Relevance**—Relevant to the subject matter and contributory to findings and conclusions that meet the objectives of the audit. Criteria can be context-sensitive; even for the same subject matter, there can be different criteria, depending on the objectives and circumstances of the IT audit. For example, the criterion is considered relevant because data transactions are in the scope of the IT audit.
- **Reliability**—Allows reasonably consistent measurement or evaluation of the underlying subject matter and the development of consistent conclusions when applied by different IT auditors in similar circumstances.
- **Measurability**—Permits consistent measurement of the subject matter and the development of consistent conclusions when applied by different IT auditors in similar circumstances, e.g., the criterion is measurable because each data transaction with unprotected personal information can be uniquely identified and thus consistently measured.
- **Understandability**—Communicated clearly and not subject to significantly different interpretations by intended users. For example, the criterion is understandable because the relevant section of the law has already been the subject of multiple court rulings, helping to establish a clear understanding about the practical execution and interpretation of the law.

An IT auditor should consider the selection of criteria carefully. Adhering to local laws and regulations is important and should be considered a mandatory requirement. However, it is recognized that many IT audits include areas—such as change management, IT general controls and access controls—that are not covered by law or regulations. In addition, some industries, such as the payment card industry, have established mandatory requirements. The relevance of local and international data protection rules and privacy and security regulations should be considered. If legislative requirements are not prescriptive, an IT auditor should ensure that criteria selected meet the audit objectives to ensure compliance with the legislation.[102]

After considering the selection of criteria, an IT auditor should have enough information to identify and select the audit approach or strategy and to start developing the audit program. Some specific activities in this step are:

- Identify and obtain departmental policies, standards and guidelines for review.
- Identify a list of individuals to interview.
- Identify methods (including tools) to perform the evaluation.
- Develop audit tools and methodologies to test and verify controls.
- Develop test scripts.
- Identify criteria for evaluating tests (similar to test scripts used by an IT auditor to conduct an evaluation).
- Define a methodology to evaluate whether a test and its results are accurate (and repeatable if necessary).

The terms audit plan and audit program are frequently used interchangeably. However, they are different types of documents that serve different purposes. The main difference between an audit plan and an audit program is the scope of the document.

ADDITIONAL GUIDANCE

For additional guidance, see ISACA Standard 1203 Engagement Planning and 1007 Criteria and Guideline 2203 Engagement Planning and 2007 Criteria.

[101] ITAF 2008.3
[102] ITAF 2008.2.2

ISACA. All Rights Reserved.

Audit Plan

An audit plan is a high-level description of the audit work to be performed in a certain period of time by the auditor or a team of auditors. An audit plan typically contains details about an audit including the:[103]

- Areas to be audited
- Type of work planned
- High-level objectives and scope of the work
- Fact-finding interviews to be conducted
- Relevant information to be obtained
- Procedures to verify or validate the information obtained and its use as audit evidence
- General topics, such as:
    - Budget
    - Resource availability and allocation
    - Schedule dates
    - Type of report
    - Intended audience
    - Deliverables
- Specific topics, such as:
    - Identification of tools needed for gathering evidence, performing tests and preparing/summarizing information for reporting
    - Assessment criteria (enterprise policies, procedures or protocols) for evaluating current practices
    - Risk assessment documentation
    - Reporting requirements and distribution
    - External reports available (information that can be relied upon, if any)
    - Reports to be requested, if necessary, such as an independent external assessment

System Information Flows

Audit planning involves gaining an understanding of the area being audited. System flowcharts—graphic representations of the sequence of operations in an information system or program—are often helpful. Information system flowcharts show how data from source documents flow through the computer to ultimately be distributed to users. Symbols used should conform to the internationally accepted standard. System flowcharts should be updated when necessary.

An IT auditor should document the system flow process by gathering information, including the computerized and manual aspects of an IT system. The focus should be on processing related to the data flows that are of significance to the audit objective. An IT auditor may find, depending upon the processes and the use of technology, that

[103] ITAF 2203.5.2

ISACA. All Rights Reserved.

documenting the transaction flow may not be practical. In that case, an IT auditor should prepare a high-level diagram or narrative and/or utilize quality system documentation, if provided.

A transaction flowchart provides information regarding key application processing controls. Points where transactions are entered, processed and posted should be reviewed for control weaknesses.

Figure 3.8 is an example of a system flowchart that documents an invoice payment process.

Figure 3.8—Invoice Payment Process Invoice Flowchart

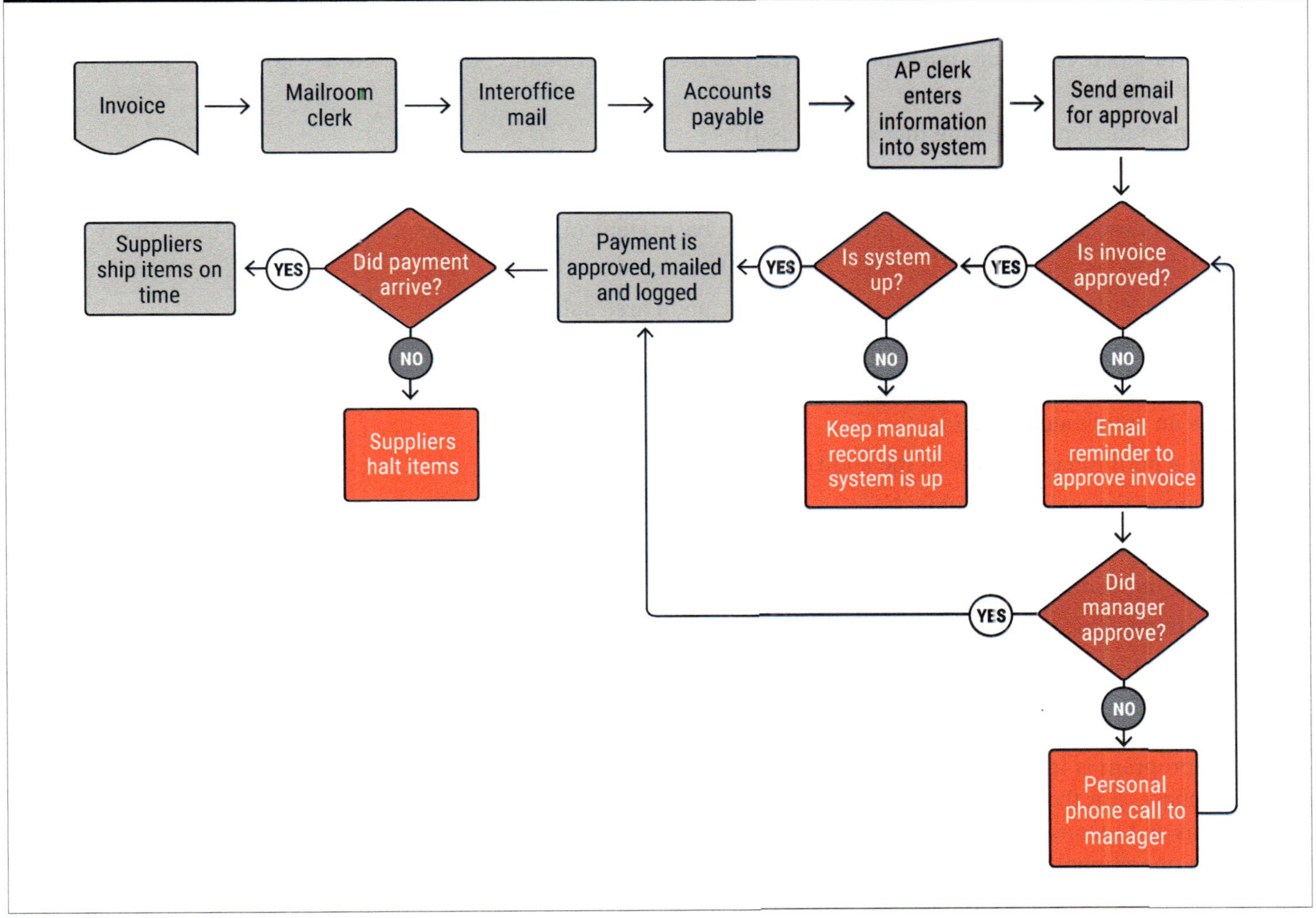

Audit expert systems are specialized tools that can be used to analyze the flow of data through the processing logic of the application software and to document the logic, paths, control conditions and processing sequences. When using audit expert systems, an IT auditor should be thoroughly knowledgeable of the operations of the system to confirm that the decision paths followed are appropriate.

Understanding the business environment can also be achieved through process mining. Process mining enables users to analyze processes from end-to-end. Data to be analyzed are independent of a specific system, therefore data extracted from a wide variety of ERP systems (e.g., SAP or Oracle) can be analyzed by a process mining tool. Examples of processes that can be analyzed using process mining include, but are not limited to, purchase-to-pay, order-to-cash and record-to-report.

ISACA. All Rights Reserved.

Audit Program

An audit program is a more granular description of the work to be performed to meet the audit objectives. An audit program is a step-by-step set of audit procedures and instructions. It includes the steps needed to test controls, evaluate results, obtain suitable evidence to form an opinion and report the findings to the stakeholders. Other details that are typically included in an audit program include the areas to be audited, high-level objectives, and the tools and techniques that will be used to test controls.[104] The primary objectives of developing and using an audit program are to:

- Formally document audit procedures and sequential steps.
- Create procedures that are repeatable and easy to use by internal or external auditors who need to perform similar audits.
- Document the type of testing that will be used.
- Meet general accepted audit standards.

General audit procedures in an audit program are the basic steps in the performance of an audit. They usually include:

- Obtaining and recording an understanding of the audit area/subject
- Creating a risk assessment and general audit plan and schedule
- Performing detailed audit planning that includes the necessary audit steps and a breakdown of the work planned across an anticipated timeline
- Doing a preliminary review of the audit area/subject
- Evaluating the audit area/subject
- Verifying and evaluating the appropriateness of controls designed to meet control objectives
- Conducting compliance testing (tests of the implementation of controls and their consistent application)
- Conducting substantive testing (confirming the accuracy of information)
- Reporting (communicating results)
- Following-up in cases with an internal audit function

The audit program is important for future audits, because it becomes one of the resources reviewed during the planning phase. For the current audit, the audit program is important because it is the source of support for the conclusions and recommendations made for the current audit. Whether the audit being performed is a compliance audit or an operational audit, the IT auditor's testing will involve consideration of controls and control objectives. When the IT auditor is documenting and analyzing system controls, identification of control objectives and understanding of control design are followed by a test of control effectiveness (i.e., does the execution of the design achieve the result intended by its design?)

Minimum Skills to Develop an Audit Program

The most important skill for an IT auditor is being able to understand the business environment and related risk to determine what to test and why.

Development of a meaningful audit program requires the ability to customize audit procedures according to the nature of the subject under review and the specific risk that must be addressed in the audit subject. Following are some skills that can enable the IT auditor to develop good audit programs:

[104] ISACA, *Information Systems Auditing: Tools and Techniques–Creating Audit Programs*, 31 March 2016, *https://store.isaca.org/s/store#/store/browse/detail/a2S4w000004KoDbEAK*

ISACA. All Rights Reserved.

- Good understanding of the nature of the enterprise and its industry to identify and categorize the types of risk and threat
- Good understanding of IT functions and components and sufficient knowledge of the technologies that affect them
- Understanding of the relationship between business risk and IT risk
- Basic knowledge of risk assessment practices
- Understanding of the different testing procedures for evaluating IT controls and identifying the best method of evaluation, for example:
  - Use of generalized audit software to survey the contents of data files (e.g., system logs, user access list)
  - Use of specialized software to assess the contents of operating systems, databases and application parameter files
  - Flowcharting techniques for documenting business processes and automated controls
  - Use of audit logs and reports to evaluate parameters
  - Review of documentation
  - Inquiry and observations
  - Walk-throughs
  - Reperformance of controls

ADDITIONAL GUIDANCE

For additional guidance, see ISACA "Information Systems Auditing: Tools and Techniques–Creating Audit Programs".

3.6.2 Proficiency

An IT auditor must possess the professional competence and have adequate knowledge of the audit subject to perform specific IT audits.[105] IT audit management should ensure that appropriate resources are available to conduct audits included in the IT audit plan. The availability of such resources should be confirmed and ensured prior to commencement of any audit. The professional and technical skills and knowledge required to carry out an audit can vary with their roles in an IT audit.[106]

An IT auditor is chosen to participate in each IT audit based on specific skills and knowledge. Factors may include the auditor's proficiency in identifying and assessing IT risk and controls specific to the audit subject or the auditor's ability to apply specific audit tools and techniques.[107]

An IT auditor should accept only roles, responsibilities and associated tasks that are consistent with the auditor's knowledge and skills. Time and cost issues might prohibit an IT auditor from acquiring all the necessary knowledge and skills before the start of an IT audit; therefore, an IT auditor can accept roles, responsibilities and associated tasks if there is a reasonable expectation that appropriate measures will be taken during the audit to ensure successful completion. The following measures allow a reasonable expectation:[108]

- **Learning on the job**—In certain circumstances, it will be possible for an IT auditor to acquire the necessary skills and knowledge during the audit itself.

[105] ITAF 1006.1 and 1006.2
[106] ITAF 2006.2 through 2006.6
[107] ITAF 2006.2.7
[108] ITAF 2204.3.3

ISACA. All Rights Reserved.

- **Supervision**—An in-charge auditor could arrange for adequate supervision, allowing the IT auditor to perform the audit.
- **External resources**—External experts can be hired for those areas of an IT audit for which there is a lack of adequate internal knowledge and skills. An in-charge auditor may choose to have an inexperienced IT auditor participate and work closely with external experts in order to acquire and/or develop the knowledge and skills required to perform future IT audits.

In addition, an IT auditor can gain competencies through internal team-building sessions, workshops, conferences, seminars, lectures and other modes of interaction.[109]

ADDITIONAL GUIDANCE

For additional guidance, see ISACA Standard 1006 Proficiency and 1204 Performance and Supervision and Guideline 2006 Proficiency and 2204 Performance and Supervision.

3.7 Audit Fieldwork

Audit fieldwork comprises obtaining, documenting and preserving sufficient and appropriate audit evidence to support audit findings and conclusions and to achieve audit objectives.[110] It is the part of the audit process during which an IT auditor executes the audit program by:

- **Assessing controls and gathering evidence**—An IT auditor should assess the controls in scope by gathering and analyzing information and evidence on the design effectiveness and operating effectiveness of the controls.
- **Documenting work performed and identifying findings**—An IT auditor should document the work performed, record the information and evidence gathered, and document any identified findings.[111]

During the course of the audit, an IT auditor should ensure that audit findings and conclusions are supported by appropriate analysis and interpretation of evidence. The audit process should be documented, describing the audit work and the audit evidence that supports the IT auditor's findings and conclusions.

Fieldwork typically begins with an entrance meeting. This is a kick-off meeting during which an IT auditor meets with the auditee. The purpose of the meeting is to ensure that all parties understand the audit process. To achieve this, an IT auditor should:

- Finalize the audit scope.
- Clarify any special concerns or underlying business issues.
- Schedule milestone dates for the audit.
- Explain the methodology of the audit.
- Identify points of contact for both the audit team and the management team.
- Describe what management can expect as the audit progresses, particularly focusing on the audit timeline and the audit report and ratings.
- Collaborate with management on any areas of concern within scope of the audit subject.

It is always a good practice to include senior management responsible for the area under audit in the entrance meeting.

[109] ITAF 2006.2.*11*
[110] ITAF 1204.4 and 1204.5
[111] ITAF 2204.2.*2*

ISACA. All Rights Reserved.

3.7.1 Common IT Considerations

There are some IT considerations (elements) that are common to any IT audit regardless of the specific audit subject. These include, but are not limited to, reviews and tests of:

- Standards, policies and procedures
- Segregation of duties
- Identity access management (authentication and authorization)
- Change management
- System information flows/data reviews and analysis
- Incident management

Standards

A standard is a mandatory requirement, code of practice or specification approved by a recognized external standards organization, such as the International Organization for Standardization (ISO). A standard mandates not only what must be done, but also the way an enterprise must comply with it. Enterprises meeting the requirements of standards may be certified as compliant. Standards can help implement policy, limit risk and support efficient business operations.

Many enterprises believe that the value of standards is the authority and perception of excellence that they provide. In lieu of formal certification, an enterprise may base its practices and operations on external standards such as an ISO standard. Alternatively, an enterprise may develop its own standards, such as requiring all staff to use the same product, operating system or desktop. Proper use of a standard facilitates support and maintenance, provides better cost control, and provides authority for the practices and procedures of the enterprise because a standard requires the implementation of certain practices.

Policies

A policy is a document that records a high-level principle or course of action that has been adopted. The intended purpose is to influence and guide both present and future decision-making to be in line with the philosophy, objectives and strategic plans established by the enterprise's management teams. Additionally, policies need to describe the consequences of failing to comply, the means for handling exceptions, and the manner in which compliance will be checked and measured.

Policies must be developed and communicated. If not, the enterprise has no means of enforcing standards of behavior, which increases the risk that the behavior that occurs may be inappropriate. A lack of enforcement may also lead to circumvention of controls or increased liability because the enterprise recognizes the need for a policy but does not follow its own rules.

An IT auditor should understand that policies are a part of the audit scope and test the policies for compliance. IT controls should flow from the enterprise's policies, and an IT auditor should use policies as a benchmark for evaluating compliance. However, any policies that hinder the achievement of business objectives must be identified and reported for improvement. An IT auditor should also consider the extent to which the policies apply to third parties or outsourcers, the extent to which third parties or outsourcers comply with the policies, and whether the policies of the third parties or outsourcers are in conflict with the enterprise's policies.

ISACA. All Rights Reserved.

Procedures

A procedure is a document containing a detailed description of the steps necessary to perform specific operations in conformance with applicable standards. A procedure is defined as a part of a process. Procedures are created to define the ways in which processes should be carried out. Procedures are invaluable as means of implementing the intent of policies because they specify the tasks that people perform. By describing actions in consistent and measurable ways, an enterprise can greatly increase the probability that an operation will be conducted according to good practice and that any abnormal operations will be detected.

Generally, procedures are more dynamic than their respective parent policies. Procedures must reflect the regular changes in business and aligned IT focus and environment. Therefore, frequent reviews and updates of procedures are essential if they are to be relevant. An IT auditor should review procedures to identify/evaluate and thereafter test controls over business and aligned IT processes. The controls embedded in procedures are evaluated to ensure they fulfill necessary control objectives while making processes as efficient and practical as possible. Where operational practices do not match documented procedures or where documented procedures do not exist, it is difficult for management and auditors to identify controls and ensure that they are in continuous operation.

Lack of procedures makes it difficult to carry out activities in a systematic manner and may result in undependable, inconsistent operations and elevated risk. Procedures should be published and used. It is common for procedures to be followed for only a short time, after which experienced staff begin to work from memory. This practice should be discouraged for any operations in which precision is important, such as shutdown procedures for power plants or industrial machinery, or complex monetary transactions. Quite often, procedures are embedded in information systems, which is an advisable practice to further integrate them within the enterprise.

Policies and Procedures as Benchmarks

The importance of policies and procedures is that they formally state the enterprise expectations. Therefore, policies and procedures become the benchmark that the IT auditor uses when assessing current practices. An IT auditor should verify that management assumes full responsibility for formulating, developing, documenting, promulgating and controlling policies covering general aims and directives. Periodic reviews of policies and procedures for appropriateness should be carried out.

When evaluating policies and related procedures, an IT auditor should:[112]

- Confirm that the most current version of the policy has been disseminated across the enterprise.
- Obtain acknowledgment of the policy if compliance is required of employees, contractors and others.
- Identify the mechanisms in place for monitoring compliance with the policy. If exceptions are noted, confirm that those exceptions are tracked until they are resolved.
- Identify the processes in place to ensure that polices are updated on a periodic basis. This is particularly important for policies that exist in support of external regulations and other requirements.
- Compare policies with actual practices. These comparisons will determine whether controls that are documented are actually being followed and will identify any gaps in controls that are not being addressed.

Section 2.3 provides IT-related risk and control standards that an IT auditor should be familiar with as part of the review for compliance with IT policies and procedures related to the audit subject.

[112] *Op cit* ISACA, *IT Audit Framework (ITAF™): A Professional Practices Framework for IT Audit*

ISACA. All Rights Reserved.

Segregation of Duties

An enterprise should have an organizational structure that provides an adequate separation or segregation of duties. An IT auditor should understand general organizational controls and be able to evaluate these controls in the enterprise. Where there is a strong emphasis on cooperative distributed processing or on end-user computing, IT functions may be organized somewhat differently from separate system and operation functions. An IT auditor should be able to review these organizational structures and assess the level of control they provide.

Segregation of duties (SoD) is a basic internal control that prevents or detects errors and irregularities by assigning to separate individuals the responsibility for initiating and recording transactions and for documenting the custody of assets. SoD avoids the possibility that a single person could be responsible for diverse and critical functions in such a way that errors or misappropriations could occur and not be detected in a timely manner during the normal course of carrying out business processes. SoD is an important means by which fraudulent and/or malicious acts can be discouraged and prevented. Duties that should be segregated include:

- Custody of assets
- Transaction authorization
- Recording transactions

If adequate SoD does not exist, the following can occur:

- Misappropriation of assets
- Misstated financial statements
- Inaccurate financial documentation (i.e., errors or irregularities)
- Undetected improper use of funds or modification of data
- Undetected unauthorized or erroneous changes or modification of data and programs

The IT and end-user departments should be organized to achieve adequate SoD. **Figure 3.9** shows an example of a guideline for the development of a SoD control matrix of job responsibilities that should not be combined.

ISACA. All Rights Reserved.

Figure 3.9—SoD Control Matrix

	Control Group	Systems Analyst	Application Programmer	Help Desk and Support Manager	End User	Data Entry	Computer Operator	Database	Network	Systems	Security Administrator	Systems Programmer	Quality Assurance
Control group		X	X	X		X	X	X	X	X		X	
Systems analyst	X			X	X		X				X		X
Application programmer	X			X	X	X	X	X	X	X	X	X	X
Help desk and support manager	X	X	X		X	X		X	X	X		X	
End user		X	X	X			X	X	X			X	X
Data entry	X		X	X			X	X	X	X	X	X	
Computer operator	X	X	X		X	X		X	X	X	X	X	
Database administrator	X		X	X	X	X	X		X	X		X	
Network administrator	X		X	X	X	X	X	X					
System administrator	X		X	X		X	X	X				X	
Security administrator		X	X			X	X					X	
Systems programmer	X		X	X	X	X	X	X		X	X		X
Quality assurance		X	X		X							X	

X—Combination of these functions may create a potential control weakness.

Source: ISACA, *CISA Review Manual, 27th Edition*, USA, 2019, figure 2.6, *https://www.isaca.org/bookstore/cisa-exam-resources/crm27ed*

SoD CONTROL MATRIX

The SoD control matrix (**figure 3.9**) is not an industry standard but a guideline indicating the positions that should be separated and those positions that require compensating controls when combined. The matrix illustrates potential SoD issues and should not be viewed or used as an absolute; rather, it should be used to help identify potential conflicts so that proper questions may be asked to identify compensating controls.

When performing an audit of segregation of duties, an IT auditor should:

- Obtain enough information to understand and document the relationships among the various job functions, responsibilities and authorities associated with the audit subject area. Inquire (or interview) key personnel about their duties. Include a review of:
  - Policies and procedures
  - Organization chart (and possibly job descriptions)
- Analyze job functions, responsibilities and authorities and assess the adequacy of the SoD to identify any potential conflicts of interest. Depending on the complexity of the applications and systems deployed, an automated tool may be required to evaluate the actual access a user has against a SoD matrix. Most tools come with a predefined SoD matrix that must be tailored to an enterprise's IT and business processes, including any additional functions or risk areas that are not included in the delivered SoD matrix.

ISACA. All Rights Reserved.

- Conduct specific tests to ensure that the SoD for personnel with access to the enterprise's data has been properly implemented. Observe personnel for SoD.
- For any potential conflicts of interest, identify and assess any compensating controls that have been designed and implemented.

Identity Access Management (IAM)

Identity access management encapsulates people, processes and products to identify and manage the data used in an information system to authenticate users and grant or deny access rights to data and system resources. The goal of IAM is to provide appropriate access to enterprise resources.

Identity management is comprised of many components that provide a collective and common infrastructure, including directory services, authentication services (validating who the user is) and authorization services (ensuring the user has appropriate privileges to access systems based on a personalized profile). It also includes user management capabilities, such as user provisioning and deprovisioning.

Identification/authentication is a critical building block of IT security because it is needed for most types of access control and is necessary for establishing user accountability. User accountability requires the linking of activities on an IT system to specific individuals and therefore requires the system to identify users. For most systems, identification and authentication constitute the first line of defense by preventing unauthorized people (or unauthorized processes) from entering an IT system or accessing an information asset. If users are not properly identified and authenticated, an enterprise has a higher exposure to risk of unauthorized access.

Common identification and authorization vulnerabilities that may be exploited to gain unauthorized system access include:

- Weak authentication methods (e.g., no enforcement of password minimum length, complexity and change frequency)
- Use of simple or easily guessed passwords
- Potential for users to bypass the authentication mechanism
- Lack of confidentiality and integrity for the stored authentication information
- Lack of encryption for authentication and protection of information transmitted over a network
- Lack of user knowledge about the risk associated with sharing authentication elements (e.g., passwords and security tokens)

If an end user is asked about authentication, discussion usually turns to passwords. Passwords may be a familiar method of authentication, but they are not the only method, and their reliability has long been the subject of debate.[113] Authentication of devices and users is performed to ensure that access to the enterprise resources is granted in accordance with the enterprise authentication policies.

When reviewing authentication an IT auditor should:

- Obtain and review the enterprise authentication policies.
- Sample the authentication methods in place to confirm alignment with the enterprise policies. Sample devices/users with access and confirm that approval documentation exists.

The authorization process used for access control requires that the system be able to identify and differentiate among users. Access rules (authorization) specify who can access what. For example, access control is often based on least privilege, which refers to granting users only the level of access required to perform their duties. Access should be on a documented on a need-to-know and need-to-do basis by type of access.

[113] Newman, L.; "Why the Password Isn't Dead Quite Yet," *Wired*, 6 July 2021, *www.wired.com/story/passwords-not-dead-yet-authentication/*

ISACA. All Rights Reserved.

Computer access can be set for various levels (i.e., files, tables, data items). When reviewing authorization, an IT auditor should review computer accessibility. An IT auditor should consider what can be done with the access and what is restricted. For example, access restrictions at the file level generally include the following:

- Read, inquire or copy only
- Write, create, update or delete only
- Execute only
- A combination of the above

The least dangerous type of access is read only, provided that the information being accessed is not sensitive or confidential. This is because the user cannot alter or use the computerized file beyond basic viewing or printing.

An IT auditor should verify system controls. The privilege of read/write and create/delete data and files should be granted on a least-privilege access basis. There should be a system in place for regular review of lists of authorized users and removal of users no longer with the enterprise or experiencing changes in job assignments or responsibilities. A good practice is to integrate the review of access rights with the human resources (HR) function. When an employee is transferred, promoted or demoted, access rights should be adjusted at the same time.

IT general controls, including logical access controls and physical access controls, are discussed in more detail in Chapter 4.

Change Management

Change management is a holistic and proactive approach to managing the transition from a current to a desired organizational state, focusing specifically on the critical human, or soft, elements of change. Change management includes activities such as culture change (values, beliefs and attitudes), development of reward systems (measures and appropriate incentives), organizational design, stakeholder management, human resources policies and procedures, executive coaching, change leadership training, team building and communication planning and execution.

Change management in IT involves use of a defined and documented process to identify and apply, at the infrastructure and application levels, technology improvements that are beneficial to the enterprise and involve all levels of the enterprise impacted by the changes.

The primary concern is ensuring that changes to the environment do not introduce stability. Accordingly, an IT auditor should verify that the enterprise has an established methodology for prioritizing and approving system change requests and preventing unauthorized changes to programs.

An IT auditor should determine whether:

- Formal change management procedures are in place to handle in a standardized manner all requests (including maintenance and patches) for changes to applications, procedures, processes, system and service parameters, and underlying platforms.
- Requests for change are categorized, prioritized and authorized.
- There is an established process for handling emergency changes that do not follow the established change process.
- There is a tracking and reporting system to document rejected changes, communicate the status of approved and in-process changes, and complete changes.
- Approved changes are implemented as planned and document and user procedures are updated accordingly.

ISACA. All Rights Reserved.

In addition to emergency changes, there are automated changes and blanket changes that the auditor should consider. Automated changes are processes that automatically generate software changes from one environment to another without human intervention. Blanket changes are a group of changes (e.g., router configuration changes, firewall rule updates) that are needed on a periodic basis.

When performing an audit of change management, an IT auditor should:

- Obtain and review the enterprise's authentication policies.
- Confirm that the authentication methods in place align with the enterprise's policy.
- Sample devices/users with access and confirm approval documentation.

In addition, an IT auditor should perform specific tests to assess if change management controls are present, including:

- Access to program libraries is restricted.
- Supervisory reviews are conducted.
- Change requests are approved and documented.
- Potential impact of changes is assessed.
- Changes are tested prior to migration to production.
- Change requests, including the following, are documented on a standardized form:
  - Description, cost analysis and target date of requested change
  - Control number
  - User approval signature (physical or digital)
  - Programming management approval
  - Assignment of work effort to an analyst, programmer and programming group leader for supervision
  - Description of the anticipated effect on other systems or programs
  - Rollback or back-out procedures to follow if a problem arises when installing the change

3.7.2 Audit Evidence

Audit evidence is the information used to support the audit opinion. During the course of an audit, an IT auditor obtains sufficient, reliable and relevant evidence to achieve the audit objectives.

- **Sufficient audit evidence**—Adequate, convincing and would lead another IT auditor to form the same conclusions.
- **Reliable audit evidence**—Valid, factual, objective and supportable.
- **Relevant audit evidence**—Pertains to the audit objectives and has a logical relationship to the findings and conclusions it is used to support.

An IT auditor gathers a variety of evidence during an audit. Some evidence may be relevant to the objectives of the audit, while other evidence may be considered peripheral. An IT auditor should focus on the overall objectives of the review and not the nature of the evidence gathered. The quality and quantity of evidence must be assessed.

Audit evidence may include:

- Observed processes and existence of physical items, such as:
  - A network security monitoring system in operation
  - An inventory of media in an offsite storage location
- Documentary evidence, such as:

ISACA. All Rights Reserved.

  - Written policies and procedures
  - Results of data extractions
  - Records of transactions
  - Program listings
  - Other documents and records produced in the ordinary course of business
  - External confirmation from third parties
- Representations, such as:
  - Written statements by management, e.g., representations about the existence and effectiveness of internal controls or plans for a new system implementation
  - Oral representations of such things as how a process works, or plans for management follow-up on actions related to the security awareness program
- The results of audit test procedures and analysis, such as:
  - Benchmarking IT performance against other enterprises or past periods
  - Comparison of error rates between applications, transactions and users
  - Reperformance of processes or controls

When gathering evidence, an IT auditor should consider the following:[114]

- The time, level of effort and cost of obtaining the evidence compared to the sufficiency of the evidence in reducing audit risk
- Significance of the matter being evaluated and of the audit procedure requiring the evidence in achieving the audit objectives and reducing audit risk
- Retrievability of electronic evidence in whole or in part after the passage of time

Although all evidence will assist an IT auditor in developing audit conclusions, some types of evidence are more reliable than others. The auditor must consider the rules of evidence and sufficiency and the competency of evidence as required by professional audit standards.

Determinants for evaluating the reliability of audit evidence include:

- **Independence of the provider of the evidence**—Evidence obtained from outside sources is more reliable than evidence from within the enterprise. This is why confirmation letters are used for verification of accounts receivable balances. Additionally, signed contracts or agreements with external parties can be considered reliable if the original documents are made available for review.
- **Qualifications of the individual providing the information/evidence**—Whether the providers of the information/evidence are inside or outside the enterprise, an IT auditor should consider the qualifications and functional responsibilities of the persons providing the information. Consideration of qualifications also applies to the IT auditor. If an IT auditor does not have a good understanding of the technical area under review, the information gathered from testing that area may not be reliable, especially if an IT auditor does not fully understand the test.
- **Objectivity of the evidence**—Objective evidence is more reliable than evidence that requires considerable judgment or interpretation. An IT auditor's review of media inventory is direct, objective evidence. An IT auditor's analysis of the efficiency of an application, based on discussions with certain personnel, may not be objective audit evidence.
- **Timing of the evidence**—An IT auditor should consider the time during which information exists or is available in determining the nature, timing and extent of compliance testing and, if applicable, substantive testing. For

[114] ITAF 2205.3.3

ISACA. All Rights Reserved.

example, audit evidence processed by dynamic systems, such as spreadsheets, may not be retrievable after a specified period of time if changes to the files are not controlled or the files are not backed up.

An IT auditor may seek corroborating evidence from different sources when forming a conclusion on the results of an IT audit procedure. The tests performed and the results obtained should be well documented to support the conclusions reached. This evidence includes:[115]

- Procedures performed
- Results of procedures performed
- Source documents (in either electronic or paper format), records and corroborating information used to support the audit
- Documentation that the work was performed and complies with applicable laws, regulations and policies

ADDITIONAL GUIDANCE

For additional guidance, see ISACA Standard 1205 Evidence and Guideline 2205 Evidence.

3.7.3 Audit Evidence Collection Techniques

Procedures used to gather evidence vary, depending on the characteristics of the audit subject and IT system being audited, the timing of the audit, the audit scope and objectives, and the auditor's professional judgment. Evidence can be gathered through the use of manual audit procedures, computer-assisted audit techniques (CAATs) or a combination of both. An IT auditor should select the most appropriate technique in relation to the IT audit objective. The following types of audit evidence collection techniques should be considered:[116]

- **Inquiry and confirmation**—The process of seeking information from experienced people who are familiar with the subject matter. The experienced people need not be members of the enterprise being audited. This procedure can range from formal written inquiries to informal oral inquiries. Interviewing techniques are an important skill for an IT auditor. Interviews should be organized in advance with objectives clearly communicated, follow a fixed outline, and be documented by interview notes. An interview form or checklist prepared by an IT auditor is a good approach. Personnel interviews are discovery in nature and should never be accusatory; the interviewer should help people feel comfortable, encouraging them to share information, ideas, concerns and knowledge. An IT auditor should verify the accuracy of the notes with the interviewee. Inquiry evidence is considered the least-creditable evidence, especially if obtained directly from the auditee. An IT auditor should seek corroborative data to reinforce the findings. Confirmation is considered creditable if acquired from an independent source (e.g., letters from banks and vendors, or system configuration data via an audit software tool).
- **Observation**—Observing a procedure or process being performed by the individuals who are typically responsible for its performance, or observing physical items such as facilities, computer hardware, or information system settings or configurations. This type of evidence is limited to the point in time when the observation takes place. An IT auditor should take into account that observing the performance of a process or procedure may affect the way the procedure or process is performed. The observation of processes is a key audit technique for many types of review. An IT auditor should be unobtrusive while making observations and should document everything in sufficient detail to be able to present it, if required, as audit evidence. In some situations, the release of the audit report may not be timely enough to use this observation as evidence. This may necessitate the issuance of an interim report to management of the area being audited. An IT auditor may also wish to consider whether documentary evidence would be useful as evidence (e.g., photograph of a server room with doors fully opened).

[115] ITAF 2205.3.1
[116] ITAF 2205.3.4

ISACA. All Rights Reserved.

- **Inspection**—Examination of internal or external documents and records. The items to be inspected can be supplied in paper or electronic form. Inspection can also include physical asset examination. The first step in reviewing the documentation for an IT system is to understand the existing documentation in place within the enterprise. This documentation could be a hard copy or an electronic file. If the latter is the case, controls to preserve the document integrity should be evaluated by an IT auditor. An IT auditor should look for a minimum level of IT documentation. Documentation may include:
  - Systems development initiating documents (e.g., feasibility study)
  - Documentation provided by external application suppliers
  - Service level agreements (SLAs) with external IT providers
  - Functional requirements and design specifications
  - Tests plans and reports
  - Program and operations documents
  - Program change logs and histories
  - User manuals
  - Operations manuals
  - Security-related documents (e.g., security plans, risk assessments)
  - Business continuity plans (BCPs)
  - Quality assurance (QA) reports
  - Reports on security metrics

The reliability of an inspection of records is dependent on the source of the records. Records that are obtained directly from the source are more reliable than records that have been handled in any way by the auditee. If the inspection is of a tangible asset, a cross-check of asset name, model, serial number or product ID should be performed against the asset register.

- **Analytical procedures**—Evaluating data by examining possible relationships within the data or between the data and other relevant information. This also includes examining fluctuations, trends and inconsistent relationships.
- **Recalculation/computation**—The process of checking the arithmetical and mathematical accuracy of documents or records either manually or through the use of CAATs. Recalculation is a reliable form of evidence, as an IT auditor can verify that the same results are reached by independent calculation. An IT auditor should confirm the formula used with an external party to ensure accuracy.
- **Reperformance**—Independent performance of procedures and/or controls that were originally executed by the information system or by the enterprise itself. The reperformance process is a key audit technique that generally provides better evidence than other techniques and, therefore, is used when a combination of inquiry, observation and examination of evidence does not provide sufficient assurance that a control is operating effectively.
- **Other generally accepted methods**—Other generally accepted procedures that an IT auditor can follow in gathering sufficient and appropriate evidence, such as engaging in social engineering, acting as a mystery guest or conducting ethical intrusion testing.

Although these evidence-gathering techniques are part of an audit, an audit is not considered review work exclusively. It includes examination, which incorporates the testing of controls and audit evidence and, therefore, includes the results of audit tests.

An IT auditor should recognize that with system development techniques, such as computer-aided software engineering (CASE) or prototyping, traditional system documentation is not required or is provided as an automated form. However, an IT auditor should look for documentation standards and practices within the IT function.

ISACA. All Rights Reserved.

An IT auditor should be able to review documentation for a given system and determine whether it follows the enterprise's documentation standards. In addition, an IT auditor should understand the current approaches to developing systems—such as object orientation and CASE tools or prototyping—and how documentation is constructed.

An IT auditor should recognize other components of IT documentation, such as database specifications, file layouts or self-documented program listings.

3.7.4 Audit Documentation (Workpapers)

Audit workpapers are the set of documents used to record all the work performed during an audit and demonstrate compliance with audit standards. They provide support for the representations and conclusions in an IT audit report.

Audit workpapers can be considered the bridge or interface between the audit objectives and the final report and are therefore vitally important to the documentation of an IT audit. Audit workpapers, along with the supporting evidence, must enable any person of the same level of proficiency to consistently achieve the same results and draw the same conclusions (i.e., be repeatable and reliable).

Workpapers at a minimum should include a record of the following:[117]

- Planning and preparation of the audit scope and objectives
- Description and/or walk-throughs on the scoped audit area
- Audit program
- Audit steps performed and audit evidence gathered
- Use of services of other auditors and experts
- Audit findings, conclusions and recommendations
- Audit documentation with document identification and dates
- Audit information that is required by laws and regulations, contractual stipulations and professional standards

It is also recommended that audit workpapers include:

- A copy of the report issued as a result of the audit work
- Evidence of audit supervisory review

Audit workpapers should be:

- Dated
- Initialed
- Relevant
- Clear
- Complete
- Self-contained
- Easily retrievable
- Sufficiently comprehensible

Audit workpapers are considered the property of the auditing entity and should be accessible only to authorized personnel. Where access to work papers is requested by external parties, the auditor should obtain appropriate prior approval of senior management and legal counsel.

[117] ITAF 2204.6.1

ISACA. All Rights Reserved.

Audit workpapers should be properly labeled, filed and maintained with a traceable chain of custody. An IT audit function should develop policies regarding custody, retention requirements and release of audit workpapers. Audit workpapers should be retained and available during a predefined time period in a format that complies with enterprise policies and relevant professional standards, laws and regulations. An IT auditor should ensure that audit workpapers are protected from unauthorized access, disclosure or modification throughout their preparation and retention. Periods of retention may be influenced by external requirements. An IT auditor should dispose of audit workpapers at the end of the established retention period.

3.7.5 Computer-Assisted Audit Techniques (CAATs)

A computer-assisted audit technique is any automated audit technique, such as generalized audit software, test data generators, computerized audit programs and specialized audit utilities.

CAATs are important tools that an IT auditor uses to gather and analyze data during an IT audit. When systems have different hardware and software environments, data structures, record formats or processing functions, it is almost impossible for an IT auditor to collect certain evidence without using CAATs.

CAATs enable an IT auditor to gather information independently. They provide a means to gain access and analyze data for a predetermined audit objective and to report the audit findings with emphasis on the reliability of the records produced and maintained in the system. The reliability of the source of the information used provides reassurance on findings generated.

CAATs include many types of tools and techniques such as generalized audit software (GAS), utility software, debugging and scanning software, test data, application software tracing and mapping, and expert systems.

CAATs can be used in performing various audit procedures, such as:

- Tests of the details of transactions and balances
- Analytical review procedures
- Compliance tests of IT general controls
- Compliance tests of IT application controls (ITACs)
- Network and OS vulnerability assessments
- Penetration testing
- Application security testing and source code security scans

An IT auditor should have a thorough understanding of CAATs and know where and when to apply them. For example, an IT auditor should review the results of audit procedures to determine whether there are indications that irregularities or illegal acts may have occurred. CAATs can be used for assisting auditors with continuous auditing and also helping management with continuous monitoring. Using CAATs can also aid significantly in the effective and efficient detection of irregularities or illegal acts.

An IT auditor should weigh the costs and benefits of using CAATs before going through the effort, time and expense of purchasing or developing them. Issues to consider include:

- Ease of use for existing and future audit staff
- Training requirements
- Complexity of coding and maintenance
- Flexibility of uses
- Installation requirements
- Processing efficiencies

ISACA. All Rights Reserved.

- Effort required to bring the source data into the CAATs for analysis
- Ensuring the integrity of imported data by safeguarding their authenticity
- Recording the time stamp of data downloaded at critical processing points to sustain the credibility of the review
- Obtaining permission to install the software on the auditee servers
- Reliability of the software
- Confidentiality of the data being processed

An IT audit using CAATs should ensure that the following documentation is retained:

- Online reports detailing high-risk issues for review
- Commented program listings
- Flowcharts
- Sample reports
- Record and file layouts
- Field definitions
- Operating instructions
- Description of applicable source documents

CAATs documentation should be referenced to the audit program and clearly identify the audit procedures and objectives being served. When requesting access to production data for use with CAATs, an IT auditor should request read-only access. Any data manipulation by an IT auditor should be applied to copies of production files in a controlled environment to ensure that production data are not exposed to unauthorized updating. Most CAATs allow for production data to be downloaded from production systems to a stand-alone platform and then analyzed from the stand-alone platform, thereby insulating the production systems from any adverse impact.

Generalized Audit Software (GAS)

Generalized audit software (GAS) is multipurpose audit software that can be used for general processes, such as record selection, matching, recalculation and reporting. GAS refers to standard software that has the capability to directly read and access data from various database platforms, flat-file systems and ASCII formats. GAS provides an IT auditor with an independent means to gain access to data for analysis and the ability to use high-level problem-solving software to invoke functions to be performed on data files. Features include mathematical computations, stratification, statistical analysis, sequence checking, duplicate checking and recomputations. The following functions are commonly supported by GAS:

- **File access**—Enables the reading of different record formats and file structures
- **File reorganization**—Enables indexing, sorting, merging and linking with another file
- **Data selection**—Enables global filtration conditions and selection criteria
- **Statistical functions**—Enables sampling, stratification and frequency analysis
- **Arithmetical functions**—Enables arithmetic operators and functions

Test Data

Test data are simulated transactions that can be used to test processing logic, computations and controls actually programmed in computer applications. Individual programs or an entire system can be tested. This technique encompasses integrated test facilities (ITFs) and base-case system evaluations (BCSEs).

ISACA. All Rights Reserved.

Test data involve an IT auditor using a sample set of data to assess whether logic errors exist in a program and whether the program meets its objectives. The review of an application system will provide information about internal controls built into the system.

3.7.6 Data Analytics and Artificial Intelligence

Data analytics is an important tool for an IT auditor. Using technology, an IT auditor can select and analyze full data sets to continuously audit or monitor key enterprise data for abnormalities or variances that can be used both to identify and evaluate enterprise risk and to assess compliance with control and regulatory requirements. An IT auditor can use data analytics for the following purposes:

- Determination of the operational effectiveness of the current control environment
- Determination of the effectiveness of antifraud procedures and controls
- Identification of business process errors
- Identification of business process improvements and inefficiencies in the control environment
- Identification of exceptions or unusual business rules
- Identification of fraud
- Identification of areas in which poor data quality exists
- Performance of risk assessment at the planning phase of an audit

The process used to collect and analyze data includes the following elements:

- Setting the scope (e.g., determining audit/review objectives; defining data needs, sources and reliability)
- Identifying and obtaining the data (e.g., requesting data from responsible sources, testing a sample of data, extracting the data for use)
- Validating the data (e.g., determining if the data are sufficient and reliable to perform audit tests) by:
  - Validating balances independent of the data set extracted
  - Reconciling detailed data to report control totals
  - Validating numeric, character and date fields
  - Verifying the time period of the data set (i.e., meets scope and purpose)
  - Verifying that all necessary fields in scoping are actually included in the acquired data set
- Executing the tests (e.g., running scripts and performing other analytical tests)
- Documenting the results (e.g., recording the testing purpose, data sources and conclusions reached)
- Reviewing the results (e.g., ensuring that the testing procedures have been adequately performed and reviewed by a qualified person)
- Retaining the results (e.g., maintaining important test elements), such as:
  - Program files
  - Scripts
  - Macros/automated command tests
  - Data files

ISACA. All Rights Reserved.

3.8 Audit Reporting

An IT auditor prepares a report to communicate the audit results. The audit report should ensure that audit findings are supported by sufficient and appropriate evidence.[118] Successful resolution of audit findings with auditees is essential so that auditees will adopt the recommendations in the report and promptly initiate corrective action. To achieve this goal, an IT auditor should be skilled in the use of techniques such as facilitation, negotiation and conflict resolution. An IT auditor should also understand the concept of materiality (i.e., the relative importance of audit findings based on business impact) when reporting audit results.

3.8.1 Report Objective

The objectives of audit reporting are:

- Formally present the audit results to the auditee (and the audit client, if different from the auditee)
- Serve as formal closure of the audit
- Provide statements of assurance and, if needed, identification of areas requiring corrective action with related recommendations
- Serve as a valued reference for any party researching the auditee or audit topic
- Serve as the basis for a follow-up audit if audit findings are presented
- Promote audit credibility through a well-developed and well-written report

Every audit report should provide unbiased, well-supported responses to the audit objectives. For example, if the audit objective is to determine whether adequate controls are in effect to provide reasonable assurance that only authorized physical access can be gained to the data center, then the report should state an IT auditor's conclusion or opinion as to the adequacy of the controls to achieve that objective. If controls need to be implemented or strengthened to achieve the objective, then the report should provide a recommendation to meet that need.

3.8.2 Report Structure

An audit report is the end product of the IT audit work. The exact format of an audit report will vary by enterprise; however, an IT auditor should understand the basic components of an audit report and how it communicates audit findings to management.

Audit reports usually have the following structure and content:

- Introduction to the report, including:
  - Statement of audit objectives
  - Scope of the audit, including a description of the audit subject or activity, the period under review and the period when the audit was performed
  - Nature and extent of the work performed
  - Qualifications or limitations to the audit and scope
  - Period of audit coverage
  - General statement on the nature and extent of audit procedures conducted and processes examined during the audit
  - Statement on the IT audit methodology and guidelines followed (For example, the report should include a statement that the audit was conducted in accordance with ISACA IT audit and assurance standards or other

[118] ITAF 1401.1 and 1401.2

ISACA. All Rights Reserved.

applicable professional standards. Any noncompliance with the standards should be explicitly mentioned in the report.[119])

- Audit findings included in separate sections and often grouped in sections by materiality and/or intended recipient
- IT auditor's overall conclusion and opinion on the adequacy of controls and procedures examined during the audit, and the actual potential risk identified as a consequence of detected deficiencies
- IT auditor's reservations or qualifications with respect to the audit (For example, the report may state that the controls or procedures examined were found to be adequate or inadequate. The balance of the audit report should support that conclusion, and the overall evidence gathered during the audit should provide an even greater level of support for the audit conclusions. Qualifications may include the professional certification of the IT auditor who performed the audit, such as ISACA Certified Information Systems Auditor (CISA) designation.)
- Detailed audit findings and recommendations based on the materiality of the findings and the intended recipient of the audit report (For example, an audit report directed to the audit committee of the board of directors should not include findings that are important only to local management but have little control significance to the overall enterprise. The decision on what to include in various levels of audit reports depends on the guidance provided by IT audit management. Findings that are minor may be presented to management in an alternate format, such as by memorandum, rather than included in the audit report.)
- Auditee management responses to findings, conclusions and recommendations for corrective action[120]

An IT auditor should provide a balanced report, describing not only negative issues in terms of findings but also positive constructive comments regarding improved processes and controls or effectiveness of controls already in place. Overall, an IT auditor should exercise objectivity in the reporting process.

An IT auditor should identify the elements of the audit report that are to remain confidential versus the elements that can be publicly disclosed. Inappropriate disclosure of sensitive information without supporting context may be detrimental to the enterprise and/or the enterprise's shareholders.

Occasionally, events occur after the testing period but prior to issuance of the audit report. Such occurrences, referred to as subsequent events, may require disclosure because they may change an assertion or a conclusion. An IT auditor should inquire whether management is aware of any subsequent events and, if not, obtain a written representation to that effect from auditee management.

3.8.3 Audit Report Communication

An audit report is issued to management of the group or subject being audited. An audit report is also shared with the audit committee of the board of directors and the enterprise external audit firm. The visibility of the report's findings and recommendations for corrective action amplifies the need for accuracy and clear communication.

An IT auditor should tailor the audit report presentation to the audience. For example, the audit committee may be well-versed in audit terminology and technical details and can be expected to understand the detail of evidential reports, but that should not be assumed. Members of the board of directors may require only an executive summary that skips over findings that are important only to auditee management with little control significance to the overall enterprise. Findings and recommendations should be presented and communicated from a business perspective.

After an IT auditor presents the auditee with detailed audit findings and recommendations, auditee management evaluates the findings, stating corrective actions to be taken and timing for implementing them. An IT auditor should discuss the recommendations and any planned implementation dates prior to release of the formal audit report. Various constraints—such as staff limitations, budgets or other projects—may limit immediate implementation.

[119] ITAF 2401.2.1
[120] ITAF 2401.2.11

ISACA. All Rights Reserved.

Auditee management should develop a firm program for taking corrective actions. The auditor should obtain a commitment from auditee management on the date of full implementation of the action plan and the manner in which it will be performed. The solution can take a long time to implement, and the corrective action may bring risk that may be avoided if identified while discussing and finalizing the audit report.

ADDITIONAL GUIDANCE

For additional guidance, see ISACA Standard 1401 Reporting and Guideline 2401 Reporting.

3.9 Audit Remediation

Audit remediation is the final stage of an audit when an IT auditor confirms that auditee management has taken the corrective action identified in the audit report. Alternatively, if auditee management has accepted the risk of not taking corrective action, an IT auditor documents and reports that fact during the remediation stage.

3.9.1 Follow-Up Process

Auditing is an ongoing process. An IT auditor is not effective if IT audits are performed and reports are issued, but no follow-up is conducted to determine whether auditee management has taken appropriate corrective actions. An IT auditor should have a follow-up program to determine if agreed-on corrective actions have been implemented. The timing of the follow-up depends on the criticality of the findings and is subject to an IT auditor's judgment.

Follow-up activities should be scheduled with the other steps necessary to perform each review. Specific follow-up activities and their timing may be influenced by the degree of difficulty, the risk and exposure involved, the results of the review, the time needed for implementing corrective actions, and other factors. An IT auditor should follow up on agreed-on outcomes relating to high-risk issues soon after the due date for action and should monitor them progressively.[121]

The results of the follow-up should be communicated to appropriate levels of management. An IT auditor should periodically report to the board of directors and/or the audit committee on management's progress in findings and implementing recommendations.

Auditee management may decide to accept the risk of not correcting a reported condition because of cost, complexity of the corrective action or other considerations. If it is determined that the risk related to a finding is greater than the enterprise's risk appetite and has been accepted by auditee management, the risk acceptance should be discussed with IT audit management. The acceptance of the risk (particularly failure to resolve the risk) should be approved by executive management and brought to the attention of the audit committee and/or the board of directors.[122]

3.9.2 Follow-Up Activities

Procedures for follow-up activities should be established, including:[123]

- Recording of a time frame within which management should respond to agreed-on recommendations
- Evaluation of management's response
- Verification of the response, if appropriate

[121] ITAF 2402.6.2 and 2402.6.3
[122] ITAF 1402.1 through 1402.1.3, 2402.4.1 and 2402.4.2
[123] ITAF 2402.5.1

ISACA. All Rights Reserved.

- Communication procedures that escalate outstanding and unsatisfactory responses and/or actions to the appropriate levels of management and to those charged with governance

An IT auditor's approach to follow-up activities should be aligned with risk management:

- **Time**—The amount of time for auditee management to act depends on the effect on the enterprise if corrective action is not taken. If risk is of significant magnitude in the absence of corrective action, corrective action is typically required within a relatively short time frame. An IT auditor should ensure that evaluation or verification of auditee management's action is conducted as soon as auditee management has completed its work. In the event that the action is unsatisfactory, an IT auditor can take further steps to ensure that auditee management implements a satisfactory solution.
- **Number of findings—I**f an auditee has many findings that are ranked other than low-risk, an IT auditor may consult with auditee management to ensure that corrective action is not hindered by limited resources as operational staff perform routine duties in addition to working on solutions for audit findings.
- **Degree of difficulty**—An IT auditor may wish to consult with auditee management if corrective action is challenging due to complexity of the solution.

In all these scenarios, an IT auditor may consider monitoring auditee management's progress in taking corrective action rather than waiting until the target date to evaluate its effectiveness.

Reporting should provide those charged with oversight (e.g., the audit committee and chief executives) with a summary of agreed-on corrective actions. Recommended activities that should be reported are the status of management's actions detailed by the observation, the recommendation, the risk ranking of the finding and the target date. Reporting should also share trends, which are equally important as status of individual audit findings. For example, an IT auditor may aggregate findings by subject area, operational area or some other category. It is recommended that the categories selected align with the classifications used in the enterprise's risk universe and risk assessment.

Another element that an IT auditor may consider reporting is the number of times a target date is extended. Also, reporting any instances of a finding being closed in one IT audit but reoccurring in a subsequent IT audit is helpful. This is an indication that the corrective action taken either was not the action needed to address the finding or that the execution of the corrective action failed in some way.

ISACA. All Rights Reserved.

3.10 Chapter Three Knowledge Check

Review Questions

1. An IT auditor is assigned to perform an audit in the same area that the auditor previously audited. Because it applies to a possible impairment of objectivity, the IT auditor should:

   A. Perform the audit as assigned because there is no threat to objectivity.
   B. Refuse to perform the audit due to an objectivity impairment.
   C. Perform the audit but disclose a possible objectivity impairment to those charged with governance.

2. What type of audit typically involves IT auditors and non-IT auditors collectively identifying, reviewing and testing key controls?

   A. Operational audit
   B. Integrated audit
   C. Specialized fraud audit

3. What type of assessment involves an IT auditor attempting to circumvent the security features of an IT system and exploit system vulnerabilities to gain access that would otherwise be unauthorized?

   A. Vulnerability scan
   B. Vulnerability assessment
   C. Penetration test

4. Which type of SOC report does an IT auditor review to identify and evaluate the detailed tests performed by an external audit firm on IT system controls relevant to security, availability, processing integrity, confidentiality or privacy?

   A. SOC 1 report
   B. SOC 2 report
   C. SOC 3 report

5. Which of the following depicts the sequence of steps in a typical individual audit planning process?

   A. Determine audit subject. → Define audit objective. → Set audit scope. → Perform preaudit planning. → Determine procedures.

   B. Determine audit subject. → Perform preaudit planning. → Define audit objective. → Set audit scope. → Determine procedures.

   C. Determine audit subject. → Set audit scope. → Perform preaudit planning. → Define audit objective. → Determine procedures.

ISACA. All Rights Reserved.

6. Which of the following types of evidence does an IT auditor consider the **MOST** reliable?
   A. A copy of a signed contract or agreement with an external party
   B. A confirmation letter received from an outside source
   C. A judgment made about the efficiency of an IT application based on a discussion with IT personnel

7. When preparing an audit report, an IT auditor should:
   A. Ensure that the audit report is succinct and includes only negative issues discovered during the audit and related recommendations for improvement.
   B. Discuss recommendations for improvement with the auditee, but independently determine the specific dates for implementation of corrective actions.
   C. Discuss what to include in various levels of audit reports with audit management.

8. The timing of a follow-up program by an IT auditor to determine if agreed-on corrective actions have been implemented by the auditee is influenced **MOST** by the:
   A. Criticality of the audit findings
   B. Number of audit findings
   C. Length of time since the completion of the audit

Answers on page 113

ISACA. All Rights Reserved.

Chapter 3 ANSWER KEY

Review Questions

1. **A. An IT auditor should perform the audit as assigned. Performing the same audit more than once is not a threat to objectivity unless an IT auditor has a long or close relationship with the auditee.**

   B. Performing the same audit more than once is not a threat to objectivity. However, an IT auditor who determines that there is a threat to objectivity should attempt to eliminate or reduce any impairment to an acceptable level or decline or terminate the audit.

   C. Performing the same audit more than once is not a threat to auditor objectivity. However, if an IT auditor determines there is a threat to objectivity but is unable to decline or terminate the audit, the IT auditor should make an appropriate disclosure of the impairment to objectivity or independence to those charged with governance.

2. A. An operational audit is designed to evaluate the various internal controls, economy and efficiency of a function or department and may or may not involve IT audit and non-IT audit professionals.

   B. An integrated audit typically combines financial, operational and IT audit procedures and professionals. An integrated audit is a team effort of audit professionals with different knowledge and skill sets.

   C. A specialized fraud audit is designed to discover fraudulent activity. It often involves the use of specific tools and data analysis techniques to discover fraud schemes and business irregularities. A specialized fraud audit may or may not involve both IT audit and non-IT audit professionals.

3. A. Vulnerability scanning is an automated process to proactively identify security weaknesses in a network or individual system. Vulnerability scanning is performed by security experts and an IT auditor is generally not involved. Vulnerability scanning entails the use of tools to search for new or known vulnerabilities without attempting to circumvent and then access an IT system.

   B. A vulnerability assessment is used to identify and classify vulnerabilities. A vulnerability assessment provides a careful examination of a target environment to discover any potential points of compromise or weakness without attempting to circumvent and then access an IT system.

   C. Penetration testing includes identifying existing IT system vulnerabilities and then using known exploit methods to confirm exposures, assess the level of effectiveness and quality of existing security controls, and identify how specific vulnerabilities expose IT resources and assets.

4. A. A SOC 1 report is relevant to enterprise internal controls over financial reporting only.

   B. A SOC 2 report is relevant to security, availability, processing integrity, confidentiality or privacy. It includes a detailed description of the design of controls and the tests performed by the external audit firm.

   C. A SOC 3 report is similar to a SOC 2 report, but does not include a detailed description of the design of controls and the tests performed by the external audit firm.

ISACA. All Rights Reserved.

5. **A. When planning a typical audit, an IT auditor takes steps in the following sequence. This sequence ensures that the audit meets its objective.**
   - **Determines the audit subject.**
   - **Defines audit objectives.**
   - **Establishes the scope of the audit work to be performed, based on the audit objectives.**
   - **Performs preaudit planning that includes identifying the resources needed to perform the audit work.**
   - **Determines the specific procedures to conduct the audit.**

   B. When planning an individual audit, an IT auditor:
   - Determines the audit subject.
   - Performs preaudit planning.
   - Defines audit objectives.
   - Sets audit scope.
   - Determines audit procedures.

   After determining the audit subject, the IT auditor should define audit objectives, establish the scope of the audit work to be performed, perform preaudit planning, and determine the specific procedures to conduct the audit.

   C. When planning an individual audit, an IT auditor:
   - Determines the audit subject.
   - Sets audit scope.
   - Performs preaudit planning.
   - Defines audit objectives.
   - Determines audit procedures.

   After determining the audit subject, the IT auditor should define audit objectives, establish the scope of the audit work to be performed, perform preaudit planning, and determine the specific procedures to conduct the audit.

6. A. A signed contract or agreement with an external party is considered reliable if the original documents are made available for review. However, a copy is considered less reliable, given that a copy could contain altered information.

   B. Evidence obtained from outside sources is more reliable than evidence from within an enterprise. This is why confirmation letters are used for verification of accounts receivable balances.

   C. Objective evidence is more reliable than evidence that requires considerable judgment or interpretation. An IT auditor's analysis of the efficiency of an IT application, based on discussions with certain personnel, may not be objective audit evidence.

7. A. When reporting or presenting audit results, an IT auditor should provide a balanced report, describing not only negative issues in terms of findings, but also positive constructive comments regarding improved processes and controls or effective controls already in place.

   B. An IT auditor should discuss the findings and recommendations and any planned implementation dates while in the process of releasing the audit report. Auditee management should evaluate the findings, stating corrective actions to be taken and timing for implementing corrective actions.

ISACA. All Rights Reserved.

C. The decision of what to include in various levels of audit reports should be discussed and guided by audit management. For example, the audit committee may be well-versed in audit terminology and technical details and can be expected to understand the detail of evidential reports, but that should not be assumed. Members of the board of directors may require only an executive summary that may skip over findings that are important only to auditee management with little control significance to the overall enterprise.

8. **A. An IT auditor should have a follow-up program to determine if agreed-on corrective actions have been implemented. The timing of the follow-up depends on the criticality of the findings and is subject to an IT auditor's judgement.**

B. The number of audit findings should not impact the timing of any follow-up activity. However, if an auditee has many findings that are ranked anything other than low-risk, an IT auditor may consult with auditee management to ensure that corrective action is not hindered by limited resources as operational staff perform routine duties in addition to working on solutions for audit findings.

C. The mere length of time that has passed since the completion of the audit should not impact the timing of any follow-up activity unless findings are significant (critical).

ISACA. All Rights Reserved.

Page intentionally left blank

ISACA. All Rights Reserved.

IT AUDIT
FUNDAMENTALS
An ISACA® Certificate

Chapter 4:

IT Environment and Components

IT Environment and Components

ISACA. All Rights Reserved.

IT Environment and Components

4.1 Learning Objectives

This chapter provides a description and review of the components of a traditional IT infrastructure and cloud computing environment. Where appropriate, controls and areas of concern are also presented and discussed. After completing this chapter, learners will be able to:

- Describe common IT infrastructure components.
- Evaluate IT infrastructure components and controls.
- Identify concerns associated with the use of hardware, software, operating systems and networks.
- Conduct periodic reviews of the enterprise IT infrastructure.
- Describe different types of operating systems.
- Evaluate database structures and management practices.
- Summarize cloud computing characteristics, risk and controls.
- Explain the objectives and deployment of IT general controls.
- Describe logical access controls and exposures.
- Evaluate change, configuration, release, and patch management policies and practices.
- Articulate data backup and recovery practices.
- Explain business continuity and disaster recovery planning practices.
- Describe systems development life cycle phases and concerns.
- Explain the purpose of application controls and how they are used.

4.2 Traditional IT Infrastructure

In the course of planning and conducting an IT audit, it is necessary for the IT auditor to understand the enterprise IT architecture. This includes developing a working knowledge of common IT components and related devices and how they function. An IT auditor is not expected or required to be a technical expert in the design, implementation or support of IT systems and applications. However, a strong knowledge of IT environment components helps an IT auditor to:

- Interact with IT staff
- Develop IT audit procedures and tests
- Determine the skills and competency required to conduct an IT audit

Computers are the fundamental building blocks of IT. Enterprises design and build networks to connect computers enable sharing of local network resources like printers and storage devices. Computers can be categorized according to several criteria—mainly their processing power, size and architecture. These categories are shown in **figure 4.1**.

Figure 4.1—Common Types of Computers	
Supercomputers	Very large and expensive computers with the highest processing speed, designed to be used for specialized purposes or fields that require extensive processing power (e.g., complex mathematical or logical calculations). They are typically dedicated to a few specific specialized system or application programs.

ISACA. All Rights Reserved.

Figure 4.1—Common Types of Computers *(cont.)*	
Mainframes	Large, general-purpose computers that are made to share their processing power and facilities with thousands of internal or external users. Mainframes accomplish this by executing a large variety of tasks almost simultaneously. The range of capabilities of these computers is extensive. A mainframe computer often has its own proprietary OS that can support background (batch) and real-time (online) programs operating parallel applications. Mainframes have traditionally been the main data processing and data warehousing resource of large organizations and, as such, have long been protected by a number of the early security and control tools.
High-end and midrange servers	Multiprocessing systems capable of supporting thousands of simultaneous users. In size and power, they can be comparable to a mainframe. High-end/midrange servers have many of the control features of mainframes such as online memory and CPU management, physical and logical partitioning, etc. Their capabilities are also comparable to mainframes in terms of speed for processing data and execution of client programs, but they cost much less than mainframes. Their OSs and system software base components are often commercial products. The higher-end devices generally use UNIX and, in many cases, are used as database servers while smaller devices are more likely to use the Windows® OS and be used as application servers and file/print servers.
Personal computers (PCs)	Small computer systems, referred to as PCs or workstations, that are designed for individual users, inexpensively priced and based on microprocessor technology. Their use includes office automation functions such as word processing, spreadsheets and email; small database management; interaction with web-based applications; and others such as personal graphics, voice, imaging, design, web access and entertainment. Although designed as single-user systems, these computers are commonly linked together to form a network.
Thin client computers	These are personal computers that are generally configured with minimal hardware features (e.g., diskless workstation) with the intent being that most processing occurs at the server level using software, such as Microsoft Terminal Services or Citrix Presentation Server, to access a suite of applications.
Laptop computers	Lightweight (under 10 pounds/5 kilograms) personal computers that are easily transportable and are powered by a normal AC connection or by a rechargeable battery pack. Similar to the desktop variety of personal computers in capability, they have similar CPUs, memory capacity and disk storage capacity, but the battery pack makes them less vulnerable to power failures. Being portable, these are vulnerable to theft. Devices may be stolen to obtain information contained therein and hijack connectivity, either within an internal local area network (LAN) or remotely.
Smartphones, tablets and other handheld devices	Handheld devices that enable their users to use a small computing device as a substitute for a laptop computer. Some of its uses include a scheduler, a telephone and address book, creating and tracking to-do lists, an expense manager, eReader, web browser, and an assortment of other functions. Such devices can also combine computing, telephone/fax and networking features so that they can be used anytime and anywhere. Handheld devices are also capable of interfacing with PCs to back up or transfer important information. Likewise, information from a PC can be downloaded to a handheld device.
Source: *CISA Review Manual, 27th Edition*, USA, 2019, figure 4.1, *https://www.isaca org/bookstore/cisa-exam-resources/crm27ed*	

Common IT components include:

- Hardware
- Platforms
- Software
- Operating Systems
- Databases
- Networks

ISACA. All Rights Reserved.

4.2.1 Hardware

IT systems and business processes rely on hardware. Hardware encompasses all the physical components of a computer system, including the equipment and devices that process, store and transmit data. Computer-system hardware consists of interdependent components that perform specific functions and can be classified as either processing or input/output.

Input/output (I/O) components are used to pass instructions/information to the computer and to display or record the output generated by the computer.

Areas of concern associated with hardware include:

- Obsolescence
- Disposal at end of service life (EOSL)
- Poor maintenance
- Misconfiguration
- Lack of documentation
- Loss or theft
- Data loss due to insecure disposal
- Sniffing (capturing traffic)
- Physical access
- Failure
- Use without authorization

Hardware Reviews

When auditing hardware, an IT auditor should review:

- Hardware acquisition plan
- Acquisition of hardware
- IT hardware asset management
- Capacity management and monitoring
- Preventive maintenance schedule
- Hardware availability and utilization reports
- Problem logs and job accounting system reports

When conducting a review of hardware, an IT auditor should consider the questions provided in **figure 4.2**.

ISACA. All Rights Reserved.

Figure 4.2—Hardware Reviews	
Areas to Review	**Questions to Consider**
• Hardware acquisition plan	• Is the plan aligned with business requirements? • Is the plan aligned with the enterprise architecture? • Is the plan compared regularly to business plans to ensure continued synchronization with business requirements? • Is the plan synchronized with IS plans? • Have criteria for the acquisition of hardware been developed? • Is the environment adequate to accommodate the currently installed hardware and new hardware to be added under the approved hardware acquisition plan? • Are the hardware and software specifications, installation requirements and the likely lead time associated with planned acquisitions adequately documented?
• Acquisition of hardware	• Is the acquisition in line with the hardware acquisition plan? • Have the IS management staff issued written policy statements regarding the acquisition and use of hardware, and have these statements been communicated to the users? • Have procedures and forms been established to facilitate the acquisition approval process? • Are requests accompanied by a cost-benefit analysis? • Are purchases routed through the purchasing department to streamline the process, avoid duplications, ensure compliance with tendering requirements and legislation and to take advantage of quantity and quality benefits such as volume discounts?
• IT asset management	• Has the hardware been tagged? • Has an owner been designated? • Where will the hardware be located? • Have we retained a copy of the contracts/SLAs?
• Capacity management and monitoring	• Are criteria used in the hardware performance monitoring plan based on historical data and analysis obtained from the IS trouble logs, processing schedules, job accounting system reports, preventive maintenance schedules and reports? • Is continuous review performed of hardware and system software performance and capacity? • Is monitoring adequate for equipment that has been programmed to contact its manufacturer (without manual or human intervention) in the case of equipment failure?
• Preventive maintenance schedule	• Is the prescribed maintenance frequency recommended by the respective hardware vendors being observed? • Is maintenance performed during off-peak workload periods? • Is preventive maintenance performed at times other than when the system is processing critical or sensitive applications?
• Hardware availability and utilization reports	• Is scheduling adequate to meet workload schedules and user requirements? • Is scheduling sufficiently flexible to accommodate required hardware preventive maintenance? • Are IS resources readily available for critical application programs?
• Problem logs • Job accounting system reports	• Have IS management staff reviewed hardware malfunctions, reruns, abnormal system terminations and operator actions?
Source: ISACA, *CISA Review Manual, 27th Edition*, USA, 2019, figure 4.2, *https://www.isaca.org/bookstore/cisa-exam-resources/crm27ed*	

ISACA. All Rights Reserved.

4.2.2 Software

Software refers to the programs and supporting documentation that enable and facilitate use of the computer. Software provides an interface to hardware and processes transactions on behalf of the user.

Areas of concern associated with software include:

- Logic flaws or semantic errors
- Bugs (faults in a program that causes the program to perform in an unintended or unanticipated manner)
- Lack of patching
- Lack of access control
- Disclosure of sensitive information
- Improper modification of information
- Loss of source code
- Lack of version control
- Lack of input and output validation

System Software

The architecture of most computers can be viewed as layers of circuitry and logic arranged in a hierarchical structure to interact with the computer OS. System software is a collection of computer programs used in the design, processing and control of all the computer applications that operate and maintain the computer system. Comprising system utilities and programs, the system software ensures the integrity of the system, controls the flow of programs and events in the computer, and manages the interfaces with the computer. Software developed for the computer must be compatible with its OS.

Examples of system software, which may be built into the OS, include:

- Access control software
- Data communications software
- Database management software
- Program library management systems
- Tape and disk management systems
- Network management software
- Job scheduling software
- Utility programs

Areas of concern associated with software utilities and drivers include:

- Use of outdated drivers
- Unavailability of drivers
- Unpatched drivers
- Use of insecure components (older encryption algorithms)
- Unpatched vulnerabilities

ISACA. All Rights Reserved.

Source Code Management

Source code is the language in which a software program is written. It is translated into object code by assemblers and compilers and tells the computer what to do. By its very nature, source code may contain intellectual property. It should be protected, and access should be restricted.

The actual source code should be managed using a version control system (VCS), often called revision control software (RCS). The code is maintained in a central repository, which allows programmers to check out a program source to make changes to it. Checking in the source creates a new revision of the program. A VCS enables the synchronization of source changes with changes from other developers, including conflict resolution when changes are made to the same section of source code. A VCS also allows branching—that is, creating a copy of the trunk (original main code) that exists independently and allows customization for different customers, countries, locations etc.

The advantages of VCSs include:

- Control of source code access
- Tracking of source code changes
- Allowing for concurrent development
- Allowing rollback to earlier versions
- Allowing branching

An IT auditor should always be aware of the following regarding source code:

- Who has access to the source code?
- Who can commit the code (push the code to production)?
- Is there an alignment of program source code with program objects?
- Is there an alignment with change and release management?
- Are there backups of source code (including code maintained offsite) and escrow agreements?

4.2.3 Operating System

The most significant system software related to a computer is its operating system (OS). The OS contains programs that provide interfaces between the user, processor and applications software. The OS is a master control program that runs the computer and acts as a scheduler and traffic controller. It provides the primary means of managing the sharing and use of computer resources, such as processors, real memory (e.g., RAM), auxiliary memory (e.g., disk storage) and I/O devices.

It is common for OSs to run on virtual servers. In a virtual environment, software is used to partition one physical server into multiple independent virtual servers. Each of these environments can then run its own (often different) OS. To the operator, the OS behaves as if it is running on a physical server.

Operating System Types

Following are the major types of OSs used in computer systems:

- Microsoft® offers entire families of Windows operating systems that are specific to types of enterprises and uses.
- Apple® makes macOS®, which evolved from OS X®.
- Linux® is a family of open-source OSs based on the Linux kernel.

ISACA. All Rights Reserved.

Auditors may also encounter older, legacy operating systems, such as IBM Resource Access Control Facility (RACF®/zOS®) and AS400.

Operating System Reviews

When auditing operating software development, acquisition or maintenance, an IT auditor should consider certain operating system concerns:[124]

- Unpatched vulnerabilities
- Complexity
- Lack of interoperability
- Uncontrolled changes
- Misconfiguration
- Weak access controls
- Poorly written code (buffer overflows, etc.)

During the review, the auditor should check the following:

- System software selection procedures
- Selection process (feasibility study)
- System software security
- IT asset management
- System software implementation
- System documentation
- System software maintenance activities
- System software change controls
- Controls over the installation of changed system software

When conducting a review of operating software development, acquisition or maintenance, an IT auditor should consider the questions in **figure 4.3**

Figure 4.3—Operating System Review	
Areas to Review	**Questions to Consider**
• System software selection procedures	• Do they align with the enterprise architecture? • Do they comply with short- and long-range IS plans? • Do they meet the IS requirements? • Are they properly aligned with the objectives of the business? • Do they include IS processing and control requirements? • Do they include an overview of the capabilities of the software and control options?
• Feasibility study • Selection process	• Are same selection criteria applied to all proposals? • Has the cost-benefit analysis of system software procedures addressed: ▪ Direct financial costs associated with the product? ▪ Cost of product maintenance? ▪ Hardware requirements and capacity of the product? ▪ Training and technical support requirements? ▪ Impact of the product on processing reliability? ▪ Impact on data security? ▪ Financial stability of the vendor's operations?

[124] ISACA, *CRISC® Review Manual, 7th Edition*, USA,2021, *https://store.isaca.org/s/store#/store/browse/detail/a2S4w000004Km3qEAC*

ISACA. All Rights Reserved.

Figure 4.3—Operating System Review *(cont.)*	
Areas to Review	**Questions to Consider**
• System software security	• Have procedures been established to restrict the ability to circumvent logical security access controls? • Have procedures been implemented to limit access to the system interrupt capability? • Have procedures been implemented to manage software patches and keep the system software up-to-date? • Are existing physical and logical security provisions adequate to restrict access to the master consoles? • Were vendor-supplied installation passwords for the system software changed at the time of installation?
• IT asset management	• Has an owner been designated? • Have we retained a copy of the contracts/SLAs? • What is the license agreement? Are we in compliance with it?
• System software implementation	• Are controls adequate in: ▪ Change procedures? ▪ Authorization procedures? ▪ Access security features? ▪ Documentation requirements? ▪ Documentation of system testing? ▪ Audit trails? ▪ Access controls over the software in production?
• Authorization documentation	• Have additions, deletions or changes to access authorization been documented? • Does documentation exist of any attempted violations? If so, has there been follow-up?
• System documentation	• Are the following areas adequately documented: ▪ Installation control statements? ▪ Parameter tables? ▪ Exit definitions? ▪ Activity logs/reports?
• System software maintenance activities	• Is documentation available for changes made to the system software? • Are current versions of the software supported by the vendor? • Is there a defined patching process?
• System software change controls	• Is access to the libraries containing the system software limited to individual(s) needing to have such access? • Are changes to the software adequately documented and tested prior to implementation? • Is software authorized properly prior to moving from the test environment to the production environment?
Source: ISACA, *CISA Review Manual, 27th Edition*, USA, 2019, figure 4.5, *https://www.isaca.org/bookstore/cisa-exam-resources/crm27ed*	

ISACA. All Rights Reserved.

4.2.4 Database Management

A DBMS enables the creation and maintenance of a well-organized database. Primary functions include reduced data redundancy, decreased access time and basic security over sensitive data.

DBMS data are organized in multilevel schemes, with basic data elements (e.g., fields) at the lowest level. The levels above each field have differing properties depending on the architecture of the database.

The DBMS can include a data dictionary that identifies the fields, their characteristics and their use. Active data dictionaries require entries for all data elements and assist application processing of data elements, such as providing validation characteristics or print formats. Passive dictionaries are a repository of information that can only be viewed or printed.

A DBMS can control user access at the following levels:

- User and the database
- Program and the database
- Transaction and the database
- Program and data field
- User and transaction
- User and data field

DBMS software aids in organizing, controlling and using the data needed by application programs.

Data Elements

Data elements required to define a database are called metadata. Metadata include data about data elements used to define logical and physical fields, files, data relationships, queries, etc. There are three types of metadata: conceptual schema, external schema and internal schema. If the schemas (i.e., the database configurations) are not adjusted to smoothly work together, the DBMS may not be adequate to meet user needs.

Database Controls

Maintaining database integrity and availability is critical and is ensured through the following controls:

- Define and enforce database standards (e.g., naming conventions and roles/responsibilities).
- Establish and implement data backup and recovery procedures to ensure database availability.
- Establish the necessary levels of access controls, including privileged access, for data items, tables and files to prevent inadvertent or unauthorized access.
- Establish controls to ensure that only authorized personnel can update the database.
- Establish controls to handle concurrent access problems, such as multiple users desiring to update the same data elements at the same time (i.e., transaction commit, locking of records/files).

ISACA. All Rights Reserved.

- Establish controls to ensure accuracy, completeness and consistency of data elements and relationships in the database. These controls, if possible, should be contained in the table/columns definitions to eliminate any possibility that these rules will be violated because of programming flaws or through the use of utilities in manipulating data.
- Use database checkpoints at junctures in the job stream that minimize data loss and recovery efforts to restart processing after a system failure.
- Perform database reorganization to reduce unused disk space and verify defined data relationships.
- Follow database restructuring procedures when making logical, physical and procedural changes.
- Use database performance reporting tools to monitor and maintain database efficiency (e.g., available storage space, buffer size, CPU usage, disk storage configuration and deadlock conditions).
- Minimize the ability to use nonsystem tools or other utilities (i.e., those outside security control, to access the database).

Database Reviews

When auditing a database, an IT auditor should review:

- Logical schema
- Physical schema
- Access time reports
- Database security controls
- Interfaces with programs/software
- Backup and disaster recovery procedures and controls
- Database-supported IT controls
- IT asset management

When conducting a review of a database, an IT auditor should consider the questions provided in **figure 4.4**.

Figure 4.4—Database Reviews

Areas to Review	Questions to Consider
• Logical schema	• Do all entities in the entity-relation diagram exist as tables or views? • Are all relations represented through foreign keys? • Are constraints specified clearly? • Are nulls for foreign keys allowed only when they are in accordance with the cardinality expressed in the entity-relation model?
• Physical schema	• Has allocation of initial and extension space (storage) for tables, logs, indexes and temporary areas been executed based on the requirements? • Are indexes by primary key or keys of frequent access present? • If the database is not normalized, is justification accepted?
• Access time reports	• Are indexes used to minimize access time? • Have indexes been constructed correctly? • If open searches not based on indexes are used, are they justified?

ISACA. All Rights Reserved.

Figure 4.4—Database Reviews *(cont.)*	
Areas to Review	**Questions to Consider**
• Database security controls	• Are security levels for all users and their roles identified within the database and access rights for all users and/ or groups of users justified? • Do referential integrity rules exist and are they followed? • How is a trigger created and when does it fire? • Is there a system for setting passwords? Does change of passwords exist and is it followed? • How many users have been given system administrator privileges? Do these users require the privilege to execute their job function? • Has an auditing utility been enabled? Are audit trails being monitored? • Can database resources be accessed without using DBMS commands and SQL statements? • Is system administrator authority granted to job scheduler? • Are actual passwords embedded into database utility jobs and scripts? • Has encryption been enabled where required? • Are copies of production data authorized? • Are copies of production data altered or masked to protected sensitive data?
• Interfaces with other programs/software	• Are integrity and confidentiality of data not affected by data import and export procedures? • Have mechanisms and procedures been put in place to ensure the adequate handling of consistency and integrity during concurrent accesses?
• Backup and disaster recovery procedures and controls	• Do backup and disaster recovery procedures exist to ensure the reliability and availability of the database? • Are there technical controls to ensure high availability and/or fast recovery of the database?
• Database-supported IS controls	• Is access to shared data appropriate? • Are adequate change procedures utilized to ensure the integrity of the database management software? • Is data redundancy minimized by the database management system? Where redundant data exist, is appropriate cross-referencing maintained within the system's data dictionary or other documentation? • Is the integrity of the database management system's data dictionary maintained?
• IT asset management	• Has an owner been designated? • Have we retained a copy of the contracts/SLAs? • What is the license agreement? Are we in compliance with it?

Source: ISACA, *CISA Review Manual, 27th Edition*, USA, 2019, figure 4.20, *https://www.isaca.org/bookstore/cisa-exam-resources/crm27ed*

4.3 Cloud Computing

Cloud computing is convenient, scalable on-demand network access to a shared pool of resources that can be provisioned rapidly and released with minimal management effort or service-provider interaction.

Another way to describe services offered in the cloud is to liken them to those of a utility. Just as enterprises pay for the electricity, gas and water that they use, they now have the option of paying for IT services on a consumption basis.

ISACA. All Rights Reserved.

4.3.1 Cloud Service/Delivery Models

A cloud service model, also known as cloud delivery model, specifies the capabilities offered to users and the applications supported. There are three basic cloud models, each offering a distinct computing service to the enterprise that uses it.

- **Software as a Service (SaaS)**—Offers the capability to use the provider's applications running on cloud infrastructure. The applications are accessible from various client devices through a thin client interface such as a web browser (e.g., web-based email). Provides a business application that is used by many individuals or enterprises concurrently.
- **Platform as a Service (PaaS)**—Offers the capability to deploy onto the cloud infrastructure customer-created or -acquired applications that use programming languages and tools supported by the provider. Provides an application development sandbox in the cloud.
- **Infrastructure as a Service (IaaS)**—Offers the capability to provision processing, storage, networks and other fundamental computing resources, enabling the customer to deploy and run arbitrary software, which can include operating systems and applications. Provides online processing or data storage capacity.

The capabilities of each cloud service model and issues that an IT auditor should consider when reviewing or auditing each service model are shown in **figure 4.5**

Figure 4.5—Cloud Delivery Methods

Service Model	Description	Considerations
SaaS	Capability to use the provider's applications running on cloud infrastructure. The applications are accessible from various client devices through a thin client interface such as a web browser (e.g., web-based email).	SaaS provides applications that are complete and available on demand to the end customer. Traditional licensing and asset management are changed.
PaaS	Capability to deploy onto the cloud infrastructure customer-created or customer-acquired applications developed using programming languages and tools supported by the provider.	PaaS provides an application development sandbox and is specifically designed for developers.
IaaS	Capability to provision processing, storage, networks and other fundamental computing resources, offering the customer the ability to deploy and run arbitrary software, which can include OSs and applications. IaaS put these IT operations into the hands of a third party.	IaaS can provide infrastructure services such as servers, disk space, network devices and memory and is designed for users wanting complete freedom with regard to the OS and applications they use.

Source: ISACA, *Cloud Fundamentals Study Guide*, USA, 2021, page 25, figure 2.1, *https://store.isaca.org/s/store#/store/browse/detail/a2S4w000004KoIJEAS*

4.3.2 Cloud Deployment Models

There are four cloud deployment models:

- **Private cloud**—This offering consists of one client (i.e., one individual or one enterprise). Several departments or divisions may be represented, but all exist within the same enterprise. Private clouds often employ virtualization within an enterprise's existing computer servers to improve computer utilization. A private cloud also typically involves provisioning and metering components, enabling rapid deployment and chargeback where appropriate. This model is most closely related to traditional IT outsourcing models in the marketplace, but it can

ISACA. All Rights Reserved.

also be an enterprise's internal delivery model. Because of this, the private model tends to offer the least amount of new risk and security challenge.

- **Public cloud**—An offering from one cloud service provider (CSP) to many clients who share the cloud processing power and storage capacity concurrently. Public cloud clients share applications, processing power and data storage space communally. Client data are commingled but segregated, e.g., through the use of metatags. This model tends to present the greatest assurance challenges for security and risk managers.
- **Community cloud**—A private-public cloud with clients that have a common connection or affiliation, such as a trade association, industry or locality. The community cloud business model allows a CSP to provide cloud tools and applications that are specific to the needs of the community.
- **Hybrid cloud**—A combination of two or more of the previously defined deployment models. Each of the three cloud deployment models has specific advantages and disadvantages that are relative to the other deployment models. A hybrid cloud leverages the advantage of the other cloud models, providing an optimal user experience.

A summary of the cloud infrastructure and issues that an IT auditor should consider for each deployment model is provided in **figure 4.6**.

Figure 4.6—Cloud Deployment Model Infrastructure and Considerations

Deployment Model	Description of Cloud Infrastructure	To Be Considered
Private cloud	• Operated solely for an organization • May be managed by the organization or a third party • May exist on-premise or off-premise	• Cloud services with minimum risk • May not provide the scalability and agility of public cloud services
Community cloud	• Shared by several organizations • Supports a specific community that has shared mission or interest. • May be managed by the organizations or a third party • May reside on-premise or off-premise	• Same as private cloud, plus: • Data may be stored with the data of competitors.
Public cloud	• Made available to the general public or a large industry group • Owned by an organization selling cloud services	• Same as community cloud, plus: • Data may be stored in unknown locations and may not be easily retrievable.
Hybrid cloud	• A composition of two or more clouds (private, community or public) that remain unique entities but are bound together by standardized or proprietary technology that enables data and application portability (e.g., cloud bursting for load balancing between clouds)	• Aggregate risk of merging different deployment models • Classification and labeling of data will be beneficial to the security manager to ensure that data are assigned to the correct cloud type.

Source: ISACA, *CISA Review Manual, 27th Edition*, USA, 2019, figure 5.26, *https://www.isaca.org/bookstore/cisa-exam-resources/crm27ed*

4.3.3 Cloud Essential Characteristics

Although cloud deployment models and types of cloud services vary significantly, they share five essential characteristics:

- **On-demand self-service**—Computing capabilities can be provisioned without human interaction from the service provider.

ISACA. All Rights Reserved.

- **Broad network access**—Computing capabilities are available over the network and can be accessed by diverse client platforms.
- **Resource pooling**—Computer resources are pooled to support a multi-tenant model.
- **Rapid elasticity**—Resources can scale up or down rapidly—and, in some cases, automatically—in response to business demands.
- **Measured service**—Resource utilization can be optimized by leveraging charge-per-use capabilities.

Cloud computing is often categorized as exclusively an IT issue, but that categorization underplays the potential impact of cloud computing. It also represents a weighty business decision for an enterprise,—one that requires consideration and input from many stakeholders.

4.3.4 Cloud Risk and Controls

Overall risk and benefits differ per model. When considering different types of service and deployment models, enterprises should consider the risk that accompanies them. Regardless of the models deployed, the security objectives required to meet enterprise business requirements must still be met. These include:

- Ensure the continued availability of information systems and data.
- Ensure the integrity and preserve the confidentiality of information and sensitive data while stored and in transit.
- Ensure conformity to applicable laws, regulations and standards.
- Ensure adherence to trust and obligation requirements applicable to any information relating to an identified or identifiable individual (i.e., data subject) in accordance with the enterprise's privacy policy or applicable privacy laws and regulations.

An IT auditor should be familiar with the risk associated with cloud computing and associated controls as described in **figure 4.7**. When performing a cloud computing review or audit, an IT auditor should consider:

- Data ownership, data custody and security administration related to cloud deployment models.
- Legal requirements and unique risk in the cloud environment. Regulations, such as the General Data Protection Regulation (GDPR), can present unique challenges for data stored in the cloud.
- Potential limitations to the right to audit in a cloud environment. For example, an IT auditor may not be able to physically investigate a vendor's facilities.

Figure 4.7—Risk Associated with Cloud Computing

Risk	Description	Control
Legal transborder requirements	Cloud service providers (CSPs) are often transborder, and different countries have different legal requirements, especially concerning personal private information. The enterprise might be committing: a violation of regulations in other countries when storing, processing or transmitting data within the CSP's infrastructure without the necessary compliance controls. Furthermore, government entities in the hosting country may require access to the enterprise's information with or without proper notification.	• Request the CSP's list of infrastructure locations and verify that regulation in those locations is aligned with the enterprise's requirements. • Include terms in the contract to restrict the moving of enterprise assets to only those areas known to be compliant with the enterprise's own regulation. • Prevent disclosure, encrypt any asset prior to migration to the CSP and ensure proper key management is in place.

ISACA. All Rights Reserved.

Figure 4.7—Risk Associated with Cloud Computing *(cont.)*		
Risk	**Description**	**Control**
Physical security	Physical security is required in any infrastructure. When the enterprise moves assets to a cloud infrastructure, those assets are still subject to the corporate security policy, but they can also be physically accessed by the CSP's staff, which is subject to the CSP's security policy. There could be a gap between the security measures provided by the CSP and the requirements of the enterprise.	• Request the CSP's physical security policy and ensure that it is aligned with the enterprise's security policy. • Request that the CSP provide proof of independent security reviews or certification reports that meet the enterprise's compliance requirements (e.g., SOC reports, SOX, PCI DSS, HIPAA, ISO certification). • Include in the contract language that requires the CSP to be aligned with the enterprise's security policy and to implement necessary controls to ensure it. • Request the CSP's disaster recovery plans and ensure that they contain the necessary countermeasures to protect physical assets during and after a disaster.
Data disposal	Proper disposal of data is imperative to prevent unauthorized disclosure. If appropriate measures are not taken by the CSP, information assets could be sent (without approval) to countries where the data can be legally disclosed due to different regulations concerning sensitive data. Disks could be replaced, recycled or upgraded without proper cleaning so that the information still remains within storage and can later be retrieved. When a contract expires, CSPs should ensure the safe disposal or destruction of any previous backups. Any of the data fed into the CSP's application must be erased immediately using the necessary tools to avoid disclosures and confidentiality breaches (forensic cleaning may be required for sensitive data).	• Request CSP's technical specifications and controls that ensure that data are properly wiped and backup media are destroyed when requested. • Include terms in the contract that require, upon contract expiration or any event ending the contract, a mandatory data wipe carried out under the enterprise's supervision.
Multitenancy and isolation failure	One of the primary benefits of the cloud is the ability to perform dynamic allocation of physical resources when required. The most common approach is a multitenant environment (public cloud), where different entities share a pool of resources, including storage, hardware and network components. For example, when allocated storage is no longer needed by a client it can be freely reallocated to another enterprise. In that case, sensitive data could be disclosed if the storage has not been scrubbed thoroughly (e.g., using forensic software). Furthermore, malicious entities in the cloud could take advantage of shared information—for example, by utilizing shared routing tables to map the internal network topology of an enterprise, preparing the way for an internal attack.	• Request the CSP's technical details for approval and require additional controls to ensure data privacy, when necessary. • A contractual agreement is necessary to officially clarify who is allowed to access the enterprise's information, naming specific roles for CSP employees and external partners. All controls protecting the enterprise's information assets must be clearly documented in the contract agreement or service level agreement (SLA). • Use a private cloud deployment model (no multitenancy).

ISACA. All Rights Reserved.

Figure 4.7—Risk Associated with Cloud Computing *(cont.)*		
Risk	**Description**	**Control**
Application disposal	When applications are developed in a PaaS environment, originals and backups should always be available. In the event of a contract termination, the details of the application could be disclosed and used to create more selective attacks on applications or could be copied violating the enterprise's IP.	• Include terms in the contract that require the proper disposal of applications including objects, source and backups. • Include non-compete clauses in the contract.
Lack of visibility into software system development life cycle (SDLC)	Enterprises that use cloud applications have little visibility into the software SDLC. Customers do not know in detail how the applications were developed and what security considerations were taken into account during the SDLC. This could lead to an imbalance between the security provided by the application and the security required by customers/users.	• If possible include a right of audit in the contract. • Include in the contract language that requires the CSP to be aligned with the enterprise's security policy and to implement necessary controls to ensure it. • Require SLAs that include a schedule of software changes.
Lack of control of the release management process	CSPs are able to introduce patches in their applications quickly. These deployments are often done without the approval (or even the knowledge) of the application users for practical reasons: If an application is used by hundreds of different enterprises, it would take an extremely long time for a CSP to look for the formal approval of every customer. In this case, the enterprise could have no control (or no view) of the release management process and could be subject to unexpected side effects.	• If possible, include a right of audit in the contract. • Include in the contract language that requires the CSP to be aligned with the enterprise's security policy and to implement necessary controls to ensure it. • Require SLAs that include a schedule of patches and software releases.
Identity and access management (IAM)	Information assets could be accessed by unauthorized entities due to faulty or vulnerable access management measures or processes. This could result from a forgery/theft of legitimate credentials or a common technical practice (e.g., administrator permissions override).	• If possible, include a right of audit in the contract. • Include in the contract language that requires the CSP to be aligned with the enterprise's security policy and to implement necessary controls to ensure it. • Request that the CSP provide proof of independent security reviews or certification reports that meet the enterprise's compliance requirements (e.g., SOC reports, SOX, PCI DSS, HIPAA, ISO certification).
Service Orientated Architecture (SOA)–related vulnerabilities	Security for SOA presents new challenges because vulnerabilities arise not only from the individual elements, but also from their mutual interaction. Because the SOA libraries are under the responsibility of the CSP and are not completely visible to the enterprise, there may be unnoticed application vulnerabilities.	• If possible include a right of audit in the contract. • Include in the contract language that requires the CSP to be aligned with the enterprise's security policy and to implement necessary controls to ensure it. • Request that the CSP provide proof of independent security reviews or certification reports that meet the enterprise's compliance requirements (e.g., SOC reports, SOX, PCI, DSS, HIPAA, ISO certification).

ISACA. All Rights Reserved.

Figure 4.7—Risk Associated with Cloud Computing *(cont.)*

Risk	Description	Control
Exit strategy	CSP tools facilitate bring data to the cloud or CSP but rarely the other way around. This can make it very difficult for the enterprise to migrate from one CSP to another or to bring services back in-house. It can also result in serious business disruption or failure should the CSP go bankrupt, face legal action or be the potential target for an acquisition (with the likelihood of sudden changes in CSP policies and any agreements in place). If the organization decides to bring the data back in-house, the question of how to securely render the data becomes critical because the in-house applications may have been decommissioned (i.e., sunset) and there is no application available to render the data. Another possibility is the run-on-the-banks scenario, in which there is a crisis of confidence in the CSP financial position, resulting in a mass exit and withdrawal on a first-come, first-served basis. If there are limits to the amount of content that can be withdrawn in a given time frame, then the enterprise might not be able to retrieve all its data in the time specified.	• Ensure by contract or SLA with the CSP an exit strategy that specifies the terms that should trigger the retrieval of the enterprise's assets in the time frame required by the enterprise. • Implement a disaster recovery plan, taking into account the possibility of complete CSP disruption.
Ease to contract SaaS	Business organizations may contract cloud applications without proper procurement and approval oversight, thus bypassing compliance with internal enterprise policies.	• Require that the purchase of cloud services follow the established procedures. Ensure executive management support for this.
Collateral damage	If one tenant of a public cloud is attacked, there could be an impact to the other tenants of the same CSP, even if they are not the intended target (e.g., DDoS). Another possible scenario of collateral damage could be a public cloud IaaS that is affected by an attack exploiting vulnerabilities of software installed by one of the tenants.	• Ask the CSP to include the enterprise in its incident management process that deals with notification of collateral events. • Include contract clauses and controls to ensure that the enterprise contracted capacity is always available and cannot be directed to other tenants without approval. • Use a private cloud deployment model (no multi-tenancy).
Hypervisor attacks	Hypervisors are vital for server virtualization. They provide the link between virtual machines and the underlying physical resources required to run the machines by using hypercalls (similar to system calls, but for virtualized systems). An attacker using a virtual machine in the same cloud could fake hypercalls to inject malicious code or trigger bugs in the hypervisor. This could potentially be used to violate confidentiality or integrity of other virtual machines or crash the hypervisor (similar to a DDoS attack).	• If possible, include a right of audit in the contract. • Include in the contract language that requires the CSP to be aligned with the enterprise security policy and to implement necessary controls to ensure it.

ISACA. All Rights Reserved.

Figure 4.7—Risk Associated with Cloud Computing *(cont.)*		
Risk	**Description**	**Control**
Support for audit and forensic investigations	Security audits and forensic investigations are vital to the enterprise to evaluate the security measures of the CSP (preventive and corrective), and in some cases the CSP itself (for example, to authenticate the CSP). This raises several issues because performing these actions requires extensive access to the CSP infrastructure and monitoring capabilities, which are often shared with other CSP customers.	• Request the CSP the right to audit as part of the contract or SLA. If this is not possible, request security audit reports by trusted third parties. • Request that the CSP provide appropriate and timely support (logs, traces, hard disk images, etc.) for forensic analysis as part of the contract or SLA. If this is not possible, request to authorize trusted third parties to perform forensic analysis when necessary.

Source: ISACA, *CISA Review Manual, 27th Edition*, USA, 2019, figure 5.28, *https://www.isaca.org/bookstore/cisa-exam-resources/crm27ed*

4.4 IT General Controls

A general computer (IT) control is a control, other than an application control, that relates to the environment within which computer-based application systems are developed, maintained and operated, and that is, therefore, applicable to all applications. The objectives of general controls are to ensure the proper development and implementation of applications and the integrity of program and data files and of computer operations. Like application controls, general controls may be either manual or programmed.

General controls support the entire enterprise in a centralized fashion as a part of the IT infrastructure. Because the IT infrastructure is often shared among different departments in the same enterprise, the term general controls is often used to describe all controls in the infrastructure, including the controls that support an operating system, network or facility. These controls typically include centralized user administration policies, standards and procedures, and technical elements such as access controls, firewalls and intrusion detection systems.

A review and evaluation of general controls is typically part of an IT audit. Common IT general controls include:

- Logical access controls
- Change, patch, release and configuration management controls
- Data backup, storage and recovery controls
- Business continuity and disaster recovery controls
- IT operations controls
- Physical access and environmental controls
- System development life cycle (SDLC) controls

4.4.1 Logical Access Controls

Logical access controls are the policies, procedures, organizational structure and electronic access controls designed to restrict access to computer software and data files. Logical access to interact with computer resources is granted using identification, authentication and authorization. The success of logical access controls is tied to the strength of the authentication method. All user access to systems and data should be appropriately authorized, commensurate with the role of the individual. Authorization generally takes the form of signatures (physical or electronic) of relevant management. The strength of the authentication is proportional to the quality of the method used.

ISACA. All Rights Reserved.

Logical Access Exposures

An IT auditor should be able to analyze and evaluate the effectiveness of a logical access control in accomplishing IT control and security objectives and avoiding losses resulting from exposures. Consequences of exposures can range from minor inconveniences to a total shutdown of computer functions.

Logical Access Points of Entry and Paths

Access or points of entry to an enterprise IT infrastructure can be gained through several avenues. Each avenue is subject to appropriate levels of access security.

Access to an enterprise's information resources (e.g., applications, databases, facilities and networks) from its networking or telecommunications infrastructure is controlled at general points of entry to either front- or back-end systems. The approach followed is based on a client-server model. A large enterprise can have thousands of interconnected network servers. Connectivity in such an environment needs to be controlled through a smaller set of primary domain controllers (servers) that enable a user to obtain access to specific secondary points of entry (e.g., application servers and databases).

General modes of access include:

- **Network connectivity**—Access is gained by linking a PC to a segment of an enterprise's network infrastructure, either through a physical or a wireless connection. At a minimum, such access requires user identification and authentication to a domain-controlling server. Specific access to a particular application or database may also require that users identify and authenticate themselves to that particular server (secondary point of entry). Access to the infrastructure also can occur through network management devices, such as routers and firewalls, which should be strictly controlled.
- **Remote access**—Connecting remotely to an enterprise server generally requires that users identify and authenticate themselves to the server for access to specific functions that can be performed remotely (e.g., email, file transfer protocol [FTP] or some application-specific function). Complete access to view all network resources usually requires a virtual private network (VPN), which allows secure authentication and connection into resources after privileges have been granted. Remote access points of entry can be extensive and should be centrally controlled, if possible.

Access Control Software

Access control software is used to prevent unauthorized access and modification to enterprise sensitive data or use of system critical functions. It requires the application of access controls across all layers of enterprise IT architecture, including networks, platforms or OSs, databases and application systems. Each control typically features some form of identification and authentication, access authorization, checking of specific information resources, and logging and reporting of user activities.

The greatest degree of protection in applying access control software against unauthorized internal and external access is at the network and platform/OS levels. These systems, which are referred to as general support systems, make up the primary infrastructure on which applications and database systems reside.

Most access control software has security features that enable a security administrator to automatically log and report all levels of access attempts—successes and failures. For example, access control software can log computer activity initiated through a logon ID or computer terminal. This information provides an audit trail that enables management to monitor activities of a suspicious nature, such as a hacker attempting brute force attacks on a privileged logon ID. Also, keystroke logging can be turned on for users who have sensitive access privileges. What is logged is

ISACA. All Rights Reserved.

determined by the action of the enterprise. Issues include what is logged, who/what has access to the logs and how long logs are retained (record-retention item).

OS Access Control

OS access control software is typically restricted to privileged users and interfaces with network access control software. It resides on network layer devices (e.g., routers and firewalls) that manage and control external access to enterprise networks. Additionally, OS access control software interfaces with database and/or application systems access controls to protect system libraries and user data sets.

General operating and/or application systems access control functions include:

- Creating or changing/disabling user profiles when users are transferred or separated from the enterprise
- Applying user logon limitation rules
- Ensuring access is commensurate with users' job responsibilities
- Ensuring notification concerning proper use and access prior to initial logon
- Establishing rules for access to specific information resources (e.g., system-level application resources and data)
- Reviewing access of users, administrators and third-party vendors on a periodic basis
- Reporting access attempts and other user activities
- Assigning user identification and authentication (e.g., multifactor authentication or MFA)

Single sign on (SSO) is a single-point authentication system used by multiple systems and applications. It is often viewed as a control since end users do not have to authenticate to each system/application individually. SSO prevents users from forgetting passwords and mitigates re-use of passwords. There is an alternative view, however, that SSO presents security challenges. For example, if a malicious actor gains access to an authenticated SSO account, access to all systems and applications associated with the account is also achieved.

Database and/or application-level access control functions include the following:

- Create or change data files and database profiles.
- Verify user authorization at the application and transaction level.
- Verify user authorization within the application.
- Verify user authorization at the field level for changes within a database.
- Verify subsystem authorization for the user at the file level.
- Log database/data communications access activities for monitoring access violations.

Access control software is provided at different levels within an IT architecture, with each level providing a specified degree of security.

Identification and Authorization

Logical access capabilities are implemented by security administration in a set of access rules that stipulate which users (or groups of users) are authorized to access a resource at a particular level (e.g., read-, update- or execute-only) and under which conditions (e.g., time of the day or a subset of computer terminals). The security administrator invokes the appropriate system access control mechanism upon receipt of a proper authorization request from the information owner or manager to grant a specified user the right to access, or use, a protected resource. An IT auditor should be aware that access is granted to the enterprise's IT systems using the principles of need-to-know, least privilege and SoD.

ISACA. All Rights Reserved.

Personnel and departmental changes, malicious efforts and carelessness result in authorization creep and can impact the effectiveness of access controls. Many times, access is not removed when personnel leave an enterprise, thus increasing the risk of unauthorized access. The information asset owner should review access controls periodically with a predetermined authorization matrix that defines the least-privileged access level and authority for an individual with reference to job role and responsibilities. An IT auditor should evaluate reviews of access authorizations to ensure that they are still valid.

Nonemployees with access to enterprise IT resources should also be held responsible for security compliance and be accountable for security breaches. Nonemployees include contract employees, vendor programmers/analysts, maintenance personnel, clients, external auditors, visitors and consultants. Nonemployees should be advised of their accountability to the enterprise's security requirements.

In addition to the Identity access management (IAM) overview presented in section 3.7.1, an IT auditor should be familiar with IAM concepts (processes). **Figure 4.8** presents key IAM concepts, associated access control issues (gaps) and security concerns, and recommended good practices an enterprise should consider to address any gaps.

Figure 4.8—IAM Concepts, Gaps/Security Concerns and Good Practices/Recommendations

Key Concepts of IAM	Identified Gaps and Security Concerns	Good Practices/Recommendations
Identify creation and access request	Authorized approval not in place	• The user's manager, the resource owner or the security officer, as necessary, should authorize the user for access to be granted.
	Privileged access granted without analyzing the need	• To justify its need, privileged access is to be provided after two levels of approval—the reporting manager and the reporting manager's manager or application, database or server owner.
	Group shared access	• To justify its need, group shared access is to be provided after two levels of approval—the reporting manager and the reporting manager or application, database or server owner. • Utilize the principle of least privilege (i.e., just enough access should be given as needed). • Limit the servers on which the account can exist. • Ensure and preapprove the list of users who would be sharing the account. • Account owners should maintain and publish a list of users who have access to the shared account. • Validate the logging activities for shared accounts. • Passwords should be changed on a regular basis. The frequency should be defined in the process document. • If it is found that someone obtains unauthorized access, the password must be change immediately.
Transfer request	Authorized approval not in place	• The user's manager, the resource owner or the security officer, as necessary, should authorize access.
Access termination request	User IDs not revoked immediately after termination	• At minimum, access termination should be done in one working day (at maximum, five working days).
Password communication	Unsecure means to communicate passwords	• Passwords can be communicated via user email in encrypted format. • Passwords must be stored in a sealed envelope.

ISACA. All Rights Reserved.

Figure 4.8—IAM Concepts, Gaps/Security Concerns and Good Practices/Recommendations *(cont.)*

Key Concepts of IAM	Identified Gaps and Security Concerns	Good Practices/Recommendations

Password management	Password parameters not followed
	
	Password complexity not met
	
	Nonexistent password policies, standards and guidelines
	
	Use of shared passwords
		• The password should be a minimum of eight characters in length.
		• Passwords should contain a mix of lower- and uppercase letters, numbers and punctuation. Passwords should be difficult to guess. The following should not be used:
		  ▪ Words found in the dictionary
		  ▪ Derivatives of the user ID
		  ▪ Common character sequences
		  ▪ Personal details, such as first name, last name, birth date, etc.
		• An encrypted history file should be maintained and should, at a minimum, retain the last 13 passwords for each user ID.
		• Educate and make users aware of password confidentiality to hinder displaying and printing of passwords.
		• Password changes should be enforced: 30 days for privileged access IDs and 90 days for regular access.
		• At first login, a mandatory password change should be enforced.
		• At a minimum, five consecutive unsuccessful attempts should lead to suspension of the account until it is reset by the system administrator.
		• A time-out feature or screensaver should be enabled after 15 minutes of inactivity.
		• Passwords must always be encrypted when held in storage for any significant period of time or when transmitted over networks.
		• The password must be changed promptly when disclosure is suspected.
		• Each user ID should be uniquely identifiable, preferably to the username.
		• The last login date and time should be displayed for the user at the time of login

Policy administration	Lack of documented processes, policies and procedures
	
	Lack of timely process review
		• Document review should be done on regular basis—preferably yearly. The document must have:
		  ▪ The next review date
		  ▪ The name of the owner of the process
		  ▪ The name of the process approver
		  ▪ The scope of the process
		  ▪ Roles and responsibilities
		  ▪ Measurements (key performance indicators)
		  ▪ Workflows
		  ▪ Templates, forms and formats

Validation	Validation process not in place/not adhered to Timely action not taken for accounts that are not validated in the process	• Each user account should be reevaluated by the user's manager at a fixed frequency—preferably six months for normal user accounts and three months for privileged user accounts. • Validations should be reviewed by the user's manager or the resource, application or data owner.

ISACA. All Rights Reserved.

Figure 4.8—IAM Concepts, Gaps/Security Concerns and Good Practices/Recommendations *(cont.)*

Key Concepts of IAM	Identified Gaps and Security Concerns	Good Practices/Recommendations
Reinstatement	Reinstatement without valid authorization	• All requests should be checked for valid, granted approvals. Lack of approvals/incorrect authorization requests should be reinstated.
Authorization subprocess	Access given without authorization	• All requests should be checked for valid granted approvals. Lack of approvals/incorrect authorization requests should be blocked at the access request stage. • The user's manager, the resource owner or the security officer, as necessary, should authorize the user for access to be granted
SoD	Lack of SoD	• All requests passing through the IAM process should be validated for SoD policy checking. Requests that fail the SoD check should be blocked at the access request stage.
Log management	Lack of logging, auditing and reviewing of events	• A log management process should be in place.
Privileged access	Access provided to users without validating the needs of access	• To justify its need, privileged access is to be provided after two levels of approval—the reporting manager and the reporting manager's manager or application, database or server owner.
	Periodic revalidation process not in place	
	Revalidation process in place although the nonvalidated accounts are not terminated	• Documented processes must be in place. • Revalidation of privilege accounts must be conducted on a quarterly basis.
		• At a minimum, nonvalidated accounts should be terminated/locked in one working day (at maximum, five working days)
Dormant/orphan user accounts	Owners or custodians not identified for user accounts	• All accounts without an owner or custodian need to be identified and highlighted so that they can be assigned or removed.

Source: *CISA Review Manual, 27th Edition*, USA, 2019, figure 5.9, *https://www.isaca.org/bookstore/cisa-exam-resources/crm27ed*

Auditing Logical Access Controls

When evaluating logical access controls, an IT auditor should:

- Obtain a general understanding of the IT environment and security risk facing IT processing, through a review of relevant documentation, inquiry, observation, risk assessment and evaluation techniques.
- Document and evaluate controls over potential access paths into the system to assess their adequacy, efficiency and effectiveness by reviewing appropriate hardware and software security features and identifying any deficiencies or redundancies.
- Test controls over access paths to determine whether they are functioning and effective by applying appropriate audit techniques.
- Evaluate the access control environment to determine if the control objectives are achieved by analyzing test results and other audit evidence.
- Evaluate the security environment to assess its adequacy by reviewing written policies, observing practices and procedures, and comparing them with appropriate security standards or practices and procedures used by other enterprises.

ISACA. All Rights Reserved.

Assessing and Documenting the Access Paths

The access path is the logical route an end user takes to access computerized information, starting from a terminal/workstation and typically ending with access to the data. Along the way, numerous hardware and software components are encountered. An IT auditor should evaluate each component for proper implementation and physical and logical access security.

Special consideration should be given to the:

- Origination and authorization of the data
- Validity and correctness of the input data
- Maintenance of the affected OSs (patching, hardening and closing the unnecessarily open ports)

Reviewing Reports From Access Control Software

The reporting features of access control software provide the security administrator with the opportunity to monitor adherence to security policies. By reviewing a sample of security reports, an IT auditor can determine whether enough information is provided to support an investigation and if the security administrator is performing an effective review of the report. Unsuccessful access attempts should be reported and should identify the time, terminal, logon and file or data element for which access was attempted.

Reviewing Application Systems Operations Manual

An application systems operations manual should contain documentation on the programs that generally are used throughout a data processing installation to support the development, implementation, operations and use of application systems. The manual should include information about the platform on which the application system can run, DBMSs, compilers, interpreters, telecommunication monitors and other applications that can run with the application system.

4.4.2 Patch, Change and Configuration Management Controls

The effective and efficient development and maintenance of complicated IT systems requires that rigorous change, patch, release and configuration management processes be implemented and adhered to within an enterprise. These processes provide systematic, consistent and unambiguous control over attributes of IT components comprising the system (hardware, software, firmware and network connectivity, including physical connecting media wire, fiber and radio frequency [RF]). Knowledge of the configuration status of computing environments is critical to system reliability, availability and security. It is also critical to timely maintenance of IT systems. Changes to systems must be carefully assessed, planned, tested, approved, documented and communicated to minimize any undesirable consequences to business processes.

Patch Management

Patch management is an area of systems management that involves acquiring, testing and installing multiple patches (code changes) to an administered computer system to maintain up-to-date software and, often, to address security risk. Although the auditor does not perform this process, understanding it is valuable to the audit function. During the patch management process, the initial step is assessment of the environment to be patched, which consists of creating/maintaining the baseline of systems, evaluating the patch management architecture, and then reviewing the infrastructure configuration. Following are the next steps:

- Identifying the new patch

ISACA. All Rights Reserved.

  - Determining patch relevance (includes threat assessment)
  - Verifying patch authenticity and integrity
- Evaluating and planning the patch deployment
  - Obtaining approval to deploy patch
  - Performing risk assessment
  - Planning patch release process
- Completing patch acceptance testing
  - Deploying the patch
  - Distributing and installing the patch
  - Reporting on progress
  - Addressing exceptions
- Reviewing deployment

Change Management

For an overview of change management and audit tests, see Section 3.7.1. Change management, with respect to IT, involves the use of a defined and documented process to identify and apply technology improvements that are beneficial to the enterprise at the infrastructure and application levels, and to involve all levels of the enterprise impacted by the changes.

Change control procedures, which are a part of the change management function, are established by IT management to control the movement of application changes (programs, jobs, configurations, parameters, etc.) from the test environment, where development and maintenance occur; to the quality assurance (QA) environment, where thorough testing occurs; to the production environment. Typically, IT management is responsible for ensuring the integrity of the production environment and often gives final approval for any changes to production.

Change management is used when changing hardware, installing or upgrading to new releases of off-the-shelf applications, installing a software patch, and configuring various network devices (e.g., firewalls, routers and switches). The procedures associated with change management ensure that:

- All relevant personnel have been informed of the change and when it becomes effective.
- System, operations and program documentation have been completed, updated and found in compliance with established standards.
- Job preparation, scheduling and operating instructions have been established.
- System and program test results have been reviewed and approved by user and project management.
- Data file conversion, if necessary, has been carried out accurately and completely as evidenced by review and approval by user management.
- System conversion has been carried out accurately and completely as evidenced by review and approval by user management.
- All aspects of jobs turned over have been tested, reviewed and approved by control/operations personnel.
- Legal or compliance aspects have been considered.
- The risk of adversely affecting the business operations have been reviewed and a rollback plan developed to back out changes, if necessary.

Apart from change control, standardized methods and procedures for change management are used to ensure and maintain agreed-on levels in quality service. These methods are aimed at minimizing the adverse impact of any probable incidents triggered by change that may arise. This outcome is achieved by formalizing and documenting the

ISACA. All Rights Reserved.

process of change request, authorization, testing, implementation and communication to the users. Change requests are often categorized into emergency changes, major changes and minor changes, and there may be different change management procedures in place for each type of change.

Configuration Management

Devices and systems typically must be configured after installation to support communications, to provide interfaces with other enterprise systems, and to secure operations directed by policy. The goal of configuration management is to have a single approved method for use by the enterprise to configure particular systems or devices intended for a particular role. Use of a common configuration approach makes it easier to deploy new systems, test patches and upgrades, identify the presence of malware and manage the enterprise.

Configuration management involves procedures throughout the system hardware and software life cycle (from requirements analysis to maintenance) to identify, define and establish baselines for software items in the system and thus provide a basis for problem management, change management and release management.

From an IT audit perspective, effective use of configuration management software provides important evidence of management's commitment to carefully control the maintenance process.

4.4.3 Data Backup, Storage and Recovery Controls

Data backup, storage and recovery are key considerations for an enterprise. Laws and regulations may impact how an enterprise can handle its data and should be considered by an enterprise as it develops methods for data handling.

To ensure that the critical activities of an enterprise (and their supporting applications) are not interrupted in the event of a disaster, secondary storage media are used to store software application files and associated data for backup purposes. As the amount of information increases, keeping manual inventories of tape backups (whether local or remote) becomes increasingly difficult. Manual processes are gradually being replaced by newer backup methods such as advanced disk-based backup solutions and cloud storage.

Remote (Offsite) Storage Library Controls

Offsite storage is located in a facility away from the building housing the primary information processing facility (IPF) used for storage of computer media, such as offline backup data and storage files.

An enterprise must implement strict controls over the offsite storage of its data. Unauthorized access, loss or tampering with data (either onsite or while in transit) could impact the IT system's ability to provide support for critical business processes, putting the future of the enterprise at risk.

Controls over the offsite storage library include:

- Securing physical access to library contents, ensuring that only authorized personnel have access
- Encrypting backup media, especially when in transit; encrypting data at rest, depending on criticality and classification
- Ensuring that physical construction can withstand fire/heat/water
- Locating the library away from the data center, preferably in a facility that will not be subject to the same disaster event, to avoid the risk of a disaster affecting both facilities
- Ensuring that an inventory of all storage media and files stored in the library is maintained for the specified retention time

ISACA. All Rights Reserved.

- Ensuring that a record of all storage media and files moved into and out of the library is maintained for the specified retention/expiration time
- Ensuring that a catalog of information regarding the versions and location of data files is maintained for the specified retention time and that the catalog is protected from unauthorized disclosure

The retention time for the different records must be in accordance with the enterprise retention policy.

An offsite facility must be as secure and controlled as the originating site. Requirements include:

- Having adequate physical access controls, such as locked doors, no windows and active surveillance
- Being located in an area that is not likely to be subject to the same disaster event that could affect the originating site
- Having proper environmental controls
- Having additional controls required by specific legal, regulatory or business requirements

Backup Device and Media Types

There are many backup devices and media types available. The technology chosen must be adequate to meet the business needs of the enterprise.

Backup Procedures and Frequency

Both data and software files should be backed up on a periodic basis in accordance with a defined recovery point objective (RPO). An RPO is determined based on the acceptable data loss in case of disruption of operations. It indicates the earliest acceptable point in time to recover the data. The RPO effectively quantifies the permissible amount of data loss in case of interruption.

Scheduling periodic backups can often be easily accomplished using an automated backup/media management system and automated job scheduling software. Use of an integrated solution for backup/recovery procedures and media management will prevent erroneous or missed backup cycles due to operator error. Schedules describing backup of certain data are included in the backup procedures.

Procedures for data and software backup must allow for the continuing occurrence of changes. A copy of a file or record, as of some point in time, is retained for backup purposes. All changes or transactions that occur during the interval between the copy and the current time also are retained.

Backup Documentation

An enterprise should have a written policy to govern what is stored and for how long. Any documentation required for the consistent and continuous operation of the enterprise, including source documents required for restoration of the production database. should be preserved in an offsite backup facility. Like data files, the offsite copies should be kept up to date to ensure their usefulness.

Backup Approaches

The three primary approaches for backup are:

- Full
- Incremental

ISACA. All Rights Reserved.

- Differential

Typically, these approaches are combined to complement each other.

- **Full backup**–All files and folders are copied to the backup media, resulting in one backup set (with one or more media, depending on media capacity). The main advantage is having a unique repository in case of restoration, but it requires more time and media capacity.
- **Incremental backup**–Files and folders that are new or changed since the last incremental or full backup are copied. Incremental backup is a faster method of backup and requires less media capacity, but it requires that all backup sets restore all changes that occurred since a full backup, and restoration takes more time.
- **Differential backup**–Files and folders added or changed since the last full backup are copied. This type of backup is faster and requires less media capacity than a full backup and requires only the last full and differential backup sets to make a full restoration. It also requires less time to restore than incremental backups, but it is slower and requires more media capacity than incremental backups because data that are backed up are cumulative.

Backup Testing

Backup testing is important to ensure the successful recovery of the infrastructure and critical business processes. Testing should focus on:

- Identifying gaps
- Verifying assumptions
- Testing timelines
- Ensuring effectiveness of strategies
- Evaluating performance of personnel
- Checking accuracy and currency of the backup and recovery plan

Testing must be carefully planned and controlled to avoid placing the enterprise at increased risk. To ensure that all plans are regularly tested, an IT auditor should be aware of the testing schedule and tests to be conducted for all critical functions.

All tests must be fully documented with pretest, test and posttest reports. Test documentation should be reviewed by an IT auditor. Information security should also be validated during the test to ensure that it is not being compromised. A key element to this approach is that backups rotated offsite should not be returned for reuse until their replacement has been sent offsite. Variations of this method can be used depending on whether quarterly backups are required and on the amount of redundancy an enterprise may wish to have.

Offsite Facility Reviews

An offsite storage facility should be evaluated to ensure the presence, synchronization and currency of critical media and documentation. This includes data files, applications software, applications documentation, systems software, systems documentation, operations documentation, necessary supplies, special forms and a copy of the BCP. For verification, an IT auditor should perform a detailed inventory review, including testing for correct dataset names, volume serial numbers, accounting periods and bin locations of media.

An IT auditor should also review the documentation, compare it for currency with production documentation, evaluate the availability of the facility and ensure it conforms with management's requirements.

When performing a review or audit of backup, storage and recovery controls, an IT auditor should also:

ISACA. All Rights Reserved.

- Evaluate offsite storage to ensure its adequacy, by inspecting the facility and reviewing its contents and security and environmental controls.
- Verify the arrangements for transporting backup media to ensure that they meet the appropriate security requirements.
- Evaluate the ability of personnel to respond effectively in emergency situations, by reviewing emergency procedures, employee training and results of employee tests and drills.
- Ensure that a process for maintaining backup, storage and recovery plans is in place and effective, and that it covers both periodic and unscheduled revisions.
- Review backup and recovery procedures to determine if they are being followed.

4.4.4 Business Continuity and Disaster Recovery Controls

The purpose of business continuity/disaster recovery is to enable a business to continue offering critical services in the event of a disruption and to survive a disastrous interruption to activities. Rigorous planning and commitment of resources are necessary to adequately prepare for such an event.

Business Continuity Plan

A business continuity plan (BCP) is used by an enterprise to respond to disruption of critical business processes. BCP is primarily the responsibility of senior management, as it is entrusted with safeguarding the assets and the viability of the enterprise, as defined in the BCP/DRP policy. The BCP is generally followed by the business and supporting units to enable a reduced but sufficient level of functionality in business operations in response to an interruption, while recovery activities are taking place. The plan should address all functions and assets required for the enterprise to remain viable and specify the continuity procedures necessary to minimize the consequences of business interruption.

Depending on the complexity of the enterprise, there can be one or more plans. These plans do not have to be integrated into a single plan. However, all plans must be consistent with one another to enable a viable BCP strategy.

Business Continuity Plan Components

Whether a BCP consists of more than one plan document depends on the size and/or requirements of an enterprise. A BCP should address continuity of operations, disaster recovery and business resumption. A BCP may also address:

- Continuity of support/IT contingencies
- Crisis communications
- Incident response
- Transportation issues
- Occupant emergencies
- Evacuation and emergency relocation

Most BCPs include procedures that accommodate recovery of information systems (i.e., data storage, servers, etc.), user workstations, selected equipment (card readers, barcode scanners, printers, etc.) and network infrastructure (channels, equipment). Copies of the plan should be kept offsite—at the recovery facility, at the media storage facility and possibly at the homes of key decision-making personnel. Many enterprises place electronic versions of their plans on mirrored websites.

ISACA. All Rights Reserved.

Business Continuity Plan Testing

Most business continuity tests fall short of full-scale testing of all operational portions of the enterprise, if operations are tested at all. However, full or partial testing is necessary to determine how well the plan works or which portions of the plan need improvement. The BCP test should be scheduled during a time that will minimize disruptions to normal operations. The test should address all critical components and simulate actual primetime processing conditions.

The test should be designed to:

- Verify the completeness and precision of the BCP.
- Evaluate the performance of the personnel involved in the exercise.
- Appraise the training and awareness of employees who are not members of the business continuity team.
- Evaluate the coordination between business continuity team members and external vendors and suppliers.
- Measure the ability and capacity of the backup site to perform prescribed processing.
- Assess the vital records retrieval capability.
- Evaluate the state and quantity of equipment and supplies that have been relocated to the recovery site.
- Measure the overall performance of operational and IT processing activities related to maintaining the business entity.

Assessing the results and the value of BCP tests is an important IT auditor responsibility.

Auditing Business Continuity

When performing a review or audit of business continuity, an IT auditor should:

- Understand and evaluate business continuity strategy and its connection to business objectives.
- Review the business impact analysis (BIA) findings to ensure they reflect current business priorities and controls.
- Evaluate the BCPs to determine their adequacy and currency by reviewing the plans and comparing them to appropriate standards and/or government regulations—e.g., recovery time objective (RTO), recovery point objective (RPO)—as defined in the business impact analysis (BIA).
- Verify that the BCPs are effective by reviewing the results of previous tests performed by IT and end-user personnel.
- Evaluate cloud-based mechanisms.
- Evaluate offsite storage to ensure its adequacy by inspecting the facility and reviewing its contents, security and environmental controls (as part of data backup, storage and recovery).
- Verify the arrangements for transporting backup media to ensure they meet the appropriate security requirements (as part of data backup, storage and recovery).
- Evaluate the ability of personnel to respond effectively in emergency situations by reviewing emergency procedures, employee training and results of employee tests and drills.
- Ensure that the process of maintaining plans is in place and effective and covers both periodic and unscheduled revisions.
- Evaluate whether the business continuity manuals and procedures are written in a simple and easy to understand manner. This can be achieved by interviewing stakeholders to determine whether they understand their roles and responsibilities with respect to business continuity strategies.

ISACA. All Rights Reserved.

Disaster Recovery Planning

A disaster recovery plan (DRP) is a set of human, physical, technical and procedural resources needed to recover, within a defined time and cost, an activity interrupted by an emergency or disaster.

Disaster recovery planning, in support of business operations/IT service provisioning, is an element of an internal control system established to manage availability and restore critical processes/IT services in the event of interruption. The purpose of this continuous planning process is to ensure that cost-effective controls are in place to prevent data loss and to recover the IT capacity of the enterprise in the event of a disruption. The importance of the availability of individual applications/IT services depends on the criticality of the business processes they support. The importance and urgency of restoring business processes and corresponding IT services and applications can be established through performing a BIA and assigning RPOs and RTOs. Both the availability of business data and the ability to process and handle data are vital to the sustainability and/or survival of any enterprise. Planning for disasters is, therefore, an important part of risk management and business continuity planning processes.

Disaster recovery planning is a continuous process. After initially defining the criticality of business processes and supporting IT services, systems and data, the DR team must periodically review and revisit those assessments. Following are two important outcomes of disaster recovery planning:

- **Changes**—In IT infrastructure (servers, networks, data storage systems); in supporting processes (increasing their maturity); in procedures and organizational structure (new headcount or new roles). These changes are combined into programs spanning three to five years, often called IT DR strategies.
- **Disaster recovery plans**—Developed to direct the enterprise response to incidents ranging from simple emergencies to full-blown disasters. The plans range from simple department-level procedures to modular multitiered plans for multiple locations and lines of business.

The ultimate goal of the disaster recovery planning process is to respond to incidents that may adversely impact people, impede operations to deliver goods and services to the marketplace, and hinder compliance with regulatory requirements.

Disaster recovery planning may be subject to various compliance requirements, depending on geographic location, nature of business, and the legal and regulatory framework. Most compliance requirements focus on assuring continuity of service; however, human safety is the most essential aspect of disaster planning. For example, in case of fire, safe evacuation comes first; restoration of service is secondary.

Disaster Recovery Testing

Based on the risk assessment and BIA, critical applications and infrastructure are identified and scheduled for testing. If recovery plans are not tested, the enterprise bears an unacceptable risk that the plans will not work. As testing plans requires expending time and resources, an enterprise should carefully plan and develop test objectives to ensure that measurable benefits can be achieved. Once the objectives have been defined, an independent third party, such as an IT auditor, should be present to monitor and evaluate the test and assess the results. The auditor should provide a list of recommendations to improve the plan. In summary, testing should include:

- Develop test objectives.
- Execute the test.
- Evaluate the test.
- Develop recommendations to improve the effectiveness of testing processes and recovery plans.
- Establish a follow-up process to ensure that the recommendations are implemented.

ISACA. All Rights Reserved.

4.4.5 IT Operations Controls

IT operations controls are associated with the day-to-day operation of computer programs and systems. These controls are designed to ensure that IT systems are operating efficiently and that effectiveness targets are being met.

IT operations staff are responsible for the accurate and efficient operation of the network, systems and applications, and for the delivery of high-quality IT services to business users and customers. Tasks of the IT operations staff include:

- Execute and monitor scheduled jobs
- Facilitate timely backup
- Monitor unauthorized access and use of sensitive data
- Monitor and review the extent of adherence to IT operations procedures as established by IT and business management
- Participate in tests of disaster recovery plans (DRPs)
- Monitor the performance, capacity, availability and failure of information resources
- Facilitate troubleshooting and incident handling

Procedures detailing instructions for operational tasks and procedures coupled with appropriate IT management oversight are necessary parts of the IT control environment.

This documentation should include:

- Procedures based on operating instructions and job flows for computer and peripheral equipment
- Procedures for monitoring systems and applications
- Procedures for detecting systems and applications errors and problems
- Procedures for handling information services problems and escalation of unresolved issues
- Procedures for backup and recovery

IT Operations Review and Audit

When auditing IT operations, an IT auditor should review:

- IT personnel (observation)
- Operator access
- Operator manuals
- Access to the library
- Contents and location of offline storage
- File-handling procedures
- Data entry
- Lights-out operations

When conducting a review of IT operations, an IT auditor should consider the questions provided in **figure 4.9**.

ISACA. All Rights Reserved.

Figure 4.9—IT Operations Review	
Areas to Review	**Questions to Consider**
• Observation of IT personnel	• Have controls been put in place to ensure efficiency of operations and adherence to established standards and policies? • Is adequate supervision present? • Have controls been put in place regarding IS management review, data integrity and security?
• Operator access	• Is access to files and documentation libraries restricted to operators? • Are responsibilities for the operation of computer and related peripheral equipment limited? • Is access to correcting program and data problems restricted? • Should access to utilities that allow system fixes to software and/or data be restricted? • Is access to production source code and data libraries (including run procedures) limited?
• Operator manuals	• Are instructions adequate to address: ▪ The operation of the computer and its peripheral equipment? ▪ Startup and shutdown procedures? ▪ Actions to be taken in the event of machine/program failure? ▪ Records to be retained? ▪ Routine job duties and restricted activities?
• Access to the library	• Is the librarian prevented from accessing computer hardware? • Does the librarian have access only to the tape management system? • Is access to library facilities provided to authorized staff only? • Is removal of files restricted by production scheduling software? • Does the librarian handle the receipt and return of foreign media entering the library? • Are logs of the sign-in and sign-out of data files and media maintained?
• Contents and location of offline storage	• Are offline file storage media containing production system programs and data clearly marked with their contents? • Are offline library facilities located away from the computer room? • Are policies and procedures adequate for: • Administering the offline library? • Checking out/in media, including requirements for signature authorizations? • Identifying, labeling, delivering and retrieving offsite backup files? • Encryption of offsite backup files (especially if these physically move between locations)? • Inventorying the system for onsite and offsite media, including the specific storage locations of each tape? • Secure disposal/destruction of media, including requirements for signature authorizations?
• File handling procedures	• Have procedures been established to control the receipt and release of files and secondary storage media to/ from other locations? • Are internal tape labels used to help ensure that the correct media are mounted for processing? • Are these procedures adequate and in accordance with management's intent and authorization? • Are these procedures being followed?

ISACA. All Rights Reserved.

Figure 4.9—IT Operations Review *(cont.)*	
Areas to Review	**Questions to Consider**
• Data entry	• Are input documents authorized and do the documents contain appropriate signatures? • Are batch totals reconciled? • Does segregation of duties exist between the person who keys the data and the person who reviews the keyed data for accuracy and errors? • Are control reports being produced? Are the reports accurate? Are the reports maintained and reviewed?
• Lights-out operations	• Remote access to the master console is often granted to standby operators for contingency purposes such as automated software failure. Is access to security sufficient to guard against unauthorized use? • Do contingency plans allow for the proper identification of a disaster in the unattended facility? • Are the automated operation software and manual contingency procedures documented and tested adequately at the recovery site? • Are proper program change controls and access controls present? • Are tests of the software performed on a periodic basis, especially after changes or updates are applied? • Do assurances exist that errors are not hidden by the software and that all errors result in operator notification?
Source: ISACA, *CISA Review Manual, 27th Edition*, USA, 2019, figure 4.14, *https://www.isaca.org/bookstore/cisa-exam-resources/crm27ed*	

Job Scheduling

In complex IT environments, computer systems transfer hundreds to thousands of data files daily. A schedule is typically created that lists the jobs that must be run and the order in which they are to run, including any dependencies. Due to the inherent complexity of this process, automated job scheduling software provides control over the scheduling process. In addition to the scheduling of batch jobs, job scheduling software can be used to schedule tape backups and other maintenance activities. Job scheduling is a major function of the IT department. The schedule includes the jobs that must be run, the sequence of job execution, and the conditions required for program execution. High-priority jobs should be given optimal resource availability. Maintenance functions (e.g., backups and system reorganization) should be performed during nonpeak times, if possible. Low-priority jobs can be scheduled if time becomes available.

When conducting a review of job and personnel scheduling, an IT auditor should consider the questions provided in **figure 4.10**.

ISACA. All Rights Reserved.

Figure 4.10—Scheduling Reviews	
Areas to Review	**Questions to Consider**
• Regularly scheduled applications • Input deadlines • Data preparation time • Estimated processing time • Output deadlines • Procedures for collecting, reporting and analyzing key performance indicators	• Are the items included in SLAs? • Are the items functioning according to the SLAs?
• Job schedule	• Have critical applications been identified and the highest priority assigned to them? • Have processing priorities been established for other applications and are the assigned priorities justified? • Is scheduling of rush/rerun jobs consistent with their assigned priority? • Do scheduling procedures facilitate optimal use of computer resources while meeting service requirements? • Do operators record jobs that are to be processed and the required data files? • Do operators schedule jobs for processing on a predetermined basis and perform them using either automated scheduling software or a manual schedule?
• Daily job schedule	• Is the number of personnel assigned to each shift adequate to support the workload? • Does the daily job schedule serve as an audit trail? Does the schedule provide each shift of computer operators with the work to be carried out, the sequence in which programs are to be run and indication when lower-priority work can be performed? • At the end of a shift, does each operator pass to the work scheduler or the next shift of operators a statement of the work completed and the reasons any scheduled work was not finished?
• Console log	• Were jobs run and completed according to the schedule? • If not, are the reasons valid?
• Exception processing logs	• Do operators obtain written or electronic approval from owners when scheduling request-only jobs? • Do operators record all exception processing requests? • Do operators review the exception processing request log to determine the appropriateness of procedures performed?
• Reexecuted jobs	• Are all reexecutions of jobs properly authorized and logged for IS management review? • Are procedures established for rerunning jobs to ensure that the correct input files are being used and subsequent jobs in the sequence also are rerun, if appropriate?
• Personnel	• Are personnel who are capable of assigning, changing job schedules or job priorities authorized to do so?
Source: ISACA, *CISA Review Manual, 27th Edition*, USA, 2019, figure 4.3, *https://www.isaca.org/bookstore/cisa-exam-resources/crm27ed*	

ISACA. All Rights Reserved.

4.4.6 Physical Access and Environmental Controls

Physical controls are locks, fences, closed-circuit TV (CCTV) and devices that are installed to physically restrict access to a facility or hardware. Physical controls require maintenance, monitoring and the ability to assess and react to an alert if a problem is indicated.

Physical Access Exposures

From an IT perspective, an enterprise should consider the following questions when considering physical access exposures and controls:

- Are hardware facilities reasonably protected against forced entry?
- Are keys to the computer facilities adequately controlled to reduce the risk of unauthorized access?
- Are computer terminals locked or otherwise secured to prevent removal of boards, chips and the computer itself?
- Are authorized equipment passes required before computer equipment can be removed from its normal secure surroundings?

Facilities to be protected include:

- Programming area
- Computer room
- Operator consoles and terminals
- Tape library, tapes, disks and all magnetic media
- Storage rooms and supplies
- Offsite backup file storage facility
- Input/output control room
- Communications closets
- Telecommunications equipment (including radios, satellites, wiring, modems and external network connections)
- Microcomputers and PCs
- Power sources
- Disposal sites
- Minicomputer establishments
- Dedicated telephones/telephone lines
- Control units and front-end processors
- Portable equipment (e.g., handheld scanners and coding devices, barcode readers, laptop computers, printers, pocket local area network (LAN) adapters)
- Onsite and remote printers
- Local area networks

Additionally, system, infrastructure or software application documentation should be protected against unauthorized access.

For these safeguards to be effective, they must extend beyond the computer facility to include any vulnerable access points within the entire enterprise and at organizational boundaries/interfaces with external enterprises. This may include remote locations and rented, leased or shared facilities. Additionally, an IT auditor may require assurances that similar controls exist at service provider or other third-party facilities, if they are potentially vulnerable access points to sensitive information within the enterprise.

ISACA. All Rights Reserved.

Physical Access Controls

Physical access controls are designed to protect the enterprise from unauthorized access. These controls should limit access to individuals authorized by management. This authorization may be explicit, as in a door lock for which management has authorized who may have a key, or implicit, as in a job description that implies a need to access sensitive reports and documents. The following are examples of physical access controls:

- **Bolting door locks**—Locks opened with traditional metal door keys that are stamped "do not duplicate" and stored and issued under strict management control
- **Combination door locks (cipher locks)**—Numeric keypads or dials that permit entry
- **Electronic door locks**—Magnetic or embedded chip-based plastic card keys or tokens entered into sensor readers to gain access
- **Biometric door locks**—Locks activated by individuals' unique body features, such as voice, retina, fingerprint, hand geometry or signature
- **Manual logging**—A process that requires all visitors to sign a log with their name, the enterprise they are representing, reason for visiting, person to see, and date and time of entry and departure
- **Electronic logging**—A feature of electronic and biometric security systems that logs all access attempts and highlights those that are unsuccessful
- **Identification badges (photo IDs)**—ID badges that are to be worn and displayed by all personnel
- **Video cameras**—Cameras located at strategic points and monitored by security guards
- **Security guards**—Guards located at strategic points to protect the enterprise from loss
- **Controlled visitor access**—A process that requires that all visitors be escorted by a responsible employee
- **Deadman doors (mantrap or airlock entrance)**—Two doors (typically used for entry to facilities such as computer rooms and high-security areas) that require the first entry door to close and lock with only one person permitted in the area for the second door to operate
- **Computer workstation locks**—Locks that secure a device to the desk, e.g., preventing a computer from being turned on, or disengaging keyboard recognition, thus preventing use
- **Controlled single-entry point**—A single point of entry to monitor all incoming personnel
- **Alarm system**—Alarms linked to inactive entry points, motion detectors, and the reverse flow of enter- or exit-only doors

Facilities such as computer rooms should not be visible or identifiable from the outside; there should be no windows or directional signs. The building or department directory should discreetly identify only the general location of the information processing facility. If windows are present, they should be constructed of reinforced glass and, if on the ground floor of the building, further protected, e.g., with bars.

Physical Access Review and Audit

An IT auditor should inspect (tour) computer facilities to gain an understanding of physical access controls and restrictions (e.g., control over employees, visitors, intruders and vendors). The following paths of physical entry should be evaluated for proper physical controls and security:

- All entry doors
- Emergency exit doors
- Glass windows and walls
- Movable walls and modular cubicles
- Areas above suspended ceilings and beneath raised floors

ISACA. All Rights Reserved.

- Ventilation systems
- Areas over a curtain or fake wall

Testing of physical access controls can be achieved by visually observing any previously noted safeguards to obtain evidence of compliance or to observe deviations, if any. Documents to assist with this effort include emergency evacuation procedures, fire suppression system test results, and key lock logs accounting for all keys. Testing should extend beyond the data center and include the following related facilities:

- Location of all operator consoles
- Printer rooms
- Computer storage rooms (including equipment, paper and supply rooms)
- UPS/generator
- Location of all communications equipment identified on the network diagram
- Media storage
- Offsite backup storage facility

A thorough test includes observing smoke and water detectors and checking general cleanliness. For a ground-floor computer room, an IT auditor may also consider walking around the outside of the room, viewing the location of any windows, examining emergency exit doors for evidence they are routinely used (such as the presence of cigarette stubs or litter) and examining the air conditioning units. An IT auditor should also consider whether any additional threats exist close to the room, such as storage of dangerous or flammable material.

Environmental Threats and Exposures

Typical environmental threats include:

- Floods
- Lightning
- Tornadoes
- Hurricanes
- Earthquakes
- Fire

Exposures associated with environmental threats include:

- Power interruptions
  - Loss of power (e.g., surge, spikes, sags, brownouts, faults)
  - Generators (e.g., insufficient capacity, poor maintenance)
  - Batteries (e.g., poorly maintained, outdated)
- HVAC malfunctions
  - Overheating
  - Humidity problems (e.g , corrosion and condensation (high humidity), static (low humidity)
  - Clogged filters
- Water problems
  - Loss of water (needed for cooling systems)
- Health and safety issues
- Operational security challenges

ISACA. All Rights Reserved.

- Restricting access to server rooms and wiring closets
- Securing access to power supplies, generators, elevator shafts

Environmental Controls

Environmental controls include power, heating, ventilation and air conditioning (HVAC) systems, water drainage, fire suppression, and other measures designed to ensure that the facilities in which systems are stored are designed to accommodate the physical requirements of computer system operation.

IT systems rely on controlled environmental conditions, including clean and steady power and controls over humidity and temperature. An enterprise should be prepared for power failure or other environmental disturbances in order to prepare for conditions that may lead to system failure. Having an uninterruptible power supply (UPS), backup generators and surge protectors can protect equipment from damage or failure, but such systems require more than an initial investment. For instance, a UPS must be validated to ensure it has adequate power to run critical systems until a backup generator can come online. The UPS must be tested periodically and generators must be checked for fuel and to ensure proper mechanical function.

Computing environments should incorporate systems to monitor and control factors such as temperature, humidity and electrical power quality. Without adequate environmental controls to prevent, detect and recover from physical damage to IT systems, other general and application control activities could be rendered ineffective or useless. In a large and geographically dispersed enterprise, an IT site operations manager may be assigned at each site to ensure that all equipment is inventoried and configured to policy-compliant standards.

Geographic concerns need to be considered, particularly for enterprise facilities and disaster recovery sites. Regions with a risk of earthquakes, hurricanes, flooding or other natural disasters should be avoided when selecting facility sites. Proximity to facilities that present special risk (e.g., nuclear power plants, chemical production facilities, airports) should be considered. Primary processing facilities, disaster recovery sites and offsite data storage facilities should be located far enough from one another to ensure that a disaster event does not impact more than one site.

4.4.7 System Development Life Cycle (SDLC) Controls

SDLC includes the phases deployed in the development or acquisition of a software system. SDLC is an approach used to plan, design, develop, test and implement an application system or a major modification to an application system. Typical phases of SDLC include a feasibility study, requirements study, requirements definition, detailed design, programming, testing, installation and postimplementation review. It does not include service delivery or benefits realization activities.

The control objective associated with SDLC is that SDLC processes are established, in place and operating effectively to provide reasonable assurance that business, financial and/or industrial software systems and applications are developed in a repeatable and reliable manner to ensure that business objectives are met.

SDLC Models

Several SDLC models exist, with traditional Waterfall and Agile being used most frequently. Development Operations (DevOps) is often discussed with SDLC models; however, its role relates to the planning, deployment and maintenance of the asset produced during the SDLC. Essentially, DevOps is a subset of Agile and begins when the Agile SDLC ends.

ISACA. All Rights Reserved.

Traditional Waterfall

A traditional SDLC (Waterfall) model and variants of the model normally involve a life cycle verification approach that ensures that potential mistakes are corrected early and not solely during final acceptance testing. This life cycle approach is the oldest and most widely used for developing business applications. This approach works best when project requirements are likely to be stable and well-defined. It facilitates the determination of a system architecture relatively early in the development effort. The approach is based on a systematic, sequential approach to system and/or software development. The traditional approach is useful in web applications in which prototypes of screens are necessary to aid in the completion of requirements and design.

The primary advantage of the traditional approach is that it provides a template for placing methods of meeting the requirements (e.g., definition, design, programming). However, some problems with this approach include the following:

- Unanticipated events that result in iterations, creating problems in implementing the approach
- The difficulty of obtaining an explicit set of requirements from the customer/user as the approach requires
- Managing requirements and convincing the user about the undue or unwarranted requirements in the system functionality, which may lead to conflict in the project
- The necessity of customer/user patience because a working version of the system programs are not available until late in the project life cycle
- A shifting business environment that alters or changes the customer/user requirements before they are delivered

SDLC Phases

An SDLC approach is traditionally made up of a number of distinct phases (**figure 4.11**), each with a defined set of activities and outcomes. Each phase has defined goals and activities to perform with assigned responsibilities, expected outcomes and target completion dates. There are other interpretations that use a slightly different number of phases with different names.

The actual phases for each project may vary depending on whether a developed or acquired solution is chosen. For example, system maintenance efforts may not require the same level of detail or number of phases as new applications. The phases and deliverables should be decided during the early planning stages of the project.

Over the years, business application development has occurred largely through the use of traditional SDLC phases. With purchased packages having become more common, the design and development phases of the traditional life cycle are being replaced with selection and configuration phases.

Figure 4.11—Traditional SDLC Phases and Descriptions

SDLC Phase	General Description
Phase 1—Feasibility Study	Determine the strategic benefits of implementing the system either in productivity gains or in future cost avoidance, identify and quantify the cost savings of a new system, and estimate a payback schedule for costs incurred in implementing the system. Further, intangible factors such as readiness of the business users and maturity of the business processes will also be considered and assessed. This business case provides the justification for proceeding to the next phase.
Phase 2—Requirements Definition	Define the problem or need that requires resolution and define the functional and quality requirements of the solution system. This can be either a customized approach or vendor-supplied software package, which would entail following a defined and documented acquisition process. In either case, the user needs to be actively involved.

ISACA. All Rights Reserved.

Figure 4.11—Traditional SDLC Phases and Descriptions *(cont.)*	
SDLC Phase	**General Description**
Phase 3A—Software Selection and Acquisition (purchased systems)	Based on requirements defined, prepare a request for proposal outlining the entity requirements to invite bids from prospective suppliers, in respect of those systems that are intended to be procured from vendors or solution providers.
Phase 3B—Design (in-house development)	Based on the requirements defined, establish a baseline of system and subsystem specifications that describe the parts of the system, how they interface, and how the system will be implemented using the chosen hardware, software and network facilities. Generally, the design also includes program and database specifications and will address any security considerations. Additionally, a formal change control process is established to prevent uncontrolled entry of new requirements into the development process.
Phase 4A—Configuration (purchased systems)	Configure the system, if it is a packaged system, to tailor it to organization requirements. This is best done through the configuration of system control parameters, rather than changing program code. Modern software packages are extremely flexible, making it possible for one package to suit many organizations simply by switching functionality on or off and setting parameters in tables. There may be a need to build interface programs that will connect the acquired system with existing programs and databases.
Phase 4B—Development (in-house development)	Use the design specifications to begin programming and formalizing supporting operational processes of the system. Various levels of testing also occur in this phase to verify and validate what has been developed. This generally includes all unit and system testing and several iterations of user acceptance testing.
Phase 5—Final Testing and Implementation	Establish the actual operation of the new information system, with the final iteration of user acceptance testing and user sign-off conducted in this phase. The system also may go through a certification and accreditation process to assess the effectiveness of the business application in mitigating risk to an appropriate level and providing management accountability over the effectiveness of the system in meeting its intended objectives and in establishing an appropriate level of internal control.
Phase 6—Post-implementation	Following the successful implementation of a new or extensively modified system, implement a formal process that assesses the adequacy of the system and projected cost-benefit or ROI measurements vis-à-vis the feasibility stage findings and deviations. In so doing, IS project and end-user management can provide lessons learned and/or plans for addressing system deficiencies as well as recommendations for future projects regarding system development and project management processes followed.
Source: ISACA, *CISA Review Manual, 27th Edition*, USA, 2019, figure 3.11, *https://www.isaca.org/bookstore/cisa-exam-resources/crm27ed*	

Agile

Agile development does not ignore the concerns of traditional software development but approaches them from a different perspective. Agile development:

- Plans only for the next iteration in detail, rather than planning subsequent development phases.
- Uses an adaptive approach to requirements and does not emphasize managing a requirements baseline.
- Focuses on quickly proving an architecture by building actual functionality versus formally defining software and data architecture early on and in increasingly more detailed models and descriptions.
- Assumes limits to defect testing but attempts to validate functions through a frequent-build test cycle and to correct problems in the next subproject before too much time and cost are incurred.
- Performs and adapts its development based on frequent inspections rather than emphasizing defined and repeatable processes.

ISACA. All Rights Reserved.

Auditor's Involvement in SDLC

Throughout the SDLC project management process an IT auditor should analyze the associated risk and exposures inherent in each phase of the SDLC and ensure that appropriate control mechanisms are in place to minimize risk in a cost-effective manner. Caution should be exercised to avoid recommending controls that cost more to administer than the associated risk they are designed to minimize.

When reviewing the SDLC process, an IT auditor should obtain documentation from the various phases and attend project team meetings, offering advice to the project team throughout the system development process. An IT auditor should also assess the project team's ability to produce key deliverables by the promised dates.

Typically, an IT auditor should review the adequacy of the following project management activities:

- Levels of oversight by project committee/board
- Risk management methods within the project
- Issue management
- Cost management
- Processes for planning and dependency management
- Reporting processes to senior management
- Change control processes
- Stakeholder management involvement
- Sign-off process (at a minimum, signed approvals from systems development and user management responsible for the cost of the project and/or use of the system)

Additionally, adequate and complete documentation of all phases of the SDLC process should be evident. Typical types of documentation include, but should not be limited to, the following:

- Objectives defining what is to be accomplished during that phase
- Key deliverables by phases with project personnel assigned direct responsibilities for these deliverables
- A project schedule with highlighted dates for the completion of key deliverables
- An economic forecast for that phase, defining resources and the cost of the resources required to complete the phase

4.5 Application Controls

Application controls are the policies, procedures and activities designed to provide reasonable assurance that objectives relevant to a given automated solution (application) are achieved. As such, application controls are controls over input, processing and output functions. They include methods for ensuring that:

- Only complete, accurate and valid data are entered and updated in a computer system.
- Processing accomplishes the correct task.
- Processing results meet expectations.
- Data are maintained completely and accurately and are available for reporting.

Application control issues may include:

- Data validation is not performed on data entry.
- Data in reports are incomplete/inaccurate.
- Access to sensitive areas of the application and its data is not restricted to appropriate personnel.

ISACA. All Rights Reserved.

- System calculations are performed incorrectly.
- Errors in system logic or configurations result in incorrect output of data.

To understand the relationship between general IT controls and application controls, the auditor should consider that application controls refer to a given automated solution (application), while general controls relate to the environment in which computer-based application systems are developed, maintained and operated. The general controls are applicable to all applications, and there is a correlation between a weak general control environment and failure in application controls.

4.5.1 Input/Origination Controls

Input controls are techniques and procedures used to verify, validate and edit data to ensure that only correct data are entered into the computer. Input controls must ensure that every transaction to be processed is entered, processed and recorded accurately and completely. Following are examples of input controls:

- **Input authorization**—Input authorization verifies that all transactions have been authorized and approved by management.
- **Batch Controls and Balancing**—Batch controls group input transactions to provide control totals. The batch control can be based on total monetary amount, total items, total documents or hash totals.
- **Error Reporting and Handling**—Input processing requires that controls be identified to verify that only correct data are accepted into the system and input errors are recognized and corrected.

4.5.2 Processing Controls

Processing controls are meant to ensure the reliability of application program processing. An IT auditor should understand the controls exercised over processing to evaluate the exposures covered by them and those that remain. Following are examples of processing controls:

- **Data Validation and Editing Procedures**—Procedures should be established to ensure that input data are validated and edited as close to the time and point of origination as possible. **Figure 4.12** provides various types of data validation edits and controls.
- **Processing Controls**—Processing controls are meant to ensure the completeness and accuracy of accumulated data.
- **Data File Control Procedures**—File controls should ensure that only authorized processing is performed on stored data. **Figure 4.13** provides types of data file controls.

Figure 4.12—Data Validation Edits and Controls

Edits	Description
Sequence check	The control number follows sequentially and any sequence or duplicated control numbers are rejected or noted on an exception report for follow-up purposes. For example, invoices are numbered sequentially. The day's invoices begin with 12001 and end with 15045. If any invoice larger than 15045 is encountered during processing, that invoice would be rejected as an invalid invoice number.
Limit check	Data should not exceed a predetermined amount. For example, payroll checks should not exceed US $4,000. If a check exceeds US $4,000, the data is rejected for further verification/authorization.
Range check	Data should be within a predetermined range of values. For example, product type codes range from 100 to 250. Any code outside this range should be rejected as an invalid product type.
Validity check	Programmed checking of the data validity in accordance with predetermined criteria. For example, a payroll record contains a field for marital status and the acceptable status codes are M or S. If any other code is entered, the record should be rejected.

ISACA. All Rights Reserved.

Figure 4.12—Data Validation Edits and Controls *(cont.)*	
Edits	**Description**
Reasonableness check	Input data are matched to predetermined reasonable limits or occurrence rates. For example, a widget manufacturer usually receives orders for no more than 20 widgets. If an order for more than 20 widgets is received, the computer program should be designed to print the record with a warning indicating that the order appears unreasonable.
Table lookups	Input data comply with predetermined criteria maintained in a computerized table of possible values. For example, the input clerk enters a city code of 1 to 10. This number corresponds with a computerized table that matches the code to a city name.
Existence check	Data are entered correctly and agree with valid predetermined criteria. For example, a valid transaction code must be entered in the transaction code field.
Key verification	The keying process is repeated by a separate individual using a machine that compares the original keystrokes to the repeated keyed input. For example, the worker number is keyed twice and compared to verify the keying process.
Check digit	A numeric value that has been calculated mathematically is added to data to ensure that the original data have not been altered or an incorrect, but valid, value substituted. This control is effective in detecting transposition and transcription errors. For example, a check digit is added to an account number so it can be checked for accuracy when it is used.
Completeness check	A field should always contain data rather than zeros or blanks. A check of each byte of that field should be performed to determine that some form of data, not blanks or zeros, is present. For example, a worker number on a new employee record is left blank. This is identified as a key field and the record would be rejected, with a request that the field be completed before the record is accepted for processing.
Duplicate check	New transactions are matched to those previously input to ensure that they have not already been entered. For example, a vendor invoice number agrees with previously recorded invoices to ensure that the current order is not a duplicate and, therefore, the vendor will not be paid twice.
Logical relationship check	If a particular condition is true, then one or more additional conditions or data input relationships may be required to be true and consider the input valid. For example, the hire date of an employee may be required to be more than 16 years past his/her date of birth.
Source: *CISA Review Manual, 27th Edition*, USA, 2019, figure 3.18, *https://www.isaca.org/bookstore/cisa-exam-resources/crm27ed*	

Figure 4.13—Data File Controls	
Method	**Description**
Before and after image reporting	Computer data in a file prior to and after a transaction is processed can be recorded and reported. The before and after images make it possible to trace the impact transactions have on computer records.
Maintenance error reporting and handling	Control procedures should be in place to ensure that all error reports are properly reconciled and corrections are submitted on a timely basis. To ensure SoD, error corrections should be reviewed properly and authorized by personnel who did not initiate the transaction.
Source documentation retention	Source documentation should be retained for an adequate time period to enable retrieval, reconstruction or verification of data. Policies regarding the retention of source documentation should be enforced. Originating departments should maintain copies of source documentation and ensure that only authorized personnel have access. When appropriate, source documentation should be destroyed in a secure, controlled environment.
Internal and external labeling	Internal and external labeling of removable storage media is imperative to ensure that the proper data are loaded for processing. External labels provide the basic level of assurance that the correct data medium is loaded for processing. Internal labels, including file header records, provide assurance that the proper data files are used and allow for automated checking.
Version usage	It is critical that the proper version of a file be used as well as the correct file, for processing to be correct. For example, transactions should be applied to the most current database, while restart procedures should use earlier versions.

ISACA. All Rights Reserved.

Figure 4.13—Data File Controls *(cont.)*	
Method	**Description**
Data file security	Data file security controls prevent unauthorized access by unauthorized users that may have access to the application to alter data files. These controls do not provide assurances relating to the validity of data but ensure that unauthorized users who may have access to the application cannot alter stored data improperly.
One-for-one checking	Individual documents agree with a detailed listing of documents processed by the computer. It is necessary to ensure that all documents have been received for processing.
Prerecorded input	Certain information fields are preprinted on blank input forms to reduce initial input errors.
Transaction logs	All transaction input activity is recorded by the computer. A detailed listing, including date of input, time of input, user ID and terminal location, can then be generated to provide an audit trail. It also permits operations personnel to determine which transactions have been posted. This will help to decrease the research time needed to investigate exceptions and decrease recovery time if a system failure occurs.
File updating and maintenance authorization	Proper authorization for file updating and maintenance is necessary to ensure that stored data are safeguarded adequately, correct and up to date. Application programs may contain access restrictions in addition to the overall system access restrictions. The additional security may provide levels of authorization as well as an audit trail of file maintenance.
Parity checking	Data transfers in a computer system are expected to be made in a relatively error-free environment. However, when programs or vital data are transmitted, additional controls are needed. Transmission errors are controlled primarily by error-detecting or correcting codes. The former is used more often because error-correcting codes are costly to implement and are unable to correct all errors. Generally, error detection methods such as a check bit and redundant transmission are adequate. Redundancy checking is a common error-detection routine. A transmitted block of data containing one or more records or messages is checked for the number of characters or patterns of bits contained in it. If the numbers or patterns do not conform to predetermined parameters, the receiving device ignores the transmitted data and instructs the user to retransmit. Check bits are often added to the transmitted data by the telecommunications control unit and may be applied either horizontally or vertically. These checks are similar to the parity checks normally applied to data characters within on-premises equipment. A parity check on a single character generally is referred to as a vertical or column check, and a parity check on all the equivalent bits is known as a horizontal, longitudinal or row check. Use of both checks greatly improves the possibilities of detecting a transmission error, which may be missed when either of those checks is used alone.
Source: *CISA Review Manual, 27th Edition*, USA, 2019, figure 3.19, *https://www.isaca.org/bookstore/cisa-exam-resources/crm27ed*	

4.5.3 Output Controls

Output controls provide assurance that the data delivered to users are presented, formatted and delivered in a consistent and secure manner. Following are examples of output controls:

- **Logging and storage of negotiable, sensitive and critical forms in a secure place**—Negotiable, sensitive or critical forms should be properly logged and secured to provide adequate safeguards against theft, damage or disclosure.
- **Computer generation of negotiable instruments, forms and signatures**—The computer generation of negotiable instruments, forms and signatures should be properly controlled.
- **Report accuracy, completeness and timeliness**—Report design and generation specifications, templates and creation/change request processes are critical system output controls.
- **Reports generated from the system**—These represent the data that management relies upon for business decisions and review of business results.
- **Report distribution**—Output reports should be distributed according to authorized distribution parameters.

ISACA. All Rights Reserved.

- **Balancing and reconciling**—Data processing application program output should be balanced routinely to the control totals.
- **Output error handling**—Procedures for reporting and controlling errors contained in the application program output should be established.
- **Output report retention**—A record retention schedule should be adhered to firmly.
- **Verification of receipt of reports**—To provide assurance that sensitive reports are properly distributed, the recipient should sign a log as evidence of receipt of output.

4.5.4 Application Control Review and Audit

When reviewing and auditing application controls, an IT auditor should perform the following activities:

- Plan the audit, set audit objectives and identify risk associated with the application being audited.
- Identify the significant application components and the flow of transactions through the system and gain a detailed understanding of the application by reviewing the available documentation and interviewing appropriate personnel. (Section 3.7.1 provides additional information covering the flow of transactions through the system.)
- Identify the application control strengths and evaluate the impact of the control weaknesses.
- Develop a testing strategy.
- Test the controls to ensure their functionality and effectiveness by applying appropriate audit procedures.
- Evaluate the control environment by analyzing the test results and other audit evidence to determine that control objectives are achieved.
- Consider the operational aspects of the application to ensure its efficiency and effectiveness by comparing the system to efficient system design standards, analyzing procedures used, and comparing them to management's objectives for the system.

ISACA. All Rights Reserved.

Page intentionally left blank

ISACA. All Rights Reserved.

4.6 Chapter Four Knowledge Check

Review Questions

1. What type of software is used to transmit messages or data from one point to another either locally or remotely?

   A. Access control software
   B. Data communications software
   C. Application software

2. Which of the following cloud models, when deployed, offers the **GREATEST** amount of new risk and security challenge to an enterprise?

   A. Private cloud
   B. Public cloud
   C. Hybrid cloud

3. Which of the following would an IT auditor be concerned about regarding enterprise use of a private cloud?

   A. Data may be stored in unknown locations.
   B. Data may not be easily retrievable.
   C. Services may not be scalable or agile enough to meet enterprise needs.

4. When evaluating logical access controls associated with group shared access to an account, an IT auditor should ensure that:

   A. The greatest level (highest privilege) of access has been provided to all users.
   B. Passwords are changed at the end of the day in which it is determined that an unauthorized access has occurred.
   C. The need for shared access has been properly justified and approved.

5. When reviewing an enterprise SDLC process, an IT auditor should:

   A. Analyze the associated risk and exposures inherent in each phase of the SDLC.
   B. Recommend controls to minimize risk throughout the SDLC process, regardless of the cost to implement.
   C. Avoid attending SDLC project team meetings to ensure auditor objectivity.

6. Which of the following data validation controls use a numeric calculated value that is added to data to ensure that the original data have not been altered and is effective in detecting transposition and transcription errors?

   A. Key verification
   B. Check digit
   C. Validity check

Answers on page 166

ISACA. All Rights Reserved.

Chapter 4 ANSWER KEY

Review Questions

1. A. Access control software is designed to prevent unauthorized access to data, unauthorized use of system functions and programs, and unauthorized updates/changes to data, and to detect or prevent unauthorized attempts to access computer resources.
   B. Data communications software is used to transmit messages or data from one point to another either locally or remotely. The data communication system is concerned only with the correct transmission between two points.
   C. Application software refers to applications written for a computer for end users to use and produce work.

2. A. A private cloud model is most closely related to traditional IT-outsourcing models. However, it can also be an enterprise's internal delivery model. Because of this, the private model tends to offer the least amount of new risk and security challenge.
   B. Public cloud clients share applications, processing power and data storage space communally. Client data are commingled but segregated, e.g., through the use of metatags. This model tends to present the greatest assurance challenges for security and risk managers.
   C. A hybrid cloud is a combination of two or more deployment models. Because it may contain a public cloud component, it will also present assurance challenges for security and risk managers, but not to the same extent as a purely public cloud deployment.

3. A. Data stored in unknown locations is a concern primarily associated with the deployment of a public cloud and not a private cloud.
   B. Difficulty retrieving data is a concern primarily associated with the deployment of a public cloud and not a private cloud.
   C. An area of concern for an IT auditor associated with a private cloud deployment is that it may not provide the same degree of scalability and agility that cloud public services provide.

4. A. It is good practice to utilize the principle of least privilege (i.e., giving just enough access as needed), not most, when allowing group shared access to an account.
   B. If it is found that someone has obtained unauthorized access to a group account, the password should be changed immediately—not put off until the end of the day—to prevent any further unauthorized access.
   C. The need for group shared access should be justified, and it should have two levels of approval—from the reporting manager and from the application, database or server owner.

5. **A. Throughout the SDLC project management process, an IT auditor should analyze the associated risk and exposures inherent in each phase of the SDLC.**
   B. An IT auditor should ensure that the appropriate control mechanisms are in place throughout the SDLC process to minimize risk in a cost-effective manner. Caution should be exercised to avoid recommending controls that cost more to administer than the associated risk that they are designed to minimize.
   C. When reviewing the SDLC process, an IT auditor should obtain documentation from the various phases and attend project team meetings, offering advice to the project team throughout the system development process.

6. A. With key verification, the keying process is repeated by a separate individual using a machine that compares the original keystrokes to the repeated keyed input. For example, the worker number is keyed twice and compared to verify the keying process.
   B. A check digit is a numeric value that has been calculated mathematically and added to data to ensure that the original data have not been altered, or that a valid but incorrect value has not been substituted. This control is effective in detecting transposition and transcription errors. For example, a check digit is added to an account number so it can be checked for accuracy when it is used.
   C. A validity check is the programmed checking of the data validity in accordance with predetermined criteria. For example, a payroll record contains a field for marital status and the acceptable status codes are M or S. If any other code is entered, the record should be rejected.

ISACA. All Rights Reserved.

IT AUDIT FUNDAMENTALS
An ISACA® Certificate

Chapter 5:

Specific Audit Subjects

Specific Audit Subjects

ISACA. All Rights Reserved.

Specific Audit Subjects

5.1 Learning Objectives

After completing this chapter, learners will be able to:

- Describe how network perimeter security protects enterprise data, assets and information.
- Articulate the risk and controls associated with Windows and UNIX®/Linux operating systems.
- Explain how to audit application container deployments.
- Summarize security vulnerabilities and risk associated with mobile (web) apps.
- Describe security concerns and risk associated with the use of Windows Active Directory and Oracle databases.
- Evaluate enterprise information security and privacy policies and practices.
- Identify how to assess the protection of an enterprise's mobile computing media and devices.

5.2 Network Infrastructure

Network perimeter security is a proactive process to ensure the protection of enterprise data, assets and information that are stored on computer equipment residing on a network, and the information flowing through the network.

Network perimeter security is built on the concept that layers of security components, when aggregated, provide the necessary protection from unauthorized access to the network. This process includes:[125]

- Security policy built on good practices using recognized standards
- Authorization and access controls addressed by identity management
- External perimeter control through the use of firewalls to protect the internal network from external intrusion
- Virtual private networks (VPNs) to allow authorized traffic through the firewall, using encryption techniques to prevent eavesdropping and physical devices (tokens) in the user's custody to further enhance authentication
- Intrusion detection tools to identify suspect network activity and issue alerts
- Penetration testing to ensure that firewalls are securely configured
- Internal security assessments to evaluate policy and procedures
- Risk management to evaluate and identify networks and resources requiring enhanced security
- Internal network segmentation, limiting access of data in certain locations to authorized users, and restricting that area from others within the enterprise

5.2.1 Network Perimeter Risk

The enterprise network is the primary communications channel because:[126]

- Key business processes (applications) function through the network.
- Financial transactions are stored and processed.
- Email containing privileged information is exchanged.

[125] ISACA, *Network Perimeter Security Audit/Assurance Program*, USA, 2009, *https://store.isaca.org/s/store#/store/browse/detail/a2S4w000004KoDdEAK*
[126] *Ibid.*

ISACA. All Rights Reserved.

- Analysis, business strategy, intellectual property, presentations, etc., are stored and exchanged.
- Personal identification information may be stored and transmitted.

The failure to provide adequate network security can result in:[127]

- Disclosure of privileged information
- Loss of physical assets
- Loss of intellectual property
- Loss of competitive advantage
- Loss of customer confidence
- Violation of regulatory requirements
- Disruption of network traffic, resulting in the inability to perform critical business functions
- Infection of computer systems with viruses and other malware that disrupt processing and require costly disinfection
- Use of the network as a launching pad for malicious activity against other enterprises (and the potential to be held liable for damages)

With the advent of the Internet, outsourcing, mobile devices, cloud and other hosted services, the concept of a perimeter changed considerably. Consequently, significant new risk and vulnerability needs to be addressed in a network environment. The perimeter is an important line of defense that protects the enterprise against external threats, and its design should reflect a proactive stance toward preventing potential risk.

An important component of the security perimeter is the Internet perimeter. This perimeter ensures secure access to the Internet for enterprise employees and guest users residing at all locations, including those involved in telecommuting or remote work. In order to provide security of email, front-end mobile and web apps, domain name system (DNS), etc., the Internet perimeter should:

- Route traffic between the enterprise and the Internet.
- Prevent executable files from being transferred through email attachments or web browsing.
- Monitor internal and external network ports for rogue activity.
- Detect and block traffic from infected internal endpoints.
- Control user traffic bound toward the Internet.
- Identify and block anomalous traffic and malicious packets recognized as potential attacks.
- Eliminate threats such as email spam, viruses and worms.
- Enforce filtering policies to block access to websites containing malware or questionable content.

The perimeter should also provide protection for virtual private networks (VPNs), wide area networks (WANs) and wireless local area networks (WLANs). Failure to design and harden the perimeter may allow access to unauthorized parties and possibly increase the effort required to isolate anomalies.

5.2.2 Network Perimeter Audit and Controls

When performing an audit of the network perimeter, an IT auditor should:[128]

- Provide management with an independent assessment relating to the effectiveness of the network perimeter security and its alignment with the IT security architecture and policy.

[127] *Ibid.*
[128] *Ibid.*

ISACA. All Rights Reserved.

- Provide management with an evaluation of the preparedness of the IT function in the event of an intrusion.
- Identify issues that affect the security of the enterprise network.

The audit should focus on the network perimeter security—including associated policies, standards and procedures—and on the effectiveness of the security implementation. The audit should also describe which networks within the enterprise will be reviewed and if independent penetration and intrusion testing will be included.

An audit of the network perimeter should review the following controls and test to ensure that the enterprise has implemented them:[129]

Network Security Components

- Networks are segmented by trust levels, with appropriately configured routers, and default password settings are changed from the factory defaults.
- The firewall rule requirements are assessed and documented.
- The firewall configuration reflects the rule-set requirements.
- Virtual private networks (VPNs) are required to access sensitive enterprise information.
- The VPN configuration provides communication security through encryption and ensures authentication.
- Remote dial-up access is secured through configuration controls, use is limited to necessary functions, encryption is utilized where possible, and availability of workstations for remote dial-up access is restricted.
- Encryption and user authentication are required for wireless networks. Use of tokens is strongly recommended.
- Intrusion detection software is installed and monitored, and intrusion alerts are researched.

5.2.3 Virtual Private Network

A virtual private network (VPN) is a secure private network that uses the public telecommunications infrastructure to transmit data. VPNs are used by enterprises for both extranets and wide areas of intranets. Using encryption and authentication, a VPN encrypts all data that pass between two Internet points, maintaining privacy and security.

A VPN extends the enterprise network securely via encrypted packets sent via virtual connections over the public Internet to distant offices, home workers, salespeople and business partners. Rather than using expensive dedicated leased lines, VPNs take advantage of the public worldwide IP infrastructure (thereby enabling remote users to make a local call versus dialing-in at long distance rates), or they use Internet cable modems or DSL connections for inexpensive public network connectivity.

VPNs are platform-independent. Any computer system that is configured to run on an IP network can be connected through a VPN with no modifications except for the installation of remote software.

The types of VPN are:

- **Remote-access VPN**—Connects telecommuters and mobile users to the enterprise WAN in a secure manner. It lowers the barrier to telecommuting by ensuring that information is reasonably protected on the open Internet. Also known as user-to gateway or client-to-gateway VPN.
- **Gateway-to-gateway VPN**—Forms a secure connection between two networks. Also known as site-to-site VPN.

[129] *Ibid.*

ISACA. All Rights Reserved.

Independent of the connectivity type, the primary issues associated with a VPN include:

- Security of transmissions, including preventing hijacking of transmissions and preventing malware from entering the network
- Technology management
- Configuration management
- Ensuring information is unaltered and maintains accuracy and reliability

5.3 Commonly Used Operating Systems

Operating system types, software integrity issues, activity logging and issues that an IT auditor should consider when conducting an audit or review of operating software development, acquisition or maintenance is discussed and described in Section 4.2.4. This section covers commonly used operating systems.

5.3.1 Microsoft Windows

Microsoft develops entire families of Windows operating systems that are specific to types of enterprises and uses. Current products include:

- **Windows**—The operating system for mainstream personal computers, tablets and smartphones. The latest version is Windows 11.
- **Windows Server®**—The operating system for server computers. The latest version is Windows Server 2022.
- **Windows PE**—A lightweight version used for installing Windows on bare-metal computers and for recovery or troubleshooting purposes. The latest version is Windows PE 10.
- **Windows IoT**—previously Windows Embedded

5.3.2 UNIX/Linux Operating System

UNIX® is one of the longest enduring operating systems in existence. Developed in 1969 by Bell Labs of AT&T, the UNIX operating system has evolved as the equipment on which it runs has matured. UNIX was initially developed for internal AT&T and academic use, but commercial hardware vendors created customized versions for their specific hardware. UNIX was the first OS to operate on multiple hardware platforms. The major UNIX implementations are Oracle® Solaris, IBM® AIX® and Hewlett Packard Enterprise HP-UX®.[130]

Linux® is a family of open-source OSs based on the Linux kernel, an OS kernel first released by Linus Torvalds in 1991. Distributions include the Linux kernel, supporting system software and libraries. A distribution is a package of software that makes up the entire OS. Anyone can create a new distribution by creating a new graphical user interface (GUI) or changing the supported hardware of the OS. Many of the associated libraries and software packages for drivers and GUIs are part of the GNU Project.[131]

In an enterprise, UNIX and Linux are the underlying computing platforms for application servers that host essential business applications (both centralized and distributed), database servers that manage the massive databases used to store business data, and web servers that provide the public face of the business on the Internet and process transactions. In light of the development strategies of both UNIX and Linux, it is essential that the source of the UNIX/Linux operating system distribution be known. Further, care must be taken to ensure that only authorized and tested functions, processes and configurations are allowed to enter the production environment.

[130] ISACA, *UNIX/LINUX Operating System Security Audit/Assurance Program,* USA, 2009, *https://store.isaca.org/s/store#/store/browse/detail/a2S4w000004KoEUEA0*
[131] Stallman, R.; "Linux and the GNU System," GNU Operating System, *www.gnu.org/gnu/linux-and-gnu.html*

ISACA. All Rights Reserved.

5.3.3 Operating System Functions and Risk

OS integrity involves using specific hardware and software features to:

- Protect itself from deliberate and inadvertent modification.
- Ensure that privileged programs cannot be interfered with by user programs.
- Provide for effective process isolation to ensure that:
  - Multiple processes running concurrently will not interfere with each other by accident or by design and are protected from writing into each other's memory (e.g., changing instructions, sharing resources).
  - Least privilege is enforced so that processes have no more privilege than needed to perform functions, and modules call on more privileged routines only for as long as needed.

To maintain system and data integrity, it is necessary to correctly and consistently define, enforce and monitor the operating environment and the granted permissions. IT management is responsible for the implementation of appropriate authorization techniques to prevent nonprivileged users from gaining the ability to execute privileged instructions and thus take control of the entire machine.

PC-based client-server Windows, UNIX and Linux OSs have special system configuration files and directories. The existence of program flaws or errors in configuring, controlling and updating the systems to the latest security patches makes them vulnerable to compromise by perpetrators. Important Windows system options and parameters are set in special system configuration files, referred to as a registry. Therefore, the registry is an important aspect of an IT audit. Noting any changes that take place in the registry is crucial for maintaining the integrity, confidentiality and availability of the systems. Similarly, with UNIX-based OSs, critical system configuration files and directories related to the nucleus (kernel) operations, system startup, network file-sharing and other remote services should be appropriately secured and checked for correctness.

UNIX/Linux Risk

Risk associated with UNIX/Linux is the potential for the operating system to be improperly configured. This can result in the inability of the enterprise to execute its critical processes. The collective development of Linux adds additional risk. Unless the distribution is controlled and managed, dangerous processes could be introduced into the operating system as a result of the open nature of the operating system and its essential processes.[132]

UNIX/Linux risk resulting from ineffective or incorrect operating system configurations could permit the operating system to become compromised, resulting in:

- Disclosure of privileged information
- Loss of physical assets
- Loss of intellectual property
- Loss of competitive advantage
- Loss of customer confidence
- Violation of regulatory requirements
- Disruption of the computer infrastructure, resulting in the inability to perform critical business functions
- Infection of computer systems with viruses and other malware to disrupt processing and require costly disinfection

[132] *Op cit* ISACA, *UNIX/LINUX Operating System Security Audit/Assurance Program*

ISACA. All Rights Reserved.

- Use of computer systems as a launching pad for malicious activity against other entities (and the potential to be held liable for damages)
- Loss of data resulting from inappropriate system configuration

5.3.4 Operating System Audit and Control Objectives

Operating systems contain programs that interface between the user, processor and applications software. Because operating systems are the primary managers of the use and the sharing of computer resources, the IT auditor should be familiar with the controls and audit objectives of two prominent operating systems: Windows and Linux.

Windows (Active Directory) Audit and Control Objectives

Windows Active Directory® is the underlying technology within the Microsoft Windows operating system that provides for an integrated and single sign-on system that addresses security, access and identity management. The key issues for a secure Active Directory are the configuration settings established during its implementation and the maintenance of the configuration during the life cycle of the Active Directory. Most enterprise users require access to a computer system, whether it is a desktop computer, mobile laptop computer or a workstation connected to an enterprise resource. The single sign-on access controls and security are controlled from Active Directory.

Failure to design and manage effective Active Directory controls could result in the following risk:

- Disruption of computing services
- Destruction of enterprise data
- Disclosure of sensitive information, including identities and intellectual property
- Reputational risk and loss of confidence by stakeholders, business partners and customers due to disclosure of information or related publicity
- Fines and penalties
- Lost productivity due to inefficient security administration

The objective of a Windows Active Directory audit is to:[133]

- Provide management with an evaluation of the Active Directory implementation and management security design effectiveness.
- Provide management with an independent assessment of the operating effectiveness of the security controls.

Windows server implementations operate with various functions and software. An IT audit should evaluate the necessary secure Active Directory infrastructure to support the servers and workstations within the enterprise. The review should focus on the configuration controls relating to:

- Active Directory management
- Secure Active Directory boundaries
- Secure domain controllers
- Physical security of the domain controllers
- Secure domain and domain controller configuration settings
- Secure administrative practices

Reviews of related controls should also be conducted where they make the most sense, for example:

- Windows server configuration assessments as part of a specifically designed audit of the enterprise server functions (web, email, file/print, etc.)

[133] ISACA, *Windows® Active Directory® Audit/Assurance Program*, USA, 2010, *https://store.isaca.org/s/store#/store/browse/detail/a2S4w000004KoF8EAK*

ISACA. All Rights Reserved.

- Workstation configuration assessments as part of a specifically designed audit of the operating system and function (desktop, laptop, special applications, etc.)
- User access and identity management as part of an identity management audit
- DNS management as part of a network assessment

UNIX/Linux Audit and Control Objectives

The objective of a UNIX/Linux audit is to provide management with an independent assessment relating to the effectiveness of configuration and security of the UNIX/Linux operating systems with the enterprise computing environment. The review should focus on configuration of the relevant UNIX/Linux servers within the enterprise. Selection of the applications/functions and specific servers should be based upon the risk introduced to the enterprise by these systems.[134]

UNIX/Linux systems are subject to identity management (see section 3.7.1), superuser access (access to the operating system configuration and security mechanisms) and general user controls (excluding users from access to operating system resources).

An audit of UNIX/Linux systems should include reviews and tests that cover:[135]

- System access and authorization
- Network services and controls
- System monitoring
- System and application patches and configuration change management
- System backup and recovery

5.3.5 Application Containers

Application containerization is a mechanism that is used to isolate applications from each other within the context of a running operating system instance. In much the same way that a logical partition (LPAR) provides segmentation of system resources in mainframes, a computing environment employing containers provides segmentation and isolates the underlying system services, so that they are logically sequestered from each other.

An application container consists of an application and all of its dependencies, such as libraries and configuration files. An application container IT audit should include a review of the preservation of data integrity through all phases of application containerization (planning, development, deployment, maintenance and destruction) and tests in the following areas:[136]

- Risk analysis and management
- Security awareness and training
- Images
- Registry
- Orchestrator
- Application security during development
- Secure connections
- Hardening

[134] *Op cit* ISACA, *UNIX/LINUX Operating System Security Audit/Assurance Program*
[135] *Ibid.*
[136] ISACA, *Application Containers Audit Program*, USA, 2018, *https://store.isaca.org/s/store#/store/browse/detail/a2S4w000004KoEVEA0*

ISACA. All Rights Reserved.

- Container destruction

Application Container Risk

Application containers share the same operating system kernel; if a malicious actor gains access to the container environment, lateral movement is possible and may result in access to all containers. If an enterprise fails to monitor application container environments, unauthorized connections and/or malicious traffic may go undetected. Unauthorized access that remains undetected can result in compromise of data.[137]

Application Container Audit and Control Objectives

When auditing application container deployments an IT auditor should address the host operating system, network, container runtime and images of application containers, including, but not limited to, Docker® and Rocket®.[138]

An IT audit of application containers should review and test to ensure the enterprise is meeting the following control objectives:[139]

- Planning
    - Risk associated with containerization is commensurate with enterprise risk tolerance.
    - The enterprise's IT risk and governance program addresses containers.
    - Roles and responsibilities are clearly defined so that enterprise goals and IT objectives are met.
    - Data integrity is preserved through all phases of application containerization (planning, development, deployment, maintenance and destruction).
- Deployment and Development
    - The principle of least privilege is applied to ensure that users do not have access beyond what is required to perform their responsibilities.
    - The attack surface of the host OS is minimized by deactivation of unnecessary services.
    - Risk of using a shared kernel, which is inherent in the application container infrastructure, is mitigated by reduction in the attack surface.
    - The network type selected by the enterprise supports the enterprise's strategic objectives while ensuring confidentiality of network traffic.
    - Compromise of container runtime is mitigated to prevent exploitation of runtime software, which may allow a malicious actor to monitor container-to-container communications or even access the containers themselves.
    - Introduction of vulnerabilities (e.g., untrusted software or malware) via image downloading is minimized.
    - Security risk is minimized through the design and implementation of image configuration protocols.
    - Confidentiality and security of images are maintained.
    - Data confidentiality and security are maintained at the orchestrator level.
    - Applications are less susceptible to exploitation.
- Maintenance
    - Sensitive data related to secure connections between application container components (e.g., username and password) are not compromised while stored in the image.
    - A formal hardening program minimizes security risk.

[137] *Ibid.*
[138] *Ibid.*
[139] *Ibid.*

ISACA. All Rights Reserved.

- Changes in container runtime are minimized so that changes take place during build rather than in production.
- Built-in security is leveraged in order to reduce the node attack surface.
- Integrity is maintained throughout the life cycle of containers.

5.4 Web Applications

Application software is generally discussed and described in section 4.2.3. A web application is an application in which all or some parts of the software are downloaded from the web every time it runs.[140] Application software is one of the important components that enables mobilizing information access. Thus, securing mobile (web) apps from security vulnerabilities and risk is fundamental. In fact, many recent security breaches have exploited vulnerabilities in application layers to gain access to an enterprise's network.[141] An insecure web application can compromise the best enterprise security arrangements and can help adversaries steal data and gain a foothold into the enterprise's internal network.[142]

5.4.1 Web Application Risk

Web applications are among the most common entry points used by attackers. Many applications are written to support business functions without due regard to the security requirements of the applications and may be subject to many common vulnerabilities, including:

- Buffer overflows
- Logic flaws
- Injection attacks
- Bugs
- Incorrect control over user access

Application vulnerabilities may also result from a poorly designed network architecture. Applications that process payment card data or other sensitive information or store such data in an insecure location, such as a demilitarized zone (DMZ)—i.e., a screened (firewalled) network segment that acts as a buffer zone between a trusted and an untrusted network—may be targeted by repeat or continuous attacks, increasing the likelihood that an attacker will find a vulnerability to exploit.

Countermeasures to web application vulnerabilities are related to proper design, coding and testing. The Open Web Application Security Project® (OWASP®)[143] Top Ten list identifies the most critical security risk to common web applications (**figure 5.1**). OWASP is an open community dedicated to enabling enterprises to conceive, develop, acquire, operate and maintain applications that can be trusted.

[140] PC, "Web application," *www.pcmag.com/encyclopedia/term/web-application*
[141] Rajendran, S.; "Securing Mobile Apps," *ISACA Now Blog*, 1 May 2017, *www.isaca.org/resources/news-and-trends/isaca-now-blog/2017/securing-mobile-apps*
[142] Rajendran, S.; "Safeguarding Mobile Applications With Secure Development Life Cycle Approach," *ISACA® Journal*, 1 May 2017, *www.isaca.org/resources/isaca-journal/issues/2017/volume-3/safeguarding-mobile-applications-with-secure-development-life-cycle-approach*
[143] OWASP, "OWASP Top Ten," *https://owasp.org/www-project-top-ten/*

ISACA. All Rights Reserved.

Figure 5.1—Web Application Security Risk

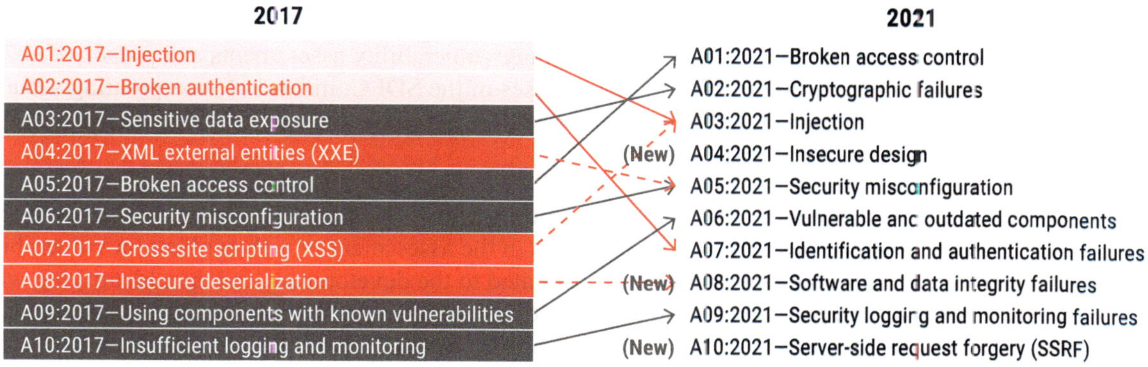

Source: OWASP, "OWASP Top Ten," *https://owasp.org/www-project-top-ten*. This figure is available under the Creative Commons Attribution 4.0 International public license.

5.4.2 Mobile Computing Audit and Control Objectives

Applications should be designed to protect information using control practices that use:

- Masking to hide sensitive data
- Menus to restrict actions that are available to the user
- Drop-down boxes to limit input options
- Range checks to ensure expected or correct data values are submitted
- Balancing to ensure proper processing of transactions
- Logs to record all activity
- Certificates to authenticate entities
- Encryption to transmit sensitive data
- Documentation to facilitate maintenance
- Coding standards to support good practice in coding
- Access controls to restrict user access

Legacy applications may have other vulnerabilities due to older standards in coding or design. These may need to be protected through the use of middleware to isolate direct access and manage data input/output, establish network isolation and secure communications channels.

A common problem with applications is the process of error handling. If error messages are too verbose, they might provide information to an attacker that can be used to modify the attack. Errors should be coded and provide the minimum necessary information to the user.

When users attempt to log in to a network, application or system, they should be required to provide a user ID and password. The use of two-factor authentication is usually desirable, especially for critical systems, and after a few invalid login attempts, the user should be denied entry. This can be accomplished by locking the user ID, disconnecting the network connection or blocking the source IP address. User IDs may remain locked for a set period of time or require resetting by an administrator.

ISACA. All Rights Reserved.

Mobile and web applications dealing with sensitive, private or other at-risk information require a secure development life cycle. Applications without security considerations may present an unexpected vulnerability to privacy. To address application security issues, developers are encouraged to consider the potential risk for each business function, code change and use of third-party frameworks and APIs, while security teams can help to improve application security through training, periodic scanning, ongoing vulnerability assessments and proactive engagement with developers. Incorporating security in all phases of the SDLC, instead of incorporating security just prior to release of the software, not only benefits the enterprise from an economic and efficiency perspective, but also ensures that business services are enabled securely.

General activities associated with the audit of application controls are discussed in section 4.5. When auditing web applications, an IT auditor should apply a risk-based approach in the assessment of web application vulnerabilities by first identifying the business goals and supporting IT goals related to the development and then identifying what can go wrong. Previous experience can be relied on to identify and assess risk related to inadequate specifications; poor coding techniques; inadequate documentation; inadequate quality control (QC) and quality assurance (QA), including testing inadequacies; lack of proper change control; lack of controls over promotion into production; and so on. Identified risk can then be placed in the context of the web application languages, development processes and deliverables—perhaps with the support of best practice material/literature on web applications development. The focus should be on application development risk, associated business risk and technical vulnerabilities, and how these can materialize and be controlled/addressed. Some controls look the same for all application development activity, but many need to reflect the way the development activity is taking place in the area under review.

5.5 Databases

Database management, including database structures, data elements, database controls and issues that an IT auditor should consider when conducting a database audit or review are described in Section 4.2.5. This section addresses database risk, security and audit approaches.

A database, like a single spreadsheet, is a table, of sorts. It has rows and columns where data can be stored. The data can be easily found using the column letter and the row number. But for different data, there might be a need for multiple spreadsheets, and a need to relate pieces of data from each of the sheets to one main item. An example of a simple database is multiple spreadsheets linking data back and forth between the spreadsheets. Keeping track of all the sheets and of which data are stored in each one requires database languages and programs that help make the process of storing, finding and organizing the data much easier.

Microsoft Windows uses a database to store all its data. The Windows database is called the registry. The Windows registry is a hierarchical database that stores low-level settings for the Microsoft Windows OS and applications that opt to use the registry. The kernel, device drivers, services, Security Account Manager and user interface can all use the registry. In other words, the Windows registry contains information, settings, options and other values for programs and hardware installed on all versions of Microsoft Windows operating systems.

Database auditing is the activity of monitoring and recording configured database actions from database users and non-database users, to ensure the security of the databases. A database administrator can audit individual actions, such as the type of Structured Query Language (SQL) statement executed, or actions performed on combinations of data. However, an IT auditor should audit both successful and failed activities and include or exclude specific users from the audit.[144]

[144] Rahman, M.; "Auditing Oracle Database," *ISACA® Journal*, 1 November 2014, *www.isaca.org/resources/isaca-journal/past-issues/2014/auditing-oracle-database*

ISACA. All Rights Reserved.

5.5.1 Database Security and Risk

Database security covers a wide range of information security controls to protect the databases in an enterprise. Database security is essential because databases contain critical and sensitive information that is required to support business operations.

Databases are vulnerable to the following types of risk:

- Unauthorized activity by authorized users
- Malware infections or interactions
- Capacity issues
- Physical damage
- Design flaws
- Data corruption
- Use of weak, unenforced or default passwords
- Use of generic or default accounts by database administrators

Database security is essential because databases contain critical and sensitive information that is required to support enterprise operations. Accordingly, database security deals with various aspects of protecting database content, owners and users. It ranges from protection against intentional authorized database uses that result in errors to unintentional database accesses by unauthorized entities.

The security areas that need to be addressed are:

- Application control
- Authentication Types
- Default configurations
- Password parameters
- Access Controls
- Roles and privileges
- Audit trails
- Recording
- Log Management
- Encryption
- Encryption Level

5.5.2 Database Audit Approaches

A database is a sensitive component of an enterprise; thus, it is important to ensure the database is configured properly to protect the security of enterprise data.

In general, the audit record should include information about the operation that was audited, the user performing the operation, and the date and time of the operation. Audit records can be stored in either a data dictionary table, called the database audit trail, or in an operating system file, called an operating system audit trail.

Following are examples of the components of a database audit of a Microsoft SQL Server® database and an Oracle database.

ISACA. All Rights Reserved.

Microsoft SQL Server Database

Ineffective or incorrect database configuration settings in a Microsoft SQL Server database can permit the restricted tables, databases and data to become compromised, resulting in, but not necessarily limited to, the following:[145]

- Disclosure of privileged information
- Loss of physical assets
- Loss of intellectual property
- Loss of competitive advantage
- Loss of customer confidence
- Violation of regulatory requirements
- Disruption of computer infrastructure that prevents performance of critical business functions

A Microsoft SQL Server database audit should provide management with an independent assessment relating to the effectiveness of configuration and security of the Microsoft SQL Server database systems within the enterprise computing environment[146] and should include reviews and tests that cover:[147]

- Access and authorization
- Security processes and monitoring
- Backup and recovery
- Encryption strategy
- Trusted relationships
- Network security

Oracle Database

An IT audit of Oracle database should include reviews and tests that cover:[148]

- Changed or disabled default accounts
- Strength of Oracle database SID (system identifier)
- Oracle critical patch updates
- PUBLIC role for identification of unnecessary privileges
- Database auditing options
- Configuration of database triggers for schema auditing and logon/logoff events
- Database activity monitoring (DAM) solutions
- Password Management for all Oracle logins
- Regular database security assessments
- Database traffic
- Security threats and countermeasures

[145] ISACA, *Microsoft SQL Server Database Audit Program*, USA, *https://store.isaca.org/s/store#/store/browse/detail/a2S4w000004KoEoEAK*
[146] *Ibid.*
[147] *Ibid.*
[148] *Op cit* Rahman

ISACA. All Rights Reserved.

5.6 Privacy

Privacy refers to the rights of individuals to trust that others will appropriately and respectfully use, store, share and dispose of their associated personal and sensitive information within the context, and according to the purposes, for which it was collected or derived. What is appropriate depends on the associated circumstances and laws, and on individuals' reasonable expectations. Individuals also have the right to reasonably control and be aware of the collection, use and disclosure of their associated personal and sensitive information.

Privacy is a significant aspect of an IT auditor's role, especially in light of global regulations, such as the General Data Protection Regulation (GDPR) in the European Union and the Health Insurance Portability and Accountability Act (HIPAA) in the United States. It is an important matter that, by its nature, requires a consistent approach throughout the enterprise.

To ensure a consistent approach, an enterprise should adopt the following good practices:

- Privacy should be considered from the outset and be built in by design. It should be systematically built into policies, standards and procedures from the beginning.
- Private data should be collected fairly in an open, transparent manner. Only data required for the purpose should be collected.
- Private data should be kept secure throughout the data life cycle.
- Private data should be used and/or disclosed only for the purpose for which the data were collected.
- Private data should be accurate, complete and up to date.
- Private data should be deleted when no longer needed.

5.6.1 Privacy Risk

Privacy is a top-of-mind risk for most enterprises. Concerns over data privacy include, but are not limited to:[149]

- Safeguarding data in transit and at rest
- Complying with external and internal requirements for personally identifiable information (PII)
- Managing risk associated with third-party data management vendors

Business risk associated with privacy issues includes:[150]

- Decline in income should customers abandon the enterprise in the event personal information is compromised
- Increase in financial liabilities if noncompliance with external requirements results in penalties and fines
- Adverse publicity, resulting in reputational damage, if a data breach occurs

5.6.2 Privacy Audit and Control Objectives

An IT auditor plays an integral role in fostering data privacy. All enterprises that collect sensitive customer data in the course of doing business rely on IT auditors to provide assurance over their information systems, ensure that compliance expectations are met and consult on emerging technologies.[151]

When performing a privacy audit an IT auditor should:[152]

- Evaluate data governance for privacy, confidentiality and compliance (DGPC) and determine whether effective data management exists.

[149] ISACA, *Data Privacy Audit Program*, USA, 2018, *https://store.isaca.org/s/store#/store/browse/detail/a2S4w000004KoDwEAK*
[150] *Ibid.*
[151] *Ibid.*
[152] *Ibid.*

ISACA. All Rights Reserved.

- Assess controls surrounding data in various phases of movement—during collection, in transit or at rest.
- Review controls around data access.
- Review third-party management of data.
- Evaluate incident-management policies and practices.

An IT audit of privacy should review and test to ensure that the enterprise is meeting the following control objectives:[153]

- Privacy Management
  - Data governance is appropriately managed across all roles and functions.
  - Clearly defined data privacy policies, procedures and guidance are appropriately addressed for enterprise usage of personally identifiable information (PII).
  - Training and awareness programs regarding data privacy, specifically handling of PII data, are consistent, up to date and disseminated in an appropriate manner.
  - Criteria exist for conducting the privacy impact assessment (PIA) for process, system and application implementation. Criteria have been incorporated into existing business processes and development processes.
- Data Management and Collection
  - Personal information is clearly defined, and appropriate tools are utilized to de-identify personal information.
  - The use, processing, storage and/or retention of personal information occurs only for legitimate business purposes or as authorized.
  - Proper processes are in place to manage the electronic and physical records containing personally identifiable information.
- Data Security
  - Access to PII is defined and enforced throughout the enterprise.
  - Suitable measures exist to prevent personal data from being read, copied, altered or deleted by unauthorized parties during data transmission or during transport of the data media.
  - Established process and procedures exist for managing security of data at rest.
- Third-Party Compliance and Contractual Agreements:
  - Information disclosed to third parties aligns with the third-parties principle.
  - A vendor-assessment tool exists for European Union (EU) affiliates that includes well-defined criteria for assessing a potential vendor's privacy and security controls during the precontracting phase.
- Incident Management and Escalation
  - Information that must be collected is documented in the appropriate form and shared with appropriate functions (e.g., incident-response team members) in the event of a privacy incident.
  - External parties managing PII for the enterprise have a proper breach-notification process in place.

Cyber liability and data breach insurance from a provider ensures coverage of costs like notification, identity-protection solutions, public relations, legal, liability, etc. An IT auditor may also provide assurance on compliance with privacy policy, laws and other regulations. To fulfill this role, an IT auditor should:

- Identify and understand compliance requirements regarding privacy established by laws, regulations and contract agreements. Depending on the assignment, an IT auditor may need to seek legal or expert opinions.

[153] *Ibid.*

ISACA. All Rights Reserved.

- Review management's privacy policy to ascertain whether it takes into consideration the requirements of privacy laws and regulations.
- Check whether personal sensitive data are correctly managed with respect to requirements.
- Verify that the correct security measures are adopted.

5.7 Mobile Computing

Mobile computing extends the concept of wireless computing to devices that expand an enterprise network to reach places, under circumstances that prohibit access by other means. Mobile computing refers to devices that are transported or moved during normal usage. Common mobile devices include tablets, smartphones, laptops, USB storage devices, digital cameras and similar technologies. Their mobility makes it more difficult to implement logical and physical access controls.

5.7.1 Mobile Computing Risk

Portable and wireless devices present a ubiquitous threat to enterprise information assets and must be properly controlled. Policies and procedures and additional protection mechanisms must be put into place to ensure that data are protected to a greater extent on portable devices, because such devices will most likely operate in environments in which physical controls are lacking or nonexistent. Mobile devices tend to be easily lost or stolen and, thus, require the use of encryption technologies and strong authentication. It also may be necessary to classify some data as inappropriate for storage on a mobile device.

An IT auditor should understand that all such media and devices can also be used by an individual to steal data and programs for personal use or gain.

Figure 5.2 presents some known vulnerabilities and associated threats that need to be understood when dealing with mobile devices.

Figure 5.2—Mobile Device Vulnerabilities, Threats and Risk

Vulnerability	Threat	Risk
Information travels across wireless networks that are often less secure than wired networks.	Malicious outsiders can do harm to the enterprise.	Information interception resulting in a breach of sensitive data, enterprise reputation, adherence to regulation or legal action
Mobility provides users with the opportunity to leave enterprise boundaries and thereby eliminates many security controls.	Mobile devices cross boundaries and network perimeters, carrying malware, and can bring this malware into the enterprise network.	Malware propagation, which may result in data leakage, data corruption and unavailability of necessary data
Bluetooth technology is very convenient for many users to have hands-free conversations; however, it is often left on and then is discoverable.	Hackers can discover the device and launch an attack.	Device corruption, lost data, call interception, possible exposure of sensitive information
Unencrypted information is stored on the device.	In the event that a malicious outsider intercepts data in transit or steals a device or if the employee loses the device, the data are readable and usable.	Exposure of sensitive data, resulting in damage to the enterprise, customers or employees

ISACA. All Rights Reserved.

Figure 5.2—Mobile Device Vulnerabilities, Threats and Risk *(cont.)*

Vulnerability	Threat	Risk
Lost data may affect employee productivity.	Mobile devices may be lost or stolen due to their portability. Data on these devices are not always backed up.	Workers dependent on mobile devices unable to work in the event of broken, lost or stolen devices and data that are not backed up
The device has no authentication requirements applied.	In the event that the device is lost or stolen, outsiders can access the device and all of its data.	Data exposure, resulting in damage to the enterprise and liability and regulation issues
The enterprise is not managing the device.	If no mobile device strategy exists, employees may choose to bring in their own unsecured devices.	Data leakage, malware propagation or unknown data loss in the case of device loss or theft.
The device allows for installation of unsigned third-party applications.	Applications may carry malware that propagates Trojans or viruses; the applications may also transform the device into a gateway for malicious outsiders to enter the enterprise network.	Malware propagation, data leakage or intrusion on enterprise network

Source: *CISA Review Manual, 27th Edition*, USA, 2019, figure 5.31, *https://www.isaca.org/bookstore/cisa-exam-resources/crm27ed*; adapted from ISACA, *Securing Mobile Devices*, USA, 2012, figure 5, *https://store.isaca.org/s/store#/store/browse/detail/a2S4w000004KoAIEA0*

Mobile device controls can reduce the risk of disclosure of sensitive data stored on mobile devices. Many can be enforced by mobile device management (MDM) systems and/or secure containers (a separately authenticated, encrypted area of the mobile device that is used to keep sensitive enterprise data segregated from the personal data) for enterprise and personal devices. Following are controls that can strengthen mobile security:

- **Device registration**—All mobile devices authorized for business use should be registered in a database. Devices that are personally owned should be flagged. An enterprise can push updates or manage authorized devices and exclude personally owned mobile devices.
- **Tagging**—Physically tagging a device with an asset ID may result in its return if it is lost; however, there is risk in identifying the enterprise that owns the device.
- **Physical security**—If the device is stationary and permits it, a cable locking system or a locking system with a motion detector can sound an audible alarm.
- **Data storage**—Only content that is absolutely needed should be stored on the device. With the ability to remotely access central servers, the requirement to store any data locally should be questioned. If data are not stored locally, then a lost or stolen device is not an issue. The data that are stored should be backed up on a regular basis, preferably to shared folders on the enterprise file server.
- **Virus detection and control**—The threat associated with viruses applies to all mobile devices. The enterprise should update the mobile device antivirus software to prevent perpetuation of malware.
- **Encryption**—Mobile devices used to store sensitive or confidential information should be encrypted in accordance with the enterprise information security policies, mandating use of a strong encryption mechanism.
- **Compliance**—Mobile devices should comply with the security requirements defined in enterprise standards. All mobile devices should require a password. Two-factor authentication can be used to further enhance security.
- **Approval**—Mobile-device use should be appropriately authorized and approved in accordance with the enterprise's policies and procedures.
- **Acceptable use policy**—A security policy should exist for mobile devices. The enterprise should have a policy that addresses mobile device use and specifies the type of information and kind of devices and information services that may be accessible through the devices.

ISACA. All Rights Reserved.

- **Due care**—Employees should exercise due care within office environments and especially during travel. Any loss or theft of a mobile device must be treated as a security breach and reported immediately in accordance with security management policies and procedures.
- **Awareness training**—Employee orientation and security awareness training should include coverage of mobile device policy and guidelines. The training allows propagation of awareness that mobile devices are important business tools when used properly but have associated risk if not managed accordingly.
- **Network authentication, authorization and accounting**—IT functions should adopt a solution that allows them to tie devices connecting to the network with each user's identity and role, and then apply role-based policies to grant proper access privileges. This approach enables IT to differentiate access for different levels of employees, guests or device types. It also lets IT take a proactive stance on tracking and monitoring how mobile devices are being used within the network.
- **Secure transmission**—Mobile devices should connect to the enterprise network via a secure connection, such as over a VPN.
- **Standard mobile device applications**—Configuration and use of mobile devices should be baselined and controlled. Only applications that either meet with the enterprise security architecture or are delivered as standard on a mobile device should be authorized for use, and all software applications must be appropriately licensed and installed by the enterprise's IT support team. MDM solutions support this.
- **Geolocation tracking**—There are many debates about the privacy concerns of GPS tracking, but location capabilities inherent in mobile devices can be invaluable in the case of loss or theft.
- **Remote wipe and lock**—Due to the nature of mobile devices, many device management solutions are focused on securing a device that is lost or stolen. Some MDM solutions allow IT to send an alarm to the device to help identify the location for a user. If a device is truly lost, IT can then remotely wipe and lock the device and/or container.
- **Secure remote support**—Employees relying on personal devices to conduct work are often out of the office. Having a secure way to support and fix mobile devices from a remote location is imperative to maintain employee satisfaction. Depending on device type, remote support solutions allow help desks to configure devices, chat, transfer files, and remotely see and control the device. It is important to select a solution that supports a wide variety of devices and keeps all access and activity logs behind the enterprise firewall to ensure security.

5.7.2 Bring Your Own Device (BYOD)

Bring your own device (BYOD) is an enterprise policy used to permit partial or full integration of user-owned mobile devices for business purposes. BYOD offers many benefits to organizations that choose to adopt the practice, including the following:

- Cost savings due to reduction of investment to procure and maintain end-user hardware and software licenses
- Increased productivity and employee satisfaction
- Increased innovation resulting from higher satisfaction and productivity

Security and control issues related to BYOD include the following:

- Protection of sensitive data and intellectual property
- Protection of networks to which BYOD devices connect
- Responsibility and accountability for devices and information contained on them
- Removal of organization data from employee-owned devices on termination of employment or loss of a device
- Malware protection

ISACA. All Rights Reserved.

Risk related to BYOD is similar to mobile computing risk. Specific BYOD-related risk includes:

- Access controls and control over device security
- Ability to eliminate sensitive enterprise data on termination of employment or loss of the device
- Management issues related to supporting many types of devices, operating systems and applications
- Assurance that employee-owned BYOD devices are properly backed up at all times

An employee BYOD agreement or acceptable use agreement (AUA) should require the employee to agree with the items in the policy before a device can be used for business purposes. The policy may state that devices can be seized, if necessary, in connection with a legal matter. An AUA ensures that maintaining security when using personal devices is a responsibility that is shared between the user and IT. In addition, BYOD should be approved by executive management and be subject to oversight and monitoring.

5.7.3 Mobile Device Access

Smartphones and other mobile devices access the Internet by connecting to wireless local area networks (WLANs). They can also connect to the Internet over mobile networks. Most mobile devices use third generation (3G) or fourth generation (4G) networks to connect to the Internet. 3G brought advances in Internet access times and download speeds, and 4G is an IP packet-switched network that adds VoIP (Voice over Internet Protocol), mobile TV and further speed increases. The newest mobile network architecture, 5G, generally includes all the features of 4G and improves on those features. It introduces new security features to better mitigate the new and existing risk of cellular technology.[154] These developments led to changes in the way Internet content is accessed, with applications that are accessed and supported via an Internet browser.

Following are general issues and exposures related to wireless and/or mobile access:

- **The interception of sensitive information**—Information is transmitted through the air, which increases the potential for unprotected information to be intercepted by unauthorized individuals.
- **The loss or theft of devices**—Devices tend to be relatively small, making them much more vulnerable to theft or loss.
- **The loss of data contained in devices**—Theft or loss can result in loss of data stored on the device. This could be several gigabytes depending on the device capacity. If encryption is weak or not applied, a hacker may access the information because it may only be protected by a password or PIN (personal identification number).
- **The misuse of devices**—Devices can be used to gather information or intercept information that is being passed over wireless networks for financial or personal benefit.
- **Distractions caused by devices**—Devices may distract the user. If they are being used in situations in which an individual's full attention is required (e.g., driving a car), they can result in an increase in the number of accidents.
- **Possible health effects of device usage**—Although unconfirmed, potential safety or health hazards include concerns with respect to electromagnetic radiation, especially for devices that must be held beside the head.
- **OS vulnerabilities**—The OS may contain vulnerabilities that allow access to the device. Vulnerabilities may allow a device to be jailbroken, meaning that restrictions are intentionally removed from a device to allow some enhancements. Jailbreaking can potentially make devices more vulnerable.
- **Applications**—Apps may contain vulnerabilities or malicious code that can allow access to data and the device itself. Jailbroken devices may be more susceptible to intrusion because the apps may not come from secure sources.

[154] ISACA, *5G Security: Addressing Risk and Threats of Mobile Network Technologies*, 26 February 2021, *https://store.isaca.org/s/store#/store/browse/detail/a2S4w000004KoEFEA0*

ISACA. All Rights Reserved.

- **Wireless user authentication**—There is a need for stronger user authentication and authorization tools at the device level.
- **File security**—Wireless phones and tablets do not use the type of file access security that other computer platforms can provide.
- **Wired equivalent privacy (WEP) security encryption**—WEP security depends particularly on the length of the encryption key and on the usage of static WEP (with many users on a WLAN sharing the same key) or dynamic WEP (with a per-user, per-session, dynamic WEP key tied to the network logon). The 64-bit encryption keys that are in use in WEP standard encryption can be easily broken with currently available computing power. Static WEP, used in many WLANs for flexibility purposes, is a serious security risk, because a static key can easily be lost or broken, exposing all the information on the device for viewing and use. An attacker possessing a WEP key can also sniff packets being transmitted and decrypt them. WEP is rarely used today because it has been deprecated. WPA2[155] is the preferred solution for wireless networks.

5.7.4 Mobile Computing Audit and Control Objectives

A mobile computing audit should cover all mobile devices that access, transmit or store enterprise data, including BYOD devices.[156]

When performing a mobile computing audit, an IT auditor should focus on the effectiveness and efficiency of controls associated with mobile computing across the following domains:

- Policies and procedures to protect data accessed by, transmitted by and stored on mobile devices
- Alignment of position responsibilities with sensitive information
- Unique identification of users who access resources remotely
- Risk associated with removable media, including disclosure, copying or modification of enterprise data
- Risk of operational disruption from malware introduced through mobile computing
- Incident-response protocols, from detection and reporting through recovery, according to the enterprise's backup policy

A mobile computing IT audit should include reviews and tests to ensure that the enterprise is meeting the following control objectives:

- **Governance**
  - Security policies address purpose, scope, roles, responsibilities, management commitment and coordination among organizational entities. Processes and procedures are maintained and applied to manage protection of information systems and assets.
  - All users are aware of relevant threats to the security of sensitive enterprise information.
  - Processes ensure that management of risk associated with mobile computing is consistent with relative importance to business processes and the enterprise's risk strategy.
- **Remote Access**
  - Technical security solutions are managed to ensure the security and resilience of systems and assets, consistent with related policies, procedures and agreements.
  - All users are uniquely identified when accessing enterprise resources, and suitable authentication is in place to substantiate the claimed identify of a user.
  - Access to systems and assets is controlled.

[155] Mitchell, B.; "An Overview of Wireless Protected Access 2 (WPA2)," Lifewire, 2 July 2021, *www.lifewire.com/what-is-wpa2-818352*
[156] ISACA, *Mobile Computing Security Audit Program*, USA, 2018, *https://store.isaca.org/s/store#/store/browse/detail/a2S4w000004KoDcEAK*

ISACA. All Rights Reserved.

- **Data Loss**
  - Appropriate security measures are adopted to protect against the risk of using mobile computing and communication facilities.
  - Removable media are protected, and their use is restricted according to policy.
  - Critical enterprise data are protected from unauthorized disclosure, copying or modification.
  - Important records are protected from loss, destruction and falsification in accordance with statutory, regulatory, contractual and business requirements.
  - Mobile devices containing sensitive enterprise information are set up according to job requirements and managed as job descriptions change or the user's employment terminates.
- **Malware**
  - Protections are in place to prevent disruptions from malware, either due to its introduction into the enterprise through mobile computing or to its infection of mobile devices.
- **Incident Response**
  - Anomalous activity is detected in a timely manner and the potential impact of events is understood.
  - A reporting facility is implemented for mobile users to report security incidents.
  - Response processes and procedures are executed and maintained to ensure timely responses to detected security incidents.
  - Backup copies of information and software are taken and tested regularly in accordance with the agreed-on backup policy.

ISACA. All Rights Reserved.

5.8 Chapter 5 Knowledge Check

Review Questions

1. What type of telecommunication infrastructure is used by a virtual private network to transmit data?

   A. Public internet
   B. Dedicated leased line
   C. Dedicated platform for VPN use only

2. An IT audit of application containers should focus on a review of the preservation of data integrity during:

   A. The planning and development phase only.
   B. The deployment, maintenance and destruction phase only.
   C. All phases of application containerization.

3. Which of the following conditions would cause an IT auditor the **MOST** concern when auditing web applications?

   A. Legacy applications are used but are protected by middleware.
   B. Two-factor authentication is used, but unsuccessful user log-in attempts are not limited.
   C. Errors messages are coded and provide the minimum necessary information to the user.

4. When performing an audit of database activities, an IT auditor should focus on:

   A. Successful activities only.
   B. Failed activities only.
   C. Both successful and failed activities.

5. When auditing enterprise privacy practices, an IT auditor should ensure that private data are:

   A. Collected fairly in an open, transparent manner.
   B. Kept indefinitely, even after they are no longer needed or required by the enterprise.
   C. Used and/or disclosed to authorized parties regardless of the purpose for which it was collected.

6. Which of the following controls can reduce the risk of disclosure of sensitive data stored on a mobile device?

   A. Requiring users to store data locally on a mobile device for immediate access
   B. Baselining and controlling the configuration and use of standard mobile device applications
   C. Providing all mobile device users with the same access privileges

Answers on page 190

ISACA. All Rights Reserved.

Chapter 5 ANSWER KEY

Review Questions

1. **A. A VPN is a secure private network that uses the public Internet telecommunications infrastructure to transmit data. VPNs are used by enterprises for both extranets and intranets. Using encryption and authentication, a VPN encrypts all data that pass between two Internet points, maintaining privacy and security.**

   B. VPNs enable remote users to make a local call (versus dialing-in at long distance rates) or use an Internet cable modem or DSL connections for inexpensive public network connectivity, rather than using expensive dedicated leased lines.

   C. VPNs are platform-independent. Any computer system that is configured to run on an IP network can be connected through a VPN with no modifications, except for the installation of remote software.

2. A. Although it is important that an IT audit of application containers includes a review of the preservation of data integrity during the planning and development phase, a proper review of the preservation of data integrity should be performed through all phases of application containerization.

   B. Although it is important that an IT audit of application containers includes a review of the preservation of data integrity during the deployment, maintenance and destruction phase, a proper review of the preservation of data integrity should be performed through all phases of application containerization.

   C. Application containers consist of an application and all the dependencies of the application, such as libraries and configuration files. An IT audit of application containers should include a review of the preservation of data integrity through all phases of application containerization (planning, development, deployment, maintenance and destruction).

3. A. Legacy applications may contain vulnerabilities due to older standards in coding or design. However, these vulnerabilities can be protected through the use of middleware to isolate direct access and manage data input/output, ensure network isolation and secure communications channels.

   B. When users attempt to log in to a mobile (web) application, they should be required to provide a user ID and password. The use of two-factor authentication is usually desirable, especially for critical systems. After a few invalid login attempts, the user should be denied entry.

   C. A common problem with applications is the process of error handling. If error messages are too verbose, they might provide information to an attacker that can be used to modify the attack. Errors should be coded and provide as little information as possible (necessary) to the user.

4. A. Databases are vulnerable to unauthorized activity by authorized database users and non-database users. Both successful and failed activities should be included in a database audit.

   B. Databases are vulnerable to unauthorized activity by authorized database users and nondatabase users. Both successful and failed activities should be included in a database audit.

   C. Database auditing is the activity of monitoring and recording configured database actions from database users and non-database users to ensure the security of the databases. An IT auditor should audit both successful and failed activities and include or exclude specific users from the audit.

5. **A. Private data should be collected fairly in an open, transparent manner. Only the data required for the purpose should be collected.**

   B. Private data should not be retained by an enterprise indefinitely. It should be deleted when it is no longer required.

   C. Private data should only be used and/or disclosed for the purposes for which they were collected.

ISACA. All Rights Reserved.

6. A. A mobile device should only store content that is absolutely needed on the device. In light of a mobile device's ability to remotely access central servers, the requirement to store any data locally should be questioned. If data are not stored locally, then a lost or stolen device will not pose a problem.

   B. The configuration and use of standard mobile device applications should be baselined and controlled. Only applications that either align with the enterprise security architecture or are delivered as standard on the mobile device should be authorized for use, and all software applications must be appropriately licensed and installed by the enterprise's IT support team.

   C. Mobile devices connecting to the network should be tied to each user's identity and role, and role-based policies should be used to grant proper access privileges. This approach enables different access permissions for different levels of employees, guests or device types.

ISACA. All Rights Reserved.

Page intentionally left blank

ISACA. All Rights Reserved.

IT AUDIT
FUNDAMENTALS
An ISACA® Certificate

Chapter 6:

Overview of Newer Technologies

Overview of Newer Technologies

ISACA. All Rights Reserved.

Overview of Newer Technologies

6.1 Learning Objectives

After completing this chapter, learners will be able to:

- Explain the basics of artificial intelligence (AI) and expert systems and associated risk.
- Describe how big data can introduce technical and operational risk to an enterprise and describe approaches for ensuring that risk is being adequately managed.
- Detail how enterprises are using blockchain methodologies and describe how to conduct an assessment of the blockchain technology control environment.
- Discuss different types of IoT devices and their unique value and risk to an enterprise.
- Identify key cybersecurity processes and related controls.

6.2 Introduction

Enterprises are exploring new opportunities driven by digital transformation and identifying technology-driven paths to deliver more value, more quickly, while also benefiting from new process efficiencies. The adoption of new and emerging technologies brings with IT technology risk, which must be sufficiently governed, controlled or integrated with the broader IT strategy.[157]

As enterprises increasingly harness new technologies, an IT auditor must understand technology topics to deliver deeper, more meaningful and value-added audits. New technology projects will benefit from an IT auditor's conscientiousness and unique ability to identify the process improvements and capability gaps that can make or break the success of a project. Most enterprises are identifying and assessing technology risk for the purposes of audit planning.[158]

Given the rise of cybersecurity as a business imperative across all industries, this chapter provides an overview of cybersecurity. An IT auditor should have a working knowledge of cybersecurity (cyberrisk) and how to better assess data protection and controls around key business processes.

6.3 Artificial Intelligence and Expert Systems

Artificial intelligence (AI) is a branch of computer science that intersects with software engineering, data science, the human sciences and business expertise (**figure 6.1**). AI enables an advanced form of software that is self-learning and autonomous; it can develop solutions to human problems and automate specific tasks previously performed by human beings.[159]

[157] ISACA, "IT Audit's Perspectives on the Top Technology Risks for 2021," December 2020, *www.isaca.org/resources/infographics/it-audits-perspectives-on-the-top-technology-risks-for-2021*
[158] *Ibid.*
[159] ISACA, *Artificial Intelligence Fundamentals Study Guide*, USA, 2021, *https://store.isaca.org/s/store#/store/browse/detail/a2S4w000004KolIEAS*

ISACA. All Rights Reserved.

Figure 6.1—AI Domains

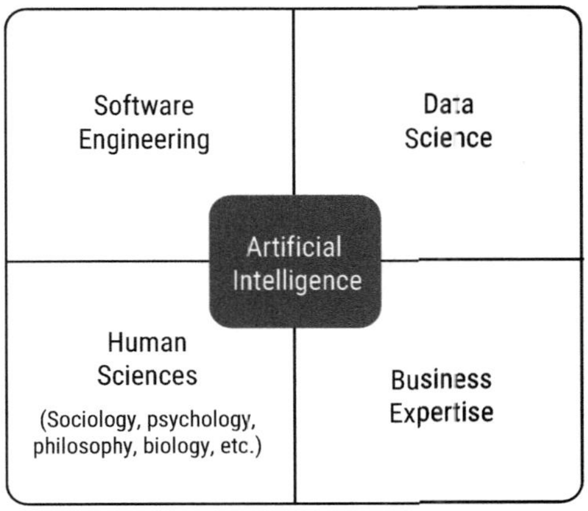

Source: ISACA, *Artificial Intelligence Fundamentals Study Guide*, USA, 2021, figure 1.1, *https://store.isaca.org/s/store#/store/browse/detail/a2S4w000004KoIIEAS*

Artificial intelligence uses raw data and looks for patterns that ultimately allow the algorithms to make good decisions. This technology makes it possible to accurately and efficiently manage and analyze huge amounts of complex data.

AI is the study and application of the principles by which:

- Knowledge is acquired and used.
- Goals are generated and achieved.
- Information is communicated.
- Collaboration is achieved.
- Concepts are formed.
- Languages are developed.

6.3.1 Enterprise Adoption and Use of AI

From driverless cars to virtual doctors, artificial intelligence (AI) is transforming the way people live, socialize, work, travel and do business. AI applications are available to help security practitioners pinpoint issues that need to be further investigated. AI can help find patterns and vulnerabilities that otherwise might not be discovered before a security incident occurs. For example, AI is used in cybersecurity detection schemes to assist with addressing common threats, while also investigating anomalies to detect new and rapidly evolving threats. Instead of presenting cybersecurity analysts with massive amounts of raw data, AI technology presents the information in more practical views and adapts quickly to new methods of attack.

Adopting AI is not as simple as adding new software or adopting a new development framework. AI—combined with big data collection, analysis and insight—requires enterprise resources, preparation and leadership commitment prior to implementation. Therefore, when considering whether to adopt AI, an enterprise should first analyze and define the reasons for wanting to incorporate it. The enterprise must define specific business cases (i.e., use cases) in terms that can equate with specific algorithms, software or tools.

ISACA. All Rights Reserved.

6.3.2 AI Risk and Control

Risk can arise directly from the development of AI solutions, from their intentional or inadvertent misapplication, or from the mishandling of the data inputs that fuel them. AI risk can be associated with superintelligence, data loss, nefarious utilization and weaponization.

Superintelligence

As an AI system becomes more autonomous and expands its ability to learn without supervision, its treatment of humans may become a concern. A superintelligent AI system can become a security and a safety threat if the AI should consider humans unable to make their own decisions and take over. Furthermore, AI potentially can duplicate itself many times over, given that it is a software application, thus ensuring its survival. A superintelligent AI might be an economic and military asset to its owner, perhaps offering a strategic advantage. However, in the hands of bad actors, such an AI system might be used in a harmful way.

For that reason, a system of manual intervention should be designed to prevent AI system override. Periodic manual reviews of transactions should be set up to ensure that those requiring manual intervention are processed as intended.[160]

Data Loss, Integrity/Reputation Loss, and Legal and Compliance Risk

AI consumes voluminous amount of data and uses that data to influence business and personal decisions for enterprises and individuals. Inaccurate data can result in any of the following:

- Libel or defamation due to distortion of individual data or information
- Litigation due to unintended bias embedded into decisions (e.g., allegations of racial discrimination based on an insurance company's increased rates for specific ZIP codes)
- Violation of regulatory compliance due to disclosure of protected consumer data
- Social backlash if algorithms cause the public to view an enterprise as intrusive or dishonest
- Data breach due to improper storage, with specific implications downstream
- Misdiagnosis of medical conditions
- Worker injury due to overreliance on predictive algorithms (e.g., machine maintenance)

Nefarious Utilization and Weaponization

Seemingly nonsensitive health, marketing and financial data that enterprises collect to fuel AI systems can be exploited by fraudsters who can weave various data threads together to create false identities. For example, a type of AI-based technology produces deepfakes, computer-generated counterfeit video representations that are extremely hard to distinguish from actual video footage.

As a control, AI algorithm logic should be documented and explained appropriately to cover all aspects of the program. AI algorithm auditability needs to be enabled at inception to understand how the algorithm reached a certain judgment.[161]

[160] Sutaria, N.; "Artificial Intelligence's Impact on Auditing Emerging Technologies," *ISACA® Journal*, 23 December 2020, *www.isaca.org/resources/isaca-journal/issues/2020/volume-6/artificial-intelligences-impact-on-auditing-emerging-technologies*

[161] *Ibid.*

ISACA. All Rights Reserved.

6.4 Big Data (Data Analytics)

Big data refers to data sets that are too large or too fast-changing to be analyzed using traditional relational or multidimensional database techniques or commonly used software tools to capture, manage and process the data within a reasonable time. Big data also refers to the ability to work with collections of data that previously was impractical because of the data volume, velocity and variety (the three Vs). A key driver of this new ability is easier distribution of storage and processing across networks of inexpensive commodity hardware (using technology such as Apache® Hadoop®) instead of requiring larger, more powerful individual computers.

The benefits of big data are plentiful. When correctly managed, big data can provide a more accurate view of the behaviors of consumers in the marketplace, operational efficiency and potential product development. Through the use of big data, predictions can be more accurate and improvement projects can target exact pain points.

An enterprise is faced with a big data issue whenever traditional techniques and tools are no longer sufficient to capture, manage and process the data in a reasonable amount of time. Challenges arise when data are:

- Spread across isolated, complex silos
- Duplicated/redundant
- Uncoordinated and lacking standardization

Issues regarding big data can be categorized according to three dimensions:

- **Variety of information**—Data comes from all types of formats. This can include data generated within an enterprise and data created from external sources.
- **Velocity of information**—Data is generated extremely quickly and generously.
- **Volume of information**—The amount of data created is vast compared to traditional sources.

Managing and processing an ever-increasing data set requires running specialized software on multiple servers. For some enterprises, big data is counted in hundreds of gigabytes. For others, it is counted in terabytes or even petabytes, with a frequent and rapid rate of growth and change (in some cases, almost in real time).

6.4.1 Big Data Risk

Advances in the ability to perform analysis of big data allow enterprises to make better business decisions and increase competitive advantages. The changes in analytics capabilities with respect to big data may introduce technical and operational risk, and enterprises should understand that risk can be incurred either through adoption or non-adoption of these capabilities.

Managers of technical and operational risk should consider that certain data elements may be governed by regulatory or contractual requirements and that data elements may need to be centralized in one place (or at least be accessible centrally) so that the data can be analyzed. In some cases, this centralization can compound technical risk.

6.4.2 Big Data IT Audit and Control Concerns

If an enterprise increases its adoption of big data solutions to drive business value and maintain a competitive advantage, it is important for an IT auditor to understand the associated risk and consider approaches to providing assurance that risk is being adequately managed.[162]

[162] McDermott, J.; "Auditing Big Data in the Enterprise," *ISACA® Journal*, 5 March 2018, *www.isaca.org/resources/isaca-journal/issues/2018/volume-2/auditing-big-data-in-the-enterprise*

ISACA. All Rights Reserved.

For example, an IT auditor should:

- Understand the enterprise overall strategy and how big data might be employed to support that strategy.
- Determine if big data solutions have been implemented using open-source technology platforms (e.g., Apache Hadoop) or within third-party cloud computing environments (e.g., Amazon Web Services® [AWS®]). These technologies present unique risk considerations for an IT auditor. For example, open-source software is highly configurable and may be more susceptible to security vulnerabilities.
- Identify if an enterprise has implemented big data in a cloud environment. If so, an IT auditor should confirm that big data cloud technology providers have adequate security controls, and that management provides sufficient oversight of the third-party vendor relationship.
- Determine if an enterprise has implemented adequate safeguards to protect data and adhere to privacy requirements, particularly for consumer information. If sensitive data are being collected and stored in the big data solution, there may be regulatory or industry-specific requirements over how those data are protected, shared, retained and purged.

6.5 Blockchain

Blockchain is a distributed, protected journaling and ledger system that can be accessed by and among multiple parties, using cryptography and peer-to-peer technology to secure data into blocks and store them in an immutable chain of transactions without any trusted central authority. By design, each participant in the blockchain possesses the same copy of this ledger and has the ability to write to or modify it, assuming the individual is properly authorized to do so. The fundamental function of blockchain is to accomplish sharing and distribution of data or value without the need for a trusted intermediary and without any enforced system management. It is the design of the software and network itself that allows participants to trust the accuracy and veracity of the information on the blockchain.

Use of blockchain technologies can enable anything from digital currency (e.g., Bitcoin) to many other value-bearing transactions.

6.5.1 Blockchain Models

Public Blockchains

Public blockchains are permissionless by design. Any person or party can:

- Join this type of blockchain network.
- Participate as a consensus participant or miner.
- Produce applications, smart contracts or transactions.
- Have a transparent view of the history of all transactions that occurred on the blockchain.

Participation simply requires the download of the particular blockchain's open-source software platform.

The foremost examples of public blockchains to date are the Bitcoin blockchain and the Ethereum® blockchain. For computationally intensive blockchains like Bitcoin, participants need the appropriate level of available memory and processing power to have a reasonable chance of success at mining and receiving the incentive reward of the network.

Public blockchains operate and are secured by the combination of cryptographic verification (e.g., proof of work, the consensus methodology used by Bitcoin) and cryptoeconomics—the combination of economic-based incentives to maintain and manage the blockchain ecosystem.

ISACA. All Rights Reserved.

Private Blockchains

Private blockchains are permissioned. Thus, they are designed and operate based on access controls that can place restrictions on the parties and types of parties that can participate, and can limit their functions and capabilities in the blockchain workflow. This is in contrast to public blockchains, in which participants are untrusted and are pseudonymous. Participants in private blockchains are typically known to the operators and inherently considered trusted participants.

In private blockchains, one or more stakeholders or administrators control the network, introducing a requirement for third-party acceptance to transact on the blockchain, which does not exist in public blockchain implementations. In the context of a private blockchain, only the parties participating in a transaction have knowledge about it. For the most part, other parties cannot have access, although many private blockchains allow for layers of different types of permissions (submit data, confirm data, view-only, etc.). Thus, although private blockchains can and usually do have a consensus methodology associated with them, trust still plays an important role in private implementations. Also, a private blockchain typically does not use a native token as an incentive to the miners to support security of the network, which is typical in a public blockchain.

Hybrid Blockchains

Hybrid blockchains are blockchain implementations in which one component is a fully public blockchain (with all the benefits and challenges) and a parallel component is a permissioned private blockchain, allowing for enterprise-level transactions that maintain regulatory compliance and access permissions. Hybrid blockchains seek to realize the best benefits of public and private blockchain technology, including not being fully open to any participant, while maintaining data immutability and transparency.

In a hybrid blockchain, although transactions are not public, they are always available to be verified when necessary.

6.5.2 Blockchain Business Risk

Blockchain is not a practical technology for all enterprises, and management must ensure that its use supports business objectives. Accordingly, a blockchain must be carefully considered, properly deployed and effectively managed. The potential risk to an enterprise can vary significantly, based on the chosen deployment model and the risk introduced when the solution is not well understood or when key safeguards are overlooked.[163]

Potential business impacts of deploying blockchain include:

- Use cases that are impractical and/or misaligned with strategic objectives
- Poor implementation or deployment that results in wasted resources due to a solution not functioning properly
- Gaps in security, including vulnerable source code, weak endpoints and theft/loss of sensitive data
- Vendors that cannot scale effectively to support blockchain at enterprise level
- Substantial impact to customers and regulatory consequence (including fines) when deployment is faulty

6.5.3 Blockchain IT Audit and Control Concerns

When conducting a review or audit of the use of blockchain, an IT auditor should focus on the following:[164]

- **Governance**—Regulatory and management oversight guidelines/requirements of the blockchain/distributed ledger technologies (BC/DLTs), networks, policies and procedures

[163] ISACA, *Blockchain Preparation Audit Program*, USA, 2019, *https://store.isaca.org/s/store#/store/browse/detail/a2S4w000004KoDOEA0*
[164] ISACA, *Blockchain Framework Audit Program*, USA, 2021, *https://store.isaca.org/s/store#/store/browse/detail/a2S4w000004KtQ8EAK*

ISACA. All Rights Reserved.

- **Infrastructure**—Any functionality or capability of a blockchain independent of the data transacting on the blockchain or among blockchains
- **Data management**—Off-chain information stored and/or transmitted in a computer-readable format that is used to transact or interact on a blockchain network, or data that are sourced from a blockchain network and treated as a source of truth for a business purpose
- **Key management**—Management of public and private keys
- **Smart contracts**—Programs self-activated when conditions are met, including DLT networks, Oracle calls, and integrated code between blockchain recording of state and other transaction data

An IT auditor should conduct an assessment of the blockchain technology control environment indicating whether it is adequately designed and operationally effective to:[165]

- Identify any governance challenges and blockchain risk that could result in reputational, legal and/or material financial impact.
- Provide management with a holistic perspective on blockchain technology that considers both technical and nontechnical factors.

A blockchain audit should consider security controls from the following perspectives:[166]

- Safeguards or countermeasures that manage the selection, development, implementation and maintenance of security measures that primarily are implemented and executed by people (as opposed to systems)
- Safeguards or countermeasures for an information system that primarily are implemented and executed by the information system through automated mechanisms contained in the hardware, software or firmware components of the system

An IT auditor's assessment of these controls will enable the enterprise to identify opportunities to strengthen the blockchain network safeguards to improve security.

6.6 The Internet of Things (IoT)

Internet of Things (IoT) refers to a collection of sensors, actuators and computing capabilities that work together to solve a problem or provide a service over the Internet. The simplest example of IoT is the connection of common everyday things to the Internet. When a thing is connected to the Internet, it has the ability to send or receive information, or both. It is this ability to send and receive information that makes things smart.[167]

This growing internetwork of things comprises physical objects with the capability to communicate in new ways—with each other, with their owners or operators, or with their manufacturers, for example—to make people's lives easier and enterprises more efficient and competitive.

6.6.1 IoT Device Types

Perhaps the single most important factor in the explosion of applications and access to connected devices is the advent of the smartphone. Because the smartphone, which can act as the user interface, often has sensors, computing functions and communication capabilities, it facilitates a significant increase in the use of other connected devices. Just as the smartphone accelerated engagement with the Internet in daily life, smartphone technology accelerates the desire and perceived need for other Internet-connected devices and their capabilities.

Common IoT devices include those listed and described in **figure 6.2**.

[165] *Ibid.*
[166] *Ibid.*
[167] ISACA, *CGEIT Review Manual, 8th Edition*, USA, 2020, *https://store.isaca.org/s/store#/store/browse/detail/a2S4w000004KolTEAS*

ISACA. All Rights Reserved.

Figure 6.2—Types of IoT Devices		
Category	**Description**	**Example IoT Device**
Type 1	Device collects and sends information	• Air quality sensor • Light sensor • Moisture sensor • Video cameras • Water sensor
Type 2	Device receives and acts on information	• 3D printer • Keyless ignition • Smart door locks
Type 3	Both Type 1 and 2 functions	• Continuous glucose monitoring and insulin pens • HVAC • Smart lights • Smart speakers • Smart television • Smart thermostat
Source: ISACA, *CGEIT Review Manual, 8th Edition*, USA, 2020, figure 4.17, *https://store.isaca.org/s/store#/store/browse/detail/a2S4w000004KoCsEAK*		

Enterprises that are considering leveraging IoT devices should address potential risk, prior to deployment within a production environment, and consider the following:

- Security-focused quality assurance testing
- Weak/hard-coded credentials
- Hardware/physical security
- Lack of secure update method
- Insecure data transfer and storage

6.6.2 IoT Risk and Controls

IoT devices are ubiquitous in personal and professional settings. Enterprises need to understand the unique risk associated with introducing IoT devices into their environment and the value to be gained.

Business value and organizational competitiveness can be gained as enterprises capitalize on the IoT capabilities of devices they purchase. Additionally, businesses can compete more effectively in the marketplace by providing IoT features in products they sell and incorporating them in service offerings.

With that additional value comes additional risk. Although specific risk depends on usage, some IoT-usage risk areas and recommended NIST controls of which an IT auditor should be aware are provided in **figure 6.3.**

ISACA. All Rights Reserved.

Figure 6.3—IoT Risk and Controls	
Potential Risk	**NIST Controls**
Business risk: • Health and safety • Regulatory compliance • User privacy • Unexpected costs	• **ID-BE.1**: The organization role in the supply chain is identified and communicated. • **ID-BE-2**: The organization place in critical infrastructure and its industry sector are identified and communicated • **ID-BE-3**: Priorities for organizational mission, objectives and activities are established and communicated • **ID-BE-4**: Dependencies and critical functions for delivery of critical services are established • **ID-BE-5**: Resilience requirements to support delivery of critical services are established for all operating states (e.g., under duress/attack, during recovery, normal operations)
Operational risk: • Inappropriate access to functionality • Shadow usage • Performance	• **PR-AC-1**: Identities and credentials are issued, managed, verified, revoked and audited for authorized devices, users, and processes • **PR-AC-2**: Physical access to assets is managed and protected • **PR-AC-3**: Remoted access is managed • **PR-AC-4**: Access permissions and authorizations are managed, incorporating the principles of least privilege and separation of duties • **PR-BE-5**: Resilience requirements to support delivery of critical services are established for all operating states (e.g., under duress/attack, during recovery, normal operations) • **PR-DS-6**: Adequate capacity to ensure availability is maintained
Source: ISACA, *Cybersecurity Audit Certificate Study Guide, 1st Edition*, USA, 2018, figure 4.10, *https://store.isaca.org/s/store#/store/browse/detail/a2S4w000004Ks06EAC*	

6.6.3 IoT Audit and Security Concerns

Audit and security concerns associated with IoT include:

- Dated software and hardware
- Unencrypted communications
- Access risk
- Device vulnerabilities

Dated Software and Hardware

Over time, as technologies improve, they require faster and more sophisticated hardware and software. Older devices, sensors and communication hardware sometimes become outdated. Updating hardware can be an expensive and logistically complicated process.

Remaining current on security patches and security upgrades is a critical part of maintaining device software. This software can often be upgraded over the same communication mechanism that the device uses to send sensor or computational data. This download of firmware of other software, when delivered via a cellular connection, is an example of an over-the-air (OTA) update. Regardless of the update mechanism used, it is important for security and operational purposes to keep hardware and software up to date.

ISACA. All Rights Reserved.

Unencrypted Communications

Encryption technologies, software and keys are critical to the safety and security of an IoT network. As computing technology improves, it is often necessary to increase the size of the key and sometimes move on from a deprecated algorithm. Keeping up with evolving encryption standards requires updates to devices. Failure to do so results in increased risk of data theft.

Access Risk

It is important to have security protocols to limit access to all layers of the IoT architecture. Devices, applications and users must be authenticated and authorized to connect to the network. Access to devices and data must be restricted to the devices and users who need them.

In addition to securing devices, it is necessary to rotate credentials, upgrade security algorithms and verify access logs. Regardless of how well a device is secured, credentials can inevitably be compromised. If a certificate has been compromised, it must be revoked.

Device Vulnerabilities

Devices are sometimes at risk of being hacked. When a device is penetrated, it can expose all its access routes and even its credentials. To protect the device from being compromised, selecting the correct hardware and operating system can be critical. A robust chipset and OS can greatly help in reducing attack vectors. For example, some chipsets provide secured random-access memory (RAM) locations for holding secrets, such as encryption keys, so that even if a device is physically hacked, its secrets remain safe.

6.7 Cybersecurity

Cybersecurity is the protection of information assets by addressing threats to information processed, stored and transported by internetworked information systems. Cybersecurity is concerned with digital assets.

Cybersecurity is one of the top overall challenges identified by IT audit leaders. Cybercriminals are continuously becoming more creative and sophisticated. New cyberthreats emerge daily, putting many business systems at risk, and enterprises face a monumental challenge to keep pace with the threats and safeguard their data.

6.7.1 Common Threat Actors/Cyberattacks

Cyberattacks typically target specific enterprises or industry sectors. Many threat actors and attack patterns have emerged, and it is essential for an IT auditor to be able to identify threats to understand key controls that mitigate them.

Common advanced threat actors include the following:

- **Competitors**—Enterprises that perform malicious acts to gain a competitive advantage
- **Cybercriminals**—Actors motivated by financial gain
- **Cyberterrorists**—Actors who frequently target critical infrastructures and/or governments
- **Hacktivists**—Politically motivated hackers who target specific individuals or enterprises to achieve ideological ends
- **Nation states**—Governments that target other states and/or private entities with a high level of sophistication to obtain intelligence or carry out other destructive activities

ISACA. All Rights Reserved.

Other threat actors include:

- **Online social hackers**—Skilled in social engineering, these attackers are frequently involved in cyberbullying, identity theft and collection of other confidential information or credentials.
- **Script kiddies**—Script kiddies are individuals who are learning to hack; they may work alone or with others and are primarily involved in code injections and distributed denial-of-service (DDoS) attacks.
- **Insider threats**—Employees, contractors, etc., who work for an enterprise. This group may include disgruntled employees.

6.7.2 Cyberattack Types

Threat actors use many types of cyberattacks.

Malware (short for malicious software) is a common type of cyberattack that is designed to infiltrate, damage or obtain information from a computer system without the owner's consent.

Common types of malware include:

- **Virus**—A computer virus is code that can replicate itself and spread from one computer to another. It requires user intervention or execution to replicate and/or cause damage.
- **Network worm**—A variant of the computer virus, a network worm is a piece of self-replicating code designed to spread itself across computer networks. It does not require intervention or execution to replicate.
- **Botnet**—Derived from robot network, a botnet is a large, automated and distributed network of previously compromised computers or devices that can be simultaneously controlled to launch large-scale attacks such as DDoS.
- **Trojan horse**—A Trojan horse is a piece of malware that gains access to a targeted system by hiding within a genuine application. Trojan horses are often broken down into categories reflecting their purposes. A common Trojan horse program is used to install remote access trojan (RAT) capabilities on the compromised target.

Some specific types of malware are characterized by their purpose:

- **Spyware**—A class of malware that gathers information about a person or enterprise without the knowledge of the person or enterprise
- **Adware**—A type of malware designed to present advertisements (generally unwanted) to users
- **Ransomware**—A kind of extortive malware (also called hostage code) that leverages cryptovirology to lock or encrypt data or functions and demand payment to unlock them
- **Keylogger**—A class of malware that secretly records user keystrokes and, in some cases, screen content
- **Rootkit**—A class of malware that hides the existence of other malware by modifying the underlying operating system

Some other common attack types follow:

- **Advanced persistent threats (APTs)**—Complex and coordinated attacks directed at a specific entity or enterprise. They require a substantial amount of research and time, often taking months or even years to fully execute. APT is a term indicating the class of complexity; however, whether a particular attack is APT cannot be tested. After an attack is discovered, and the level of complexity is determined and the amount of time and resources spent on the attack are investigated, then the attack can be classified as an attack by an APT.
- **Backdoor**—A means of regaining access to a compromised system by installing software or configuring existing software to enable remote access under attacker-defined conditions.
- **Brute force attack**—An attack made by trying all possible combinations of passwords or encryption keys until the correct one is found.

ISACA. All Rights Reserved.

- **Buffer overflow**—An attack in which a program or process tries to store more data in a buffer (temporary data storage area) than it was intended to hold. Buffer overflow is an increasingly common type of security attack on data integrity.
- **Cross-site scripting (XSS)**—A type of injection in which malicious scripts are injected into otherwise benign and trusted websites. XSS attacks occur when an attacker uses a web application to send malicious code, generally in the form of a browser-side script, to a different end user. Flaws that allow XSS attacks to succeed are widespread and occur anywhere a web application uses input from a user within the output it generates (i.e., without validating or encoding it).
- **Denial-of-service (DoS) attack**—An assault on a service from a single source that floods it with so many requests that it becomes overwhelmed and is either stopped completely or operates at a significantly reduced rate.
- **Man-in-the-middle attack**—An attack in which the actor intercepts communication between two parts of the victim system and then replaces the traffic with the intruder's own, eventually assuming control of the communication.
- **Phishing**—A type of email attack that attempts to convince a user that the originator is genuine, but with the intention of obtaining information for use in social engineering.
- **Social engineering**—An attempt to exploit social vulnerabilities to gain access to information and/or systems. It aims to trick the victim into divulging information or opening malicious software or programs.
- **Spear phishing**—An attack in which social engineering techniques are used to masquerade as a trusted party to obtain important information such as passwords from the victim.
- **Spoofing**—Faking the sending address of a transmission to gain illegal entry into a secure system.
- **Structured query language (SQL) injection**—According to OWASP, a SQL-injection attack consists of insertion or injection of a SQL query via the input data from the client to the application. This can result in the malicious actor being able to read sensitive data from the database, modify (insert/update/delete) database data, or execute administrative operations, such as shutting down the DBMS.[168]
- **Zero-day exploit**—A vulnerability that is exploited before the software creator/vendor is even aware of its existence.

6.7.3 Cybersecurity Audit and Control Concerns

The objectives of a cybersecurity audit are to:

- Provide management with an independent assessment of the effectiveness of cybersecurity processes, policies, procedures, governance and other controls.
- Identify security control concerns that could affect the confidentiality, integrity or availability of the information assets due to weaknesses and vulnerabilities in the system of internal controls, including key security controls.
- Evaluate the effectiveness of response and recovery programs.
- Evaluate compliance with cybersecurity relevant laws and regulations.

A cybersecurity audit should focus on cybersecurity standards, guidelines and procedures, and the implementation of related controls. A cybersecurity audit should include key cybersecurity processes and control areas. Examples of these processes and control areas include:

- Configuration management
- Network security server security (e.g., Windows or Linux server operating systems)
- Information security management
- Information security awareness

[168] OWASP, "SQL Injection," *https://owasp.org/www-community/attacks/SQL_Injection*

ISACA. All Rights Reserved.

- Business continuity management
- IT governance and management practices
- Business governance and management practices
- Third-party/vendor management

The primary security and control issues that enterprises face include:

- Protection of sensitive data and intellectual property
- Protection of networks to which multiple information resources are connected
- Responsibility and accountability for a network-connected device and information it contains

ISACA. All Rights Reserved.

6.8 Chapter 6 Knowledge Check

Review Questions

1. Which of the following controls should be built into an AI system?

   A. Enabling algorithm auditability at the inception of the system
   B. Disallowing a system of manual intervention to prevent AI system override
   C. Prohibiting basic assumptions and formulas from being changed

2. When providing assurance that a big data project is being adequately managed, an IT auditor should ensure that the enterprise:

   A. Views the project exclusively as a technology project.
   B. Has considered the risk associated with centralizing data in one place so that the data can be analyzed.
   C. Plans to analyze data using traditional data analysis relational or multidimensional database techniques.

3. What type of blockchain technology is not fully open to any participant, but maintains data immutability and transparency?

   A. Public blockchain
   B. Private blockchain
   C. Hybrid blockchain

4. A similarity shared by public and private blockchain models is that:

   A. Each is distributed and decentralized over a peer-to-peer network.
   B. One node contains a full copy of the ledger while other nodes only contain partial ledger copies.
   C. Both are centralized and controlled by a single entity.

5. A typical denial-of-service (DoS) attack attempts to:

   A. Penetrate an IT system.
   B. Overwhelm an IT system.
   C. Steal credentials from enterprise customers.

6. An advanced persistent threat (APT) is a type of cybersecurity attack that:

   A. Is directed against a large group of enterprises simultaneously.
   B. Requires only a small amount of time and resources to execute.
   C. Can only be classified as an APT after an attack has been investigated.

7. Which of the following NIST cybersecurity framework functions include the enterprise cybersecurity awareness and training program?

   A. Protect
   B. Detect
   C. Respond

Answers on page 208

ISACA. All Rights Reserved.

Chapter 6 ANSWER KEY

Review Questions

1. **A. As a control, AI algorithm logic should be documented and explained appropriately to cover all aspects of the program. AI algorithm auditability should be enabled at inception to understand how the algorithm reached a certain judgment.**

   B. AI potentially can duplicate itself many times over, given that it is a software application, thus ensuring its survival. For that reason, a system of manual intervention should be designed to prevent AI system override.

   C. AI basic assumptions and formulas may need to be changed as more expertise is gained.

2. A. Although an enterprise may view a big data project primarily as a technology project, it is more important that an IT auditor ensure that the enterprise big data technology initiatives are aligned with its business strategy.

   B. If data elements need to be centralized in one place so that the data can be analyzed, technical risk must be considered. For example, centralizing data may put all combined data in jeopardy, rather than a subset of the data, if an unauthorized user should gain access. Further, aggregated data may result in data privacy issues if semi-anonymous information becomes nonanonymous or identifiable due to being combined.

   C. Managing and processing big data requires running specialized software on multiple servers. Big data sets are too large or too fast-changing to be analyzed using traditional relational or multidimensional database techniques or commonly used software tools to capture manage and process the data at a reasonable elapsed time.

3. A. A public blockchain is permissionless by design, which means that any person or party can join a public blockchain network. A public blockchain has a transparent view of the history of all transactions that occurred.

   B. A private blockchain is permissioned. It can place restrictions on the parties and types of parties that can participate and limit their functions and capabilities in the blockchain workflow. In a private blockchain, only those parties participating in a transaction have knowledge about it.

   C. Hybrid blockchains are blockchain implementations in which one component is a fully public blockchain and the parallel component is a permissioned private blockchain, allowing for enterprise-level transactions that maintain regulatory compliance and access permissions. Hybrid blockchains include not being fully open to any participant, while maintaining data immutability and transparency.

4. A. Both a public and private blockchain are distributed and decentralized over a peer-to-peer network.

   B. By design, each participant in either a public or private blockchain possesses the same shared copy of a ledger and has the ability to write to or modify the ledger, assuming proper authorization to do so.

   C. Public blockchains are permissionless by design. Any person or party can join a public blockchain network and participate as a consensus participant or miner. In private blockchains, one or more stakeholders or administrators control the network.

5. A. The goal of a typical DoS attack is not to penetrate an IT system but to overwhelm the system and its security protocols to the point that normal activity cannot be carried out.

   B. A typical DoS attack overwhelms the web server resources with so many requests from one computer connected to the Internet that the server is so busy responding to the pings that it does not have enough resources to respond to legitimate requests.

   C. A DoS attack is designed not to steal customer information but to make an enterprise unable to offer its services to its customers, leading to potentially significant financial, operational, reputational and legal risk.

ISACA. All Rights Reserved.

6. A. An APT is a complex and coordinated attack directed at a specific entity or enterprise.
B. An APT requires a substantial amount of research and time, often taking months or even years to fully execute.
C. APT is a term indicating the class of complexity; however, whether a particular attack is APT cannot be tested. After an attack is discovered, the level of complexity is determined, and the amount of time and resources spent on the attack is investigated, the attack can be classified as an APT.

7. **A. The NIST cybersecurity framework includes the enterprise cybersecurity and awareness program as part of the protect function.**
B. The NIST cybersecurity framework includes anomalies and events, security continuous monitoring and detection processes as part of the detect function.
C. The NIST cybersecurity framework includes response planning, communications, analysis, mitigations, and improvements as part of the respond function.

ISACA. All Rights Reserved.

Page intentionally left blank

ISACA. All Rights Reserved.

Glossary

A

Application containerization—A mechanism that is used to isolate applications from each other within the context of a running operating system instance. In much the same way that a logical partition (LPAR) provides segmentation of system resources in mainframes, a computing environment employing containers segments and isolates the underlying system services so that they are logically sequestered from each other.

Artificial intelligence—An advanced computer system that can simulate human capabilities, such as analysis, based on a predetermined set of rules

Assertion—Any formal declaration or set of declarations about the subject matter made by management.

Scope Notes: Assertions should usually be in writing and commonly contain a list of specific attributes about the subject matter or about a process involving the subject matter.

Audit—Formal inspection and verification to check whether a standard or set of guidelines is being followed, records are accurate, or efficiency and effectiveness targets are being met

Scope Notes: May be carried out by internal or external groups

Audit accountability—Performance measurement of service delivery including cost, timeliness and quality against agreed service levels.

Audit authority—A statement of the position within the enterprise, including lines of reporting and the rights of access.

Audit charter—A document approved by those charged with governance that defines the purpose, authority and responsibility of the internal audit activity.

Scope Notes: The charter should:

- Establish the internal audit function's position within the enterprise
- Authorize access to records, personnel and physical properties relevant to the performance of IS audit and assurance engagements
- Define the scope of audit function's activities

Audit evidence—The information used to support the audit opinion.

Audit fieldwork—The process of obtaining, documenting and preserving sufficient and appropriate audit evidence to support audit findings and conclusions and achieve audit objectives.

Audit objective—The specific goal(s) of an audit.

Scope Notes: These often center on substantiating the existence of internal controls to minimize business risk.

Audit plan—1. A plan containing the nature, timing and extent of audit procedures to be performed by engagement team members in order to obtain sufficient appropriate audit evidence to form an opinion.

Scope Notes: Includes the areas to be audited, the type of work planned, the high-level objectives and scope of the work, and topics such as budget, resource allocation, schedule dates, type of report and its intended audience and other general aspects of the work

2. A high-level description of the audit work to be performed in a certain period of time.

Audit program—A step-by-step set of audit procedures and instructions that should be performed to complete an audit.

Audit responsibility—The roles, scope and objectives documented in the service level agreement (SLA) between management and audit.

Audit risk—The risk of reaching an incorrect conclusion based upon audit findings.

Scope Notes: The three components of audit risk are:

- Control risk
- Detection risk
- Inherent risk

Audit scope—The specific system, function or unit of the enterprise to be included in an audit.

Audit subject—The area to be audited.

Audit universe—An inventory of audit areas that is compiled and maintained to identify areas for audit during the audit planning process.

Scope Notes: Traditionally, the list includes all financial and key operational systems as well as other units that would be audited as part of the overall cycle of planned work. The audit universe serves as the source from which the annual audit schedule is prepared. The universe will be periodically revised to reflect changes in the overall risk profile.

ISACA. All Rights Reserved.

Audit workpapers—The set of documents used to record all work performed during an audit and to demonstrate compliance with audit standards.

B

Big data—The ability to work with collections of data that had been impractical before because of their volume, velocity, and variety ("the three Vs"). A key driver of this new ability has been easier distribution of storage and processing across networks of inexpensive commodity hardware using technology such as Hadoop instead of requiring larger, more powerful individual computers.

Blockchain —A distributed, protected journaling and ledger system. Use of blockchain technologies can enable anything from digital currency (e.g., Bitcoin) to any other value-bearing transaction

Bridge—Data link layer device developed in the early 1980s to connect local area networks (LANs) or create two separate LAN or wide area network (WAN) network segments from a single segment to reduce collision domains.

Scope Notes: A bridge acts as a store-and-forward device in moving frames toward their destination. This is achieved by analyzing the MAC header of a data packet, which represents the hardware address of an NIC.

Bug—A fault in a program that causes the program to perform in an unintended or unanticipated manner

See Anomaly, Defect, Error, Exception and Fault.

Bus—Common path or channel between hardware devices.

Scope Notes: Can be located between components internal to a computer or between external computers in a communication network.

Business case—Documentation of the rationale for making a business investment, used both to support a business decision on whether to proceed with the investment and as an operational tool to support management of the investment through its full economic life cycle

Business continuity plan (BCP)—A plan used by an enterprise to respond to disruption of critical business processes; depends on the contingency plan for restoration of critical systems

Business process—An inter-related set of cross-functional activities or events that result in the delivery of a specific product or service to a customer.

Business process owner—The individual responsible for identifying process requirements, approving process design and managing process performance.

Scope Notes: Must be at an appropriately high level in the enterprise and have authority to commit resources to process-specific risk management activities

Business risk—The probability that a situation with uncertain frequency and magnitude of loss (or gain) could prevent the enterprise from meeting its business objectives

C

Central processing unit (CPU)—Computer hardware that houses the electronic circuits that control/direct all operations of the computer system.

Chief information officer (CIO)—The most senior official of the enterprise who is accountable for IT advocacy, aligning IT and business strategies, and planning, resourcing and managing the delivery of IT services, information and the deployment of associated human resources.

Scope Notes: In some cases, the CIO role has been expanded to become the chief knowledge officer (CKO) who deals in knowledge, not just information. Also see chief technology officer (CTO).

Chief information security officer (CISO)—The person in charge of information security within the enterprise

Cloud computing—Convenient, scalable on-demand network access to a shared pool of resources that can be provisioned rapidly and released with minimal management effort or service provider interaction

Code of ethics—A document designed to influence individual and organizational behavior of employees, by defining organizational values and the rules to be applied in certain situations.

Scope Notes: A code of ethics is adopted to assist those in the enterprise called upon to make decisions understand the difference between 'right' and 'wrong' and to apply this understanding to their decisions.

COBIT 5 and COBIT 2019 perspective

Cold site—An IS backup facility that has the necessary electrical and physical components of a computer facility, but does not have the computer equipment in place.

Scope Notes: The site is ready to receive the necessary replacement computer equipment in the event that the

ISACA. All Rights Reserved.

users have to move from their main computing location to the alternative computer facility.

Compensating control—An internal control that reduces the risk of an existing or potential control weakness resulting in errors and omissions.

Compliance—Adherence to, and the ability to demonstrate adherence to, mandated requirements defined by laws and regulations, as well as voluntary requirements resulting from contractual obligations and internal policies

Compliance audit—Includes specific tests of controls to demonstrate adherence to specific regulatory or industry-specific standards or practices.

Computer forensic audit—An investigation that includes the analysis of electronic devices such as computers, smartphones, disks, switches, routers and hubs, which involves the process of collecting, assessing, classifying and documenting digital evidence to assist in the identification of an offender and the method of compromise.

Computer forensics—The application of the scientific method to digital media to establish factual information for judicial review

Scope Notes: This process often involves investigating computer systems to determine whether they are or have been used for illegal or unauthorized activities. As a discipline, it combines elements of law and computer science to collect and analyze data from information systems (e.g., personal computers, networks, wireless communication and digital storage devices) in a way that is admissible as evidence in a court of law.

Computer-assisted audit technique (CAAT)—Any automated audit technique, such as generalized audit software (GAS), test data generators, computerized audit programs and specialized audit utilities.

Configuration management—1. The control of changes to a set of configuration items over a system life cycle (ISACA)
2. The process of managing the integrity of work products using configuration identification, version control, change control and audits (CMMI)

Continuous auditing—An approach used by an IT auditor to monitor system reliability on a continuous basis and gather selective audit evidence through the computer.

Continuous IT control monitoring—A process that includes:

- Developing a strategy to regularly evaluate selected IT-related controls/metrics.
- Recording and evaluating IT-related events and the effectiveness of the enterprise in dealing with those events.
- Recording changes to IT-related controls or changes that affect IT-related risk.
- Communicating the current risk and control status to enable information-sharing decisions involving the enterprise.

Control—The means of managing risk, including policies, procedures, guidelines, practices or organizational structures, which can be of an administrative, technical, management or legal nature

Scope Notes: Also used as a synonym for safeguard or countermeasure.

See also Internal control.

Control objective—A statement of the desired result or purpose to be achieved by implementing control procedures in a particular process

Control owner—A person in whom the enterprise has invested the authority and accountability for making control-related decisions and is responsible for ensuring that the control is implemented and is operating effectively and efficiently

Control risk—Risk that assets are lost/compromised or that financial statements are materially misstated due to lack of or ineffective design and/or implementation of internal controls

Control self-assessment—An assessment of controls made by the staff and management of the unit or units involved

Control weakness—A deficiency in the design or operation of a control procedure. Control weaknesses can potentially result in risk relevant to the area of activity not being reduced to an acceptable level (relevant risk threatens achievement of the objectives relevant to the area of activity being examined). Control weaknesses can be material when the design or operation of one or more control procedures does not reduce to a relatively low level the risk that misstatements caused by illegal acts or irregularities may occur and not be detected by the related control procedures.

Corrective control—Designed to correct errors, omissions and unauthorized uses and intrusions, once they are detected.

ISACA. All Rights Reserved.

Criteria—The standards and benchmarks used to measure and present the subject matter and against which an IS auditor evaluates the subject matter.

Scope Notes: Criteria should be:

- **Objective**— free from bias
- **Measurable**— provide for consistent measurement
- **Complete**— include all relevant factors to reach a conclusion
- **Relevant**— relate to the subject matter

In an attestation engagement, benchmarks against which management's written assertion on the subject matter can be evaluated. The practitioner forms a conclusion concerning subject matter by referring to suitable criteria.

Cybersecurity—1. The protection of information assets by addressing threats to information processed, stored and transported by internetworked information systems (ISACA)

2. Protection and restoration of products, services, solutions, and supply chain; including technology, computers, telecommunications systems and services, and information; to ensure their availability, integrity, authentication, transport, confidentiality, and resilience. Cybersecurity is a part of information security. (CMMI)

D

Data leakage—Unauthorized transmission of data from an organization either electronically or physically

Demilitarized zone (DMZ)—A small, isolated network that serves as a buffer zone between trusted and untrusted networks

Scope Notes: A DMZ is typically used to house systems, such as web servers, that must be accessible from both internal networks and the Internet.

Detection risk—Risk that assets are lost/compromised or that financial statements are materially misstated due to failure of an enterprise's internal controls to detect errors or fraud in a timely manner

Detective control—Designed to detect and report when errors, omissions and unauthorized uses or entries occur

Disaster recovery plan (DRP)—A set of human, physical, technical and procedural resources to recover, within a defined time and cost, an activity interrupted by an emergency or disaster

Due professional care—Diligence that a person, who possesses a special skill, would exercise under a given set of circumstances.

F

Financial audit—An audit designed to determine the accuracy of financial records and information.

Forensic audit—A specialized audit to discover, disclose and follow up on fraud and crime.

Fraud audit—A specialized audit designed to discover fraudulent activity.

G

General computer control—A Control, other than an application control, that relates to the environment within which computer-based application systems are developed, maintained and operated, and that is therefore applicable to all applications. The objectives of general controls are to ensure the proper development and implementation of applications and the integrity of program and data files and of computer operations. Like application controls, general controls may be either manual or programmed. Examples of general controls include the development and implementation of an IS strategy and an IS security policy, the organization of IS staff to separate conflicting duties and planning for disaster prevention and recovery.

Generalized audit software (GAS)—Multipurpose audit software that can be used for general processes, such as record selection, matching, recalculation and reporting.

Governance—The method by which an enterprise ensures that stakeholder needs, conditions and options are evaluated to determine balanced, agreed-on enterprise objectives are achieved. It involves setting direction through prioritization and decision making, and monitoring performance and compliance against agreed-on direction and objectives.

H

Hardware—Physical equipment, as opposed to programs, procedures, rules and associated documentation. Contrasts with software.

Hot site—A fully operational offsite data processing facility equipped with both hardware and system software to be used in the event of a disaster.

Hub—A common connection point for devices in a network, hubs are used to connect segments of a local area network (LAN).

ISACA. All Rights Reserved.

Scope Notes: A hub contains multiple ports. When a packet arrives at one port, it is copied to the other ports so that all segments of the LAN can see all packets.

I

Identity and access management (IAM)—Encapsulates people, processes and products to identify and manage the data used in an information system to authenticate users and grant or deny access rights to data and system resources. The goal of IAM is to provide appropriate access to enterprise resources.

Impairment—A condition that causes a weakness or diminished ability to execute audit objectives

Scope Notes: Impairment to organizational independence and individual objectivity may include personal conflict of interest; scope limitations; restrictions on access to records, personnel, equipment, or facilities; and resource limitations (such as funding or staffing).

Independence in appearance—A reasonable and informed third party would be likely to conclude (weighing all the specific facts and circumstances) that an audit function's, or a member of the audit function's integrity, objectivity or professional skepticism has not been compromised.

Independence of mind—The state of mind that permits the expression of a conclusion without being affected by influences that compromise professional judgment, thereby allowing an individual to act with integrity and exercise objectivity and professional skepticism.

Information security—Ensures that, within the enterprise, information is protected against disclosure to unauthorized users (confidentiality), improper modification (integrity) and nonaccess when required (availability). Information security deals with all formats of information—paper documents, digital assets, intellectual property in people's minds, and verbal and visual communications.

Inherent risk—The risk level or exposure without taking into account the actions that management has taken or might take (e.g., implementing controls)

Input control—Techniques and procedures used to verify, validate and edit data to ensure that only correct data are entered into the computer.

Integrated audit—A process focus on risk whereby appropriate audit disciplines are combined to assess key internal controls over an operation, process or entity.

Internal controls—The policies, procedures, practices and organizational structures designed to provide reasonable assurance that business objectives will be achieved and undesired events will be prevented or detected and corrected

Internet of Things (IoT) —A collection of sensors, actuators and computing capabilities that work together to solve a problem or provide a service over the Internet

Irregularity—Violation of an established management policy or regulatory requirement. It may consist of deliberate misstatements or omission of information concerning the area under audit or the enterprise as a whole, gross negligence or unintentional illegal acts.

IT audit—The formal examination and/or testing of information systems to determine whether:

- Information systems are in compliance with applicable laws, regulations, contracts and/or industry guidelines.
- Information systems and related processes comply with governance criteria and related and relevant policies and procedures.
- Data and information have appropriate levels of confidentiality, integrity and availability.

IT operations are being accomplished efficiently and effectiveness targets are being met.

IT risk register—A repository of the key attributes of potential and known IT risk issues. Attributes may include name, description, owner, expected/actual frequency, potential/actual magnitude, potential/actual business impact, disposition.

IT steering committee—An executive-management-level committee that assists in the delivery of the IT strategy, oversees day-to-day management of IT service delivery and IT projects, and focuses on implementation aspects.

IT strategy committee—A committee at the level of the board of directors to ensure that the board is involved in major IT matters and decisions.

Scope Notes: The committee is primarily accountable for managing the portfolios of IT-enabled investments, IT services and other IT resources. The committee is the owner of the portfolio.

L

Logical access controls—The policies, procedures, organizational structure and electronic access controls

ISACA. All Rights Reserved.

designed to restrict access to computer software and data files

M

Malware—Short for malicious software. Designed to infiltrate, damage or obtain information from a computer system without the owner's consent. Examples of malware include computer viruses, worms, Trojan horses, spyware and adware.

Mobile site—The use of a mobile/temporary facility to serve as a business resumption location. The facility can usually be delivered to any site and can house information technology and staff.

Multipoint wireless—Networks that can have many attached devices that communicate with a wireless bridge.

N

Network topology—The basic configuration and architecture of a set of interconnected nodes

O

Objectivity—The ability to exercise judgment, express opinions and present recommendations with impartiality

Offsite storage—A facility located away from the building housing the primary information processing facility (IPF), used for storage of computer media such as offline backup data and storage files.

Open Systems Interconnect (OSI) model—A seven-layer conceptual model that describes functions of computer network or telecommunication systems

Open Web Application Security Project (OWASP)—An open community dedicated to enabling organizations to conceive, develop, acquire, operate and maintain applications that can be trusted

Operating system (OS)—A master control program that runs the computer and acts as a scheduler and traffic controller

Scope Notes: The operating system is the first program copied into the computer memory after the computer is turned on; it must reside in memory at all times. It is the software that interfaces between the computer hardware (disk, keyboard, mouse, network, modem and printer) and the application software (word processor, spreadsheet email) which also controls access to the devices, is partially responsible for security components and sets the standards for the application programs that run in it.

Operational audit—An audit designed to evaluate the various internal controls, economy and efficiency of a function or department.

Output controls—Processes that ensure data sent to users will be presented, formatted and delivered in a consistent and secure manner.

P

Patch management—1. An area of systems management that involves acquiring, testing and installing multiple patches (code changes) to an administered computer system to maintain up-to-date software and often to address security risk (ISACA)

Scope Notes: Patch management tasks include maintaining current knowledge of available patches, deciding what patches are appropriate for particular systems, ensuring that patches are installed properly, testing systems after installation and documenting all associated procedures, such as specific configurations required. A number of products are available to automate patch management tasks. Patches are sometimes ineffective and can sometimes cause more problems than they fix. Patch management experts suggest that system administrators take simple steps to avoid problems, such as performing backups and testing patches on noncritical systems prior to installations. Patch management can be viewed as part of change management.

2. The process to identify, acquire, install, and verify a set of changes to a computer program or its supporting data for solutions and systems. A patch is typically an isolated change of a specified scope and is sometimes referred to as a bug fix. (CMMI)

Penetration testing—A live test of the effectiveness of security defenses through mimicking the actions of real-life attackers

Physical controls—Locks, fences, closed-circuit TV (CCTV) and devices that are installed to physically restrict access to a facility or hardware.

Platform as a Service (PaaS)—Offers the capability to deploy onto the cloud infrastructure customer-created or -acquired applications that are created using programming languages and tools supported by the provider

Policy—A document that communicates required and prohibited activities and behaviors

Preventive control—An internal control that is used to avoid undesirable events, errors and other occurrences

ISACA. All Rights Reserved.

that an enterprise has determined could have a negative material effect on a process or end product

Privacy—The right of an individual to trust that others will appropriately and respectfully use, store, share and dispose of his/her associated personal and sensitive information within the context, and according to the purposes for which it was collected or derived

Procedure—A document containing a detailed description of the steps necessary to perform specific operations in conformance with applicable standards. Procedures are defined as part of processes.

Processing controls—Procedures that ensure the reliability of application program processing.

R

Reciprocal agreement—Emergency processing agreement between two or more enterprises with similar equipment or applications.

Scope Notes: Typically, participants of a reciprocal agreement promise to provide processing time to each other when an emergency arises.

Recovery point objective (RPO)—Determined based on the acceptable data loss in case of a disruption of operations. It indicates the earliest point in time that is acceptable to recover the data. The RPO effectively quantifies the permissible amount of data loss in case of interruption.

Relevant audit evidence—Audit evidence is relevant if it pertains to the audit objectives and has a logical relationship to the findings and conclusions it is used to support.

Reliable audit evidence—Audit evidence is reliable if, in the IS auditor's opinion, it is valid, factual, objective and supportable.

Residual risk—The remaining risk after management has implemented a risk response

Ring—A type of local area network (LAN) architecture in which the cable forms a loop, with stations attached at intervals around the loop.

Risk appetite—The amount of risk, on a broad level, that an entity is willing to accept in pursuit of its mission.

Risk assessment—A process used to identify and evaluate risk and its potential effects

Scope Notes: Risk assessments are used to identify those items or areas that present the highest risk, vulnerability or exposure to the enterprise for inclusion in the IS annual audit plan.

Risk assessments are also used to manage the project delivery and project benefit risk.

Risk culture—The set of shared values and beliefs that governs attitudes toward risk-taking, care and integrity, and determines how openly risk and losses are reported and discussed.

Risk management—1. The coordinated activities to direct and control an enterprise with regard to risk

Scope Notes: In the International Standard, the term "control" is used as a synonym for "measure." (ISO/IEC Guide 73:2002)

2. One of the governance objectives. Entails recognizing risk; assessing the impact and likelihood of that risk; and developing strategies, such as avoiding the risk, reducing the negative effect of the risk and/or transferring the risk, to manage it within the context of the enterprise's risk appetite.

Scope Notes: COBIT 5 perspective

Risk tolerance—The acceptable level of variation that management is willing to allow for any particular risk as the enterprise pursues its objectives

Router—A networking device that can send (route) data packets from one local area network (LAN) or wide area network (WAN) to another, based on addressing at the network layer (Layer 3) in the open systems interconnection (OSI) model

Scope Notes: Networks connected by routers can use different or similar networking protocols. Routers usually are capable of filtering packets based on parameters, such as source addresses, destination addresses, protocol and network applications (ports).

S

Segregation/separation of duties (SoD)—A basic internal control that prevents or detects errors and irregularities by assigning to separate individuals the responsibility for initiating and recording transactions and for the custody of assets.

Scope Notes: Segregation/separation of duties is commonly used in large IT organizations so that no single person is in a position to introduce fraudulent or malicious code without detection.

Software—Programs, procedures, rules and any associated documentation pertaining to the operation of a system. Contrasts with hardware.—Programs,

ISACA. All Rights Reserved.

procedures, rules and any associated documentation pertaining to the operation of a system. Contrasts with hardware.

See Application software, Operating system, System software and Utility software.

Software as a service (SaaS)—Offers the capability to use the provider's applications running on cloud infrastructure. The applications are accessible from various client devices through a thin client interface, such as a web browser (e.g., web-based email).

Software release management—The process through which software is made available to users. The term release is used to describe a collection of authorized changes.

Standard—A mandatory requirement, code of practice or specification approved by a recognized external standards organization, such as International Organization for Standardization (ISO).

Star—A type of local area network (LAN) architecture that utilizes a central controller to which all nodes are directly connected.

Strategic planning—The process of deciding on the enterprise's objectives, on changes in these objectives, and the policies to govern their acquisition and use.

Subject matter—The specific information subject to an IS auditor's report and related procedures, which can include things such as the design or operation of internal controls and compliance with privacy practices or standards or specified laws and regulations (area of activity).

Sufficient audit evidence—Audit evidence is sufficient if it is adequate, convincing and would lead another IS auditor to form the same conclusions.

Supervisory control and data acquisition (SCADA)—Systems used to control and monitor industrial and manufacturing processes, and utility facilities

Switches—Typically associated as a data link layer device, switches enable local area network (LAN) segments to be created and interconnected, which has the added benefit of reducing collision domains in Ethernet-based networks.

System development life cycle (SDLC)—The phases deployed in the development or acquisition of a software system.

Scope Notes: SDLC is an approach used to plan, design, develop, test and implement an application system or a major modification to an application system. Typical phases of SDLC include the feasibility study, requirements study, requirements definition, detailed design, programming, testing, installation and post-implementation review, but not the service delivery or benefits realization activities.

System flowchart—Graphic representations of the sequence of operations in an information system or program.

Scope Notes: Information system flowcharts show how data from source documents flow through the computer to final distribution to users. Symbols used should be the internationally accepted standard. System flowcharts should be updated when necessary.

T

Test data—Simulated transactions that can be used to test processing logic, computations and controls actually programmed in computer applications. Individual programs or an entire system can be tested.

Scope Notes: This technique includes Integrated Test Facilities (ITFs) and Base Case System Evaluations (BCSEs).

Threat event—Any event during which a threat element/actor acts against an asset in a manner that has the potential to directly result in harm

Transmission Control Protocol Internet Protocol (TCP/IP)—Provides the basis for the Internet; a set of communication protocols that encompass media access, packet transport, session communication, file transfer, electronic mail (email), terminal emulation, remote file access and network management

U

Utility software—Computer programs or routines designed to perform some general support function required by other application software, the operating system or the system users. They perform general functions, such as formatting electronic media, making copies of files or deleting files.

V

Virtual private network (VPN)—A secure private network that uses the public telecommunications infrastructure to transmit data

Scope Notes: In contrast to a much more expensive system of owned or leased lines that can only be used by one enterprise, VPNs are used by enterprises for both extranets and wide areas of intranets. Using encryption

ISACA. All Rights Reserved.

and authentication, a VPN encrypts all data that pass between two Internet points, maintaining privacy and security.

Virtualization—The process of adding a guest application and data onto a virtual server, recognizing that the guest application will ultimately be removed from this physical server

Vulnerability—A weakness in the design, implementation, operation or internal control of a process that could expose the system to adverse threats from threat events

Vulnerability analysis—A process of identifying and classifying vulnerabilities

Vulnerability scanning—An automated process to proactively identify security weaknesses in a network or individual system

W

Warm site—Similar to a hot site but not fully equipped with all of the necessary hardware needed for recovery.

Web application—An application in which all or some parts of the software are downloaded from the web every time it runs.

ISACA. All Rights Reserved.

Page intentionally left blank

ISACA. All Rights Reserved.